24⁹⁵   12⁵⁰

D1559568

THE COMPLETE GUIDE TO BUYING, SELLING AND INVESTING IN UNDEVELOPED LAND

James J. Sheerin

PROBUS PUBLISHING COMPANY
Chicago, Illinois

Library of Congress Cataloging Available

ISBN 0-917253-57-4

Printed in the United States of America

1 2 3 4 5 6 7 8 9 0

For my wife, Margaret,
   and daughter, Jamie Marie.

"To us."

Preface

This book is for the serious investor who sees opportunities for profits by investing in land. It does not offer get-rich quick strategies for the naive. Rather, it approaches investing in land like any other serious investment choice—using a methodical, deliberate and analytical system based on over twenty successful years as a buyer and seller of property.

I have written this book in such a way that it follows the land buying process itself. The opening chapter discusses the "whys" and "wherefores" of investing in raw land. Definitions and land descriptions follow. Legal issues and appraisal of land are discussed in detail. A variety of sample documents to help investors understand the sometimes complicated transactions in land investing are provided.

Finally, and most importantly, buying tips and land improvement techniques at the time of selling are offered to enhance an investor's profits. Simple rules of thumb and analytical tools are offered to make investment decisions easier. A glossary of terms will help with the seemingly private language of land investing practitioners.

The support and help of my wife and daughter made this book a reality, as did the expert advice of the professionals at Probus Publishing. Thank you all.

James J. Sheerin

CONTENTS

Contents

Contents

Contents

CHAPTER I

WHY BUY LAND?

The primary reason to invest is to make money. To do so, investors today have a broad range of investment alternatives to choose from. Stocks and bonds, precious metals, real estate, coins, stamps, gemstones and similar collectibles are but a few of the choices and, depending upon whom you talk to, all have had respectable increases in value. Astute investors don't rely upon one investment; they have a planned diversity in their portfolios. They may own stocks, some gold coins, and perhaps some of my personal preference, real estate—more specifically, land. Why land? Simply because land, particularly around major urban centers, has been incredibly consistent in its increase in value.

There are several reasons for this increase, but two are of paramount importance: (1) supply and demand, and (2) inflation.

SUPPLY AND DEMAND

There is no greater influence on supply and demand for land than the growth in population. All of us are users of land in one way or another.

Chapter I

We own it and live on it, or we rent it and live on it. We feed ourselves from its abundance, raise our families on its spaciousness, and enjoy the quality of our lives on its myriad resources. But less than one third of the earth's surface is land. Of this, the polar caps are not readily usable for everyday life, nor are the vast tundra lands and deserts, nor the lands that make up the mountain ranges. The quantity of usable land on the earth's surface is finite. Yet, of what there is, we keep using greater portions of it because the population of the world is growing at an alarming rate. In addition, nature is competing with us by taking back great amounts of acreage through erosion and the spread of desert land. And our own land use methods—clearing the land, depleting the soil, and then moving on—leave wasteland in our wake.

By the year 1830, there were one billion persons on the face of the earth (Table 1-1). It took from the dawn of time to reach this figure. One hundred years later, in 1930, the world's population reached two billion. Then, only *thirty* years later, in 1960, another billion persons was added. *Fifteen* years later (1975), we were up to four billion inhabitants. Projections are for five billion by 1987 and between six and seven billion by the year 2000. The statistics are staggering. We're adding 150 new human beings per minute, 80 million per year. If you are fifty years old now, the world's population has doubled in your lifetime (2.2 billion to 4.7 billion). By the time you're sixty-five years old, it will have tripled in your lifetime.

Table 1-1
Growth and Doubling Rate of the World's Population

Date	Population	Years to Double
Ad	250 million	————
1650	500 million	1650
1830	1 billion	180
1930	2 billion	100
1975	4 billion	45
2005	8 billion	30

Startling statistics, but how do they affect you and me? Actually, what is happening globally is also happening right in the United States. Even with our awareness of the problems of population growth, we're adding well over 2 million persons per year. Another birth every 8 seconds, a death every 16 seconds, an immigrant every 60 seconds (minus an emigrant every 15 minutes): resulting in another American every 14 seconds. And this doesn't take into consideration the fact that up to 1 million illegal aliens cross our borders annually.

At the end of the Civil War there were about 30 million persons sharing the available land in this country. Today, there are over 240 million of us. In less than 5 years there will be over 250 million, and at the turn of the century there will be at least 268 million of us (Table 1-2). We're growing at a rate of slightly over 1 percent per year.

Table 1-2
Projection of Total U.S. Population 1985 to 2025

Year	Population (millions)	Year	Population (millions)	Year	Population (millions)
1985	238	1992	254	1999	266
1986	241	1993	256	2000	268
1987	243	1994	258	2005	276
1988	245	1995	260	2010	283
1989	247	1996	261	2015	290
1990	250	1997	263	2020	297
1991	252	1998	265	2025	301

However, as rapid as population growth has been, the actual geographical area of the continental United States has changed little in more than a century. It consists of almost two billion acres:

Land owned by the federal government	408 million acres
Land owned by state & local gov'ts.	97 million acres
Indian lands	57 million acres
Privately owned lands	1,342 million acres
	1,904 million acres

Of the total 1,904 million acres, a large portion is not available to us for development. Much of it consists of waterways—lakes, ponds, rivers, swamps, bogs, bayous, and other wetlands. For example, the Okeefenokee takes up much of southern Florida, and the Mississippi delta consists of thousands of acres of submerged lands. Subtract also the barren great prairies and the desert lands of the West and Southwest, the Badlands of the Big Sky country, and the various mountain ranges. What do we have left? Whatever it is we're depleting it substantially by building 2 million new homes each year.

There are many pressures on land use. Whereas in some areas lots are as small as 2000 square feet, in other areas they are required to be 10 acres or more. (One acre is 43,560 square feet). Additional pressure on land use comes from changes in zoning requirements and environmental concerns. Zoning changes throughout the country have increased average lot sizes. In the past decade, thousands of communities have gone step by step from 10,000-square-foot lots to 60,000—and many residents want to increase the minimum lot-size requirement to 3 acres per house lot—a sixfold increase in the size of a buildable lot, with an expectable effect on prices. Environmentalists, concerned with the fragility of land, have created legislation that has removed large amounts of land from the available inventory. There is also a growing trend among cities and towns to buy up raw acreage and keep the land undeveloped, to maintain a desired standard and quality of life. Much of this is good, but what it does is significantly reduce the existing land inventory and also increase its price.

The Scottish historian Thomas Carlyle advised America over a century ago, when it was a nation of just 25 million people, that

You won't have any trouble in your country as long as you have few
people and much land, but when you have many people and little
land, your trials will begin.

In 1790 there were 484 acres of land for each person living within the
borders of what was to become the United States (Table 1-3). Today,
including acreage of all kinds, we have 8 acres per capita—about 3
acres per capita are arable. (Compare this to the 1 acre per capita of
arable land for the entire world.) Human beings can manufacture most
of their needs, but not land. Certainly, developers create new subdivisions, but they do so out of the existing supply of raw acreage. "They
ain't making any more of the stuff," as Will Rogers reportedly said.

If no more of the stuff is being made, and we're consistently using up
what there is of it, are we running out of land? The answer to this
question is a "fence straddling": it depends. It depends on the strategic
dispersal of our growing population and the proper allocation of land.
There is truly plenty of land available for our needs currently and far
into the future, but in certain geographic regions it is becoming pro-
gressively scarce. On the surface this seems contradictory: there are
land shortages in some areas and an abundance in others. Actually, less
than 6 percent of the land in this country is occupied. If you boarded a
plane in Boston, destination Los Angeles, you would see how much
open land there is. The United States Department of Agriculture estimates that urban and suburban land in the United States amounts to 94
million acres, with about 25 percent of this in open space. (Within
these 94 million acres lives 74 percent of the population.) Another 2 to
3 million acres are added each year through land development.

Why is only 5 or 6 percent of our land occupied? Being the social
animals that we are, we tend to congregate. And we tend to congregate
near our coastlines. Certainly, there are big population centers in the
heartland—Chicago, Minneapolis, St. Louis, Kansas City, etc.—but
the majority of Americans live near the Atlantic, Pacific, and Gulf
Coasts. (Buying raw land in and around urban centers along our coastlines can make you very wealthy very fast.)

But you don't have to buy just in coastal areas, because America is starting to spread out. We are a highly mobile population. Americans move often, for dozens of reasons—better opportunities, improved climate and living conditions. When Horace Greeley said "Go West, young man," he was referring to land opportunities. We have been slowly, but increasingly, following his advice. For the first time in our country's history, more people live in the South and West than in the Northeast and North Central states. Table 1-3 shows how the center of population has been shifting westward. Rural areas and small towns grew faster (15 percent) than metropolitan areas (9.5 percent) during the 1970s, reversing a 150-year trend. Most of the 30 million persons that we will be adding to our numbers in the next 15 years will be settling in and around existing urban, suburban, and small town communities. (This is where most of the profits in land investing will be made.)

As the suburbs expand, they will start connecting more populated communities to one another. Several growing areas of our country are becoming what demographers term a megalopolis—a giant, sprawling population center. If current trends continue, there will one day be a single, large megalopolis running from southern New Hampshire to the Commonwealth of Virginia. San Diego to San Francisco will be another. Several other metropolitan areas are so destined. Pundits in the business advise land investors to buy in the path of growth. In this regard, Will Rogers advised, "It's easy to make money. Just figure out where people are going, and then buy the land before they get there."

INFLATION

Inflation is the second paramount reason for land's rapid climb in value. The government cheapens the value of our dollars through the simple action of printing more of them as needed. The United States government is the largest borrower of funds, funds it needs to carry out its everyday operations. In 1984 the government spent at the astounding rate of $1.6 millions per minute. This spending is predicted to

Table 1-3
The Westward Shift

Date	Population	% Growth	Acres Per Capita	Geographic Center of Population
1790	3,929,214	--	484.6	E. of Baltimore, Md.
1800	5,308,483	35	358.7	W. of Baltimore, Md.
1810	7,239,881	36	262.9	N.W. of Wash., D.C.
1820	9,638,453	33	197.4	E. of Moorefield, W. Va.
1830	12,866,020	33	148.0	S.W. of Moorefield
1840	17,069,453	32	111.5	S. of Clarkesburg, W. Va.
1850	23,191,876	35	82.1	S.E. of Parkersburg, W. Va.
1860	31,443,321	35	60.6	S.E. of Chillicothe, Ohio
1870	39,818,449	26	47.8	N.E. of Cincinnati, Ohio
1880	50,155,783	25	37.9	S.W. of Columbus, Ohio
1890	62,947,714	25	30.2	E. of Columbus, Ind.
1900	76,094,000	20	25.0	S.E. of Columbus, Ind.
1910	92,407,000	21	20.6	Bloomington, Ind.
1920	106,461,000	15	17.9	S.E. of Spencer, Ind.
1930	123,188,000	15	15.5	N.E. of Linton, Ind.
1940	132,288,000	7	14.4	S.E. of Carlisle, Ind.
1950	151,718,000	14	12.5	N.E. of Olney, Ill.
1960	180,007,000	18	10.6	N.W. of Centralia, Ill.
1970	204,335,000	11	9.4	E.S.E. of Mascoutah, Ill.
1980	226,548,861	10	8.4	W. of DeSoto, Mo.

increase dramatically before the turn of the century, speeding up the inflationary climb.

I'm not going to explain how to control or even decrease inflation; I don't know how. Even the "experts" in the economics field and political arena differ substantially on this. Suffice it to say that inflation is an undesirable condition of modern times that is not very likely to go away. It's built into our system with historical patterns of inflationary waves. It's part of life and, with periodic interruptions, it's as much of a sure thing as the dreaded tandem of death and taxes. We have to learn to live with it.

In some parts of the world inflation is galloping well into triple digits, particularly in Argentina, Brazil, and many other Latin-American countries: many commodities increase in price daily.

In this century inflation in certain countries reached astronomical and unimaginable heights. In 1922, in post-war Germany, inflation reached a lofty 3500% and spiraled upward from there, completely destroying the German monetary system.

We're more fortunate in this country. Inflation, as undesirable as it is, is at least at palatable levels. In 1864 it was as high as 30 percent, but in recent years it has ranged from less than 2 percent to close to 14 percent.

Table 1-4
Inflation, 1960—1986

Year	Inflation Rate	Year	Inflation Rate	Year	Inflation Rate
1960	1.6%	1969	5.4%	1978	7.7%
1961	1.0%	1970	5.9%	1979	11.3%
1962	1.1%	1971	4.3%	1980	13.5%
1963	1.2%	1972	3.3%	1981	10.4%
1964	1.3%	1973	6.2%	1982	6.1%
1965	1.7%	1974	11.0%	1983	3.2%
1966	2.9%	1975	9.1%	1984	4.2%
1967	2.9%	1976	5.8%	1985	3.8%
1968	4.2%	1977	6.5%	1986	4.1% (est.)

In 1980, when we were struggling through 13.5 percent inflation, economists thought that double-digit inflation was here to stay. Instead it decreased. Yet we know that it's only a matter of time until the upward spiral recurs. It's not a matter of *if*, but rather *when*. During the twentieth century more than four out of five years have been inflationary, and since World War I nearly every year has been.

One of the most disturbing aspects of inflation is its tendency to accelerate. From 1950 to 1965 the average inflation rate was a steady and enviable 1 or 2 percent per year. The latter half of the 1960s saw it doubling to 4 percent and better. During the 1970s it first declined, then it raced into double digits. High, but definitely better than the world as a whole. In the ten leading industrial nations, the rate was 2.5 percent per year during the 1950s, up to 3.5 percent per year in the 1960s, and over 9 percent throughout the 1970s (Table 1-4).

The Consumer Price Index (CPI) is a measure of the average change in prices over time in a fixed "market basket" of goods and services purchased by a sampling of Americans. The CPI is based on prices of food, clothing, shelter, fuels, transportation fares, charges for doctors' and dentists' services, drugs, and other goods and services purchased for everyday living. Prices are gathered in 85 areas around the country from over 24,000 tenants, 18,000 housing units for property taxes, and 32,000 establishments. All taxes associated with the purchase and use of items are included in the index. Each item is weighted for its relative importance in consumers' budgets. The CPI is a statistic unto itself. It is also one of the yardsticks for measuring inflation. In this regard, the percentage of increase each year in the CPI reflects the percentage of increase in inflation.

Inflation also has a profound affect on borrowing. As inflation increases, so do all the borrowing indicators. From 1978 to 1980, as banks' prime rate doubled, housing starts fell by one-half. During an inflationary period it is advantageous to be a borrower, because inflation inflicts heavy damage upon creditors by reducing the future value of today's loans. Borrowers are ahead of the game, since they pay off their debts in dollars that have been reduced in value through inflation. The creditor's loss is the debtor's gain. Even the law, in this regard, favors debtors. The interest that debtors must pay on the loan is a deductible expense; whereas the creditor must pay an income tax on this same interest.

If you think that inflation is going to increase substantially and stay for an extended period of time, then you have to turn to investments that make you a borrower instead of a creditor. The younger segment of today's population is in a better position than the elderly to take advantage of this. When you're young, with limited erodible assets, you can borrow on your future earning capacity and pay back your debts with cheaper dollars. The elderly, on the other hand, generally have accumulated many erodible assets over their lifetime, through savings accounts, insurance policies, and similar investment and savings mediums. In doing this they have, in effect, become creditors. A savings account is really a loan to a bank for a fixed interest rate. An insurance policy, also a form of a loan, is generally paid in full by the time one becomes a senior citizen, and it will also yield cheaper dollars to its beneficiary.

Inflation also means that your dollar buys fewer goods. Stated another way, it takes more dollars to buy any good or service. If inflation should average out to 5 or 6 percent, it won't take very long for a pound of hamburger, or any meat or fish for that matter, to exceed six, seven, or eight dollars per pound. Twenty years ago you could buy a nickel candy bar; today, that same candy bar costs forty cents, and it's smaller in size (Table 1-5). The five cent newspaper of twenty years ago is now thirty cents, a 600 percent increase. The four cent stamp of that era is on its way to costing fifty cents. New cars were selling for two thousand dollars. What kind of car can you buy today for two thousand dollars? It costs practically that much for routine maintenance. A gallon of gas then was thirty cents. What is it today? Where will it be at the turn of the century if we average 5 or 6 percent inflation (which, by the way, is considered low by our economic prognosticators)?

Those of us who have been savers, thrifty as we thought we have been, are big losers too, because inflation obliterates savings account interest. An annual inflation rate of just 5 percent means that prices double in fifteen years. At 8 percent, they double in nine years. Using the Rule of 72, divide the inflation rate into 72 to see how long it will take your money to be worth half its present value in real purchasing power. Table 1-6 shows how inflation has eroded over 75 percent of the buying power of the American dollar in just the past two decades. Brace yourself: another 90 percent of today's dollar value will disap-

Table 1-5
Our Eroding Purchasing Power

Product	1967	1985	Increase
New Home	$23,000.00	$83,000.00	360%
New Car	$2,000.00	$12,000.00	600%
Postage Stamp	.05	.22	440%
Cigarettes	.35	$1.25	357%
Doctor's Visit	$6.00	$25.00	500%
Washing Machine	$220.00	$500.00	227%
One Rose	$1.00	$2.25	225%
Pound of Coffee	.49	$2.90	591%
Candy Bar	.05	.40	800%
Newspaper	.05	.30	600%

pear well within the next two decades. By the year 2000 our dollar's value will drop to a disgustingly low 2.5 cents relative to the 1967 dollar.

Not all assets are so negatively affected by our insidious enemy. Since the price of everything goes up, so too does its value. Price and value aren't always the same thing, but in this case they are virtually synonymous. Hard assets such as real estate, precious metals, and collectibles can possess enduring value and, like any other inflation-affected commodity, increase in value. It is this increase in value during inflationary times, and every other time too, that makes real estate such an ideal inflation hedge: its increase in value has historically outgained inflation's increases. Land is particularly appealing to the investor because it has proven to be an excellent investment vehicle under both favorable and adverse economic conditions.

In 1972 Homer Hoyt, a leading land economist, wrote a book titled "Investment in Vacant Land as a Hedge against Inflation." He advised

Table 1-6
Purchasing Power of the Dollar

Date	Value	Date	Value	Date	Value
1967	$1.00	1974	.67	1981	.36
1968	.96	1975	.62	1982	.34
1969	.91	1976	.58	1983	.33
1970	.86	1977	.55	1984	.32
1971	.82	1978	.51	1985	.30
1972	.79	1979	.46	1986	.29 (est.)
1973	.75	1980	.40	1987	.27 (est.)

land investors that a potential end-use must be determined for land to justify its purchase. He listed the following generalizations:

1. Vacant land that will never yield an income in the foreseeable future may have no justified value—even in times of inflation. Though speculation may increase sales prices, this possibility cannot be safely relied on for investment purposes.
2. Even in metropolitan areas there is more vacant land than can be absorbed for urban use.
3. Zero population growth lessens the total demand for land.
4. The no-growth policies of some communities prevent future building.
5. Redevelopment by building high-rise apartments, townhouses, and suburban apartments lowers the total demand for subdivision acreage.
6. The movement from metropolitan centers increases the demand for land in fringe areas.
7. Overbuilding of urban properties, offices, apartments, shopping centers, or factories decreases the short-run demand for urban land.
8. Environmental controls increase the cost of developing land, lowering vacant land values.

9. The demand for vacant land is contingent upon the availability of credit for new construction. Credit sources are scarce under inflationary conditions.

You may agree or not with any of these points made by Mr. Hoyt, but you will have to agree that inflation is on the side of the land investor and reduces his risks. As a rule, the higher the return on an investment, the greater the risk factor. Well located land is the exception. It pays a high return with a high degree of safety. It has an intrinsic security. It cannot be destroyed or stolen, and it hasn't, and won't, substantially decrease in value.

Both supply and demand and inflation are primary causes for the escalation in land values. However, there are also other sound reasons to invest in land—leverage and tax benefits, for instance.

LEVERAGE

Leverage means investing the least possible amount of your own money and borrowing the rest. Buying land with O.P.M. (other people's money) is leverage. Unlike other investments, you can buy land with a minimal down payment. You can't do that easily with gold or silver, stamps or coins, diamonds or rubies, or stocks and bonds. You can't do it with a savings account either--your interest earned is based only on what you have deposited in full. Thanks to leverage, you can control a large parcel of land with only a fraction of its worth. Land can be purchased with a 10 percent down payment and a mortgage for the rest. Each dollar of investable cash can be matched by nine dollars of mortgage money. A $10,000-dollar down payment will purchase a $100,000 parcel for you.

Leverage is a very important tactic for the investor today. It not only reduces the amount of capital that you have to commit up front, thereby allowing you to buy much larger properties than you could otherwise afford, but it allows you to get the maximum return from your committed funds. For example: if you paid $50,000 cash for a parcel of land and a year later sold it for $75,000, you would have earned a 50 percent return on your invested capital. However, had you used leverage and put down 10 percent of the purchase price ($5000) and made payments over the year towards the principal (another $5000) for a grand total of $10,000 committed, you would have earned a 250 percent return on your invested capital:

	Cash	Leverage
Profit	$\dfrac{\$25,000}{\$50,000} = 50\%$	$\dfrac{\$25,000}{\$10,000} = 250\%$
Invested		

Land is stable. There's a basic strength and soundness to it. The wind's not going to blow it away. It can't be destroyed. A thief can't take it from you. And it's always going to have some value. It has on infrequent occasions decreased in value. But it always comes back. Generally, the worst that happens is that the increase levels off periodically before resuming its rise. In the early days of our country, George Washington, in a letter to his stepson, J. P. Custis, advised

> Reflection must convince you of two things: first that lands are of permanent value;that there is scarcely a possibility of their falling in price, but almost certainty of their rising exceedingly in value.

TAX BENEFITS

The IRS is on the side of the land investor. You can deduct the mortgage interest payments and real estate taxes yearly from ordinary income, and you pay no tax on the appreciated value of the property until it's sold. In the current environment of tax reform, you have to keep abreast of any changes in tax regulations that could affect your investment activities. Installment sales too work to the benefit of the land investor by spreading out revenues and taxes over a period of time. You pay taxes only on the amount you receive, not on the full amount of the sale.

DISADVANTAGES

There are indeed some disadvantages to investing in land, some caveats that you should know about. They're truly insignificant relative to the advantages, and they are usually overstressed by those that don't fully understand land investing.

Illiquidity

Foremost among some of the negative features of land investing is its alleged illiquidity. To be liquid, an investment must be easily and readily convertible to cash. (Cash doesn't have to be converted to anything—it's our medium of exchange.) Land is difficult to convert to cash in a hurry. You have to find a buyer, ready, willing, and able; and even then there's a delay of several days, or even weeks, between the date of the sale and the closing when you receive your cash. If you own gold, silver, or similar commodities, they are very liquid and can be converted immediately to cash. In the stock market, your broker can sell your stocks in one or two days. Many investors feel that illiquidity is land's biggest drawback. However, unreasonably high pricing is the cause of much of the illiquidity. Priced reasonably and marketed aggressively, most land will sell within thirty days. If you need money in a hurry, rather than selling hastily, perhaps at a bargain price, you could remortgage the land and use this cash for your immediate needs and take your time selling the land, paying off the new mortgage with the sales proceeds.

Refinancing land to have liquid capital won't be too difficult. But for new purchases, land financing is a bit more difficult to obtain from most traditional sources. Some lenders look on raw land as being too speculative. They're used to financing homes, apartments, and similar income-producing properties. A bank, you realize, will not evaluate a parcel of raw land on the same basis as you will. You'll be considering its future value. The bank will be looking at its immediate value and income-producing capacity, if any. A bank wants to be quite sure that it can get all of its money back should you default on the loan.

Carrying Costs

Time is another negative factor to consider. While you own the land, you have to pay the carrying costs of the mortgage interest and the real estate taxes. You should buy the land, improve it, and resell it reasonably fast in order to keep carrying costs from eroding potential profits to any great extent. Also, raw land doesn't produce any income for its owner; the carrying costs must be paid out of the owner's own pocket. It would be wise to hold onto the land, however, during a high inflation period, since the value of the land will be appreciating more than enough to compensate for carrying costs.

It's important to understand the true reasons you are considering land investing. Too often, the reasons are illusory or cosmetic. It may seem to be an exciting thing to do, and it is, but this is hardly a sound reason for doing it. You also have to temper your efforts and reasons not only because of the amount of time and money that you have available for this purpose, but you have to analyze your own emotional make-up. If you're overly conservative, and always second-guessing your decisions, you may find land investing to be fraught with too many anxiety-causing elements. You should have a good rein on your nerves and an adventuresome spirit to enter into this endeavor. If you do, the seas will be relatively calm. If you tend to worry, you can still succeed very well, but the waters will be choppy and present many imaginary submerged snags. The best advice I can give is not to get too nervous about buying and selling land. You're really not spending money, you're investing it. You'll get it all back with dividends.

THE MONEYMAKING POTENTIAL OF REAL ESTATE

The single most important reason for you to commit your funds and your valuable time to investing in land is to make money. All other reasons are insignificant in comparison. You may have a full-time job that you expect to continue working at while supplementing your income with a part-time foray into land investing. With only a limited amount of time and effort, you will probably earn more from this activity than from your full-time job—unless your weekly earnings are exceptionally high. On a part-time basis you can work just the weekends, even limiting yourself to Saturdays, and still be quite successful. I've been in this business for over a decade, and from my own experience I've found that the bulk of my land buying and selling was conducted on Saturdays.

Not too many of us are disciplined enough to systematically put a sum of money away for a rainy day. There's always a need elsewhere for our discretionary income (the amount of money left over after all our bills have been paid)—the weekend trip, the ballgame, a new suit, whatever. In purchasing a parcel of land you are in effect setting up a forced savings plan for yourself. The land will have a mortgage on it, of course, and each month the bank will send you a notice reminding you to send them a payment. Naturally, you'll pay this bill. The weekend trip and the ballgame will be put off to another day. As you pay the mortgage bill, you're actually paying yourself. And some of the payment goes to interest and taxes, which are both deductible expenses. Most of the payment, however, will be applied towards reducing the principal amount of the loan. Each payment towards the principal increases your equity, or ownership, in the land. Besides the equity build-up, your land is appreciating at the same time, which further increases your equity.

CHAPTER II

REAL PROPERTY vs. PERSONAL PROPERTY

Under our legal system, property is regarded as either personal property (personalty), or real property (realty). It is important to you, the investor, to understand the differences between the two, since the classification affects a number of legal rights. I'll explain what the various classifications of real estate are later; for now, let's learn about personal property.

PERSONAL PROPERTY

Personal property are items that are not permanently affixed to, nor are a part of, land or buildings. In short, movable items—furniture, farm animals, money, clothing, and the like. In fact, leaseholds, or leases (about which you will learn shortly) are considered not as realty, but as personalty. Taking it one step further, personalty is all property that does not fit the description of realty.

It's a very simple procedure to buy or sell items of personalty. A simple handshake, or a nod of the head, coupled by the delivery of the sold item will usually suffice. For items over $500 a "bill of sale" does the job. However, when personalty and realty are mixed, it can get confusing in determining which is which. In some states a third classification called mixed property is recognized, and in those states legal decisions can certainly get quite sticky.

Personalty and realty questions always arise in the sale of a residence. If the home has a mortgage on it, the realty serves as the security for the loan, not the personalty which is kept inside the home, nor the personalty stored outside like an automobile, a wheelbarrow, or garden implements.

Some realty can become personalty and vice versa. A large tree in the back yard is part of the real estate, but if it is cut down and split into firewood, which is movable, it becomes personalty. If the tree is cut into building lumber, which is then used to add a room onto the house—it goes from realty, to personalty, and back to realty. Topsoil, which is a scarce commodity in some communities, is part of the land itself and is classified as realty. If it is scraped off and trucked away, it becomes personalty. When placed around a new homesite, it becomes realty again. Other elements of the land, trees, bushes, and natural vegetation that do not require periodic cultivation, are realty. But annual crops that a farmer plants such as corn, soybeans, wheat, and strawberries and that need cultivation are personalty and are legally defined as *emblements*. These items can be sold by a simple oral agreement. If a tenant farmer, who leases his land, is forced to vacate prior to harvesting the crops, the law will allow the tenant to return to harvest the crops under what is termed as a *tenancy at will* lease.

When a house is sold what does the new owner acquire? When you sell your home without specifically writing down what is to go along with the sale, it is generally understood that immovable items like sinks and light fixtures are included in the sale, but movable items like drapes and a washing machine are not included.

Realty is controlled by laws of the state in which the property is located. Thus the classification of whether property is realty or personalty is important in determining in which state property disputes will be settled. When items regarded as personal property are conveyed with the realty, they are classified as fixtures.

Fixtures

An item that was originally personalty is termed a fixture if it is installed or attached to the realty in a permanent manner. Built-in bookcases, for example, are a fixture because they have been installed onto the realty in a permanent manner. Plumbing and heating systems, kitchen cabinetry, and a built-in stereo system have all become part of the real estate and are now fixtures. When the realty is sold, the fixtures are included in the sale—unless specifically excepted.

Items owned and attached to a leased building by a tenant for use in conducting a business are also called fixtures, but there is a distinction—they are *trade fixtures*. Trade fixtures, also called *chattel fixtures,* are removable items of personal property that are attached to the realty, but are not considered as realty themselves and are not included in a sale of the property. Examples of trade fixtures are retail shelving, restaurant equipment, overhead cranes, and other similarly attached, but removable, equipment. A lessee is allowed, by law, to remove trade fixtures when vacating the premises any time prior to the expiration of his lease if the removal does not materially damage the real estate or the fixture itself. If a lessee, for instance, had bolted chairs to the floor in a waiting room and installed shelves on the wall to hold reading matter, he or she may remove them if their removal doesn't damage the floor or walls. Trade fixtures differ from other fixtures (*fixtures of realty*) in that trade fixtures are generally owned by the tenant, while fixtures of realty are the property of the owner of the real estate. Fixtures of realty are classified as real estate and are included in the sale of the real estate. Trade fixtures are not included in the sale of the real estate.

It is important to decide if a fixture is personalty or realty. There are many potential consequences. If the building burns down, the fixtures usually are not covered by the insurance on the building, whereas if they were part of the realty they would be. If a tenant attaches a fixture that hasn't been paid for, will the seller be able to reclaim it upon default or does it now belong to the real estate owner? When property is assessed for taxation purposes, the inclusion of the fixtures in the assessment increases the total valuation resulting in higher taxes to the real estate owner (unless they are trade fixtures, in which case they will be taxed as personal property to the lessee).

The courts, in determining what is a fixture of realty and what is a trade fixture takes into consideration the intent of the parties and the method of annexation. At the time the fixture was originally attached to the property, the intent of the parties is important in deciding the fixture's classification as realty or personalty. If a pharmacist leased a store to conduct his or her business and bolted display cases to the floor, it is his or her right to remove them when the lease expires. The display cases are a necessary and integral part of the pharmacist's business, and it was never his or her intent to make them a permanent part of the building. If the owner of a small assembly plant told a prospective buyer that the entire operation was being sold, and the buyer stated that he or she wanted a complete operation, the owner cannot later say that the assembly machinery was not part of the realty. The courts will determine from the intent of both parties that the entire operation is included in the sale—realty and machinery. Courts generally lean toward the tenant in disputes of this type. Just about anything the tenant installs may be removed if it doesn't damage the real estate or the fixture itself. If the item is not removed prior to termination of the lease, the lessee cannot later return and remove it.

In deciding upon the classification of the fixture, the court will look at the manner in which it was attached to the real estate. If it was affixed with the intent of being there permanently or until it wore out, then it would be part of the realty. A furnace, for instance, cannot be removed very well without causing substantial damage to the real estate. Other items that are simply screwed in, bolted down, or plugged in like a freezer case are not permanently affixed and are trade fixtures. If expressly agreed upon between the parties, the lessee may remove the fixture regardless of the manner of annexation. The lessee, however, is obligated to pay for any damages to the realty caused by the removal.

REAL PROPERTY

Real property has several synonyms, among the most common being land, real estate, and realty. Although they are synonymous and used interchangeably, there are essential differences between them.

Land is the solid part of the earth's crust. "Under all is the land." That's the expression used in the opening statement of the REAL-TOR'S^R Code of Ethics. Actually, land is "under all" and "over all." Legally, land is the surface, the subsurface, and the air space above the land. It is the surface of the earth, extending to its center and upward to infinity. It includes things of permanency formed by nature. This would be soil, natural vegetation like trees and bushes, waterways like ponds, lakes, and rivers, and minerals and other elements found in the ground.

Realty includes the land itself with all of its natural resources, as well as artificial additions such as houses, factories, fences, landscaping, roadways, and every other such improvement of a permanent nature.

Real estate includes all of the above physical components of the land, added by both humans and nature, as well as all its inherent interests, benefits, and rights of ownership.

Nevertheless, throughout this book *land, realty, real estate,* and *real property* will be used interchangeably.

Mineral Rights

Minerals, both solid (ore, coal, etc.) and liquid (oil and gas), all belong to the owner of the real estate. They are all classified as real property until they are removed from the ground and become personal property. When real estate is transferred, all the minerals go with the sale. Once they become personal property, however, they do not go with the sale.

A pile of coal, for instance, would not be part of the sale unless specifically included. Mineral rights can be sold or leased without selling the land. You could also sell your land to one party and the rights to the minerals to another. Or you could sell the land and retain the mineral rights. Many energy companies lease the rights to dig or drill for oil, gas, and coal on a person's land rather than buy the land outright. This way they don't tie up too much working capital. When their efforts are over, they simply vacate the premises and the owner still has possession and title to the land. Extricating liquid resources from the ground is a bit more involved. Some states, particularly the oil-producing states, apply the *rule of capture* to liquid resources. Under this rule, the landowner or an assignee (the lessee of drilling rights) takes ownership to oil and gas from wells on the land even though some of the oil or gas is being extracted from under surrounding parcels.

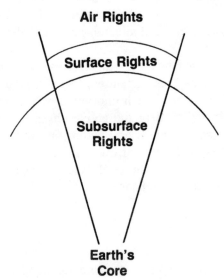

Figure 2-1. Real estate ownership rights.

Figure 2-1 shows the extent of the rights and ownership interests of real estate. The rights descend to the core of the earth and include the ownership of all minerals and substances in the ground. The rights of ownership go up to infinity also, and include the right to use the air space above the earth.

Air Rights

A landowner once owned the air space above his or her land all the way to the pearly gates. This was in effect until the advent of the airplane and, of course, orbiting satellites. The landowner now owns as much of the space above the land as can be reasonably used or occupied. The courts have decided that the air space may be entered for legitimate travel and commerce. The government has declared sovereignty over the navigable air space—it is now an aerial highway. There are many disputes today from property owners near airports over noise pollution and low-flying aircraft.

The owner may sell or lease the air space over his or her land. In many large cities around the country, air space has become a highly sought-after and marketable commodity. Often buildings and other commercial enterprises are constructed in the air space over railroad yards and highways. In Boston the multibuilding Prudential Insurance Company complex was built over the Massachusetts Turnpike. The Pan-Am Building in New York City and the Merchandise Mart in Chicago were also built in air space.

Water Rights

Laws regarding water rights were written to prevent the waste of water and to allow the public fair and equitable use of available water sources. Each state has its own water laws regarding ownership and use, and it would be a voluminous study to document them all here. What follows will be the basic theory; the readers must research the water laws of their own states.

Water is classified as *surface water* or *underground water.* In either case each is considered as part of the real estate, but because of the nature of water it doesn't adapt itself to possession as does land. In this respect, a property right in water is really only a right of use.

Surface Waters   Surface waters are lakes, ponds, rivers, streams, springs, marshes, and bogs. A landowner's rights generally depend upon whether his land fully contains the water or simply borders on it. Water that is wholly contained within a landowner's boundary lines can be used solely by the landowner. If it is not wholly contained within the boundary lines, the landowner has the right to use it in common with other water abutters. Each owner may divert some of the flow of the water onto his or her own land or slow down the flow with a dam, as long as it does not interfere with the rights of the other abutters. However, eight states follow the "natural flow" system of water rights and do not allow the abutters to interrupt or alter the flow, nor contaminate the water in any way. These states are Georgia, Maine, Mississippi, Missouri, New Jersey, Pennsylvania, South Dakota, and Virginia.

Diffused Surface Waters   Another form of surface water is surface water caused by storms, rain, snow, or spring runoff. This *diffused surface water* is defined as water that does not flow in a well-defined channel and is not confined to a well-defined basin. Naturally, it can cause serious problems for landowners, and an owner's first inclination is to get rid of the excess water. Most states will allow a landowner to alter the topography of the land so that the unwanted water will flow off. Causing the excess to run into a nearby lake or river would be, legally speaking, the ideal solution.

Alabama, California, Georgia, Illinois, Kansas, Kentucky, Pennsylvania, and Tennessee follow the "natural flow" doctrine regarding diffused surface waters, which rules that water must be allowed to flow in its natural path. Landowners are prohibited from inhibiting or interrupting the natural flow of water even if it damages their land. Several other states (Arizona, Arkansas, Hawaii, Indiana, Missouri, Nebraska, New York, North Dakota, Oklahoma, Virginia, West Virginia, and Wisconsin) follow the *common enemy* doctrine. This rule states that excess surface water is an enemy to the landowner and he or she may redirect it from damaging the land by any means available. However, the landowner must not act unreasonably or negligently in redirecting the flow of water and cause unnecessary damage to adjoining lands. If the landowner has no alternative but to direct the water onto an adjoining parcel, and it damages the neighbor's land, it is in the eyes of the law "injury without wrong." If your next-door neighbor diverts excess surface water onto your land, you, in turn, can divert it onto another neighbor's land, and that person onto another neighbor's.

Riparian Rights   If the water is nonnavigable, it is governed by the common-law doctrine of *riparian rights*. If a stream were to be one of your boundary lines, you own to the middle of the stream, as you would with a street. When you sell your property, the riparian water rights go to the new owner.

Littoral Rights   Land abutting on large, navigable waterways is governed by the doctrine of littoral rights. The coasts of the Pacific and Atlantic Oceans and the Gulf of Mexico and coastline of Alaska total more than 88,000 miles; an additional 11,000 miles border the five Great Lakes. There are also more than 100,000 natural lakes in this country. Navigable waters are regarded as public highways that the public has a right to use.

The littoral owner owns the property to the water's edge. For oceans, bay, and gulf waters the boundary is the high-water mark. The state owns the land between high and low tide—the flatlands or foreshore. The federal government owns the land under the water from the low tide mark out to the international limit of twelve miles; the rest of the world owns the land beyond this. The littoral owner has unrestricted rights to use the water as long as the owner's use does not interfere with the rights of others to use the same water.

If the boundary line of your property is on a navigable stream that may shift in direction over a period of years, your property line shifts with the stream. If soil is gradually deposited on your land during the shifting process, it becomes part of your property. This is called *accretion*. However, if the stream's change of position was caused by a sudden storm, or by some other sudden act of nature, then the accretion doctrine does not apply and the boundary lines do not legally change.

You can also lose land through an act of nature called *erosion*.

Underground Waters   Underground waters, except those flowing in underground streams, are termed *percolating waters*. The right to use subsurface water is similar to the rights to extract liquid minerals like oil and gas. Ground water is rainwater that has filtered through the surface of the land and is stored in geological formations. The larger formations are called aquifers.

It takes a long time for the rainwater to get underground. Most ground waters move horizontally at a rate of between 10 and 100 feet per year. The United States Department of Agriculture estimates the average age of underground water (the amount of time it has been underground) to be about 150 years. Some is as old as 20,000 years.

Aquifers supply wells. Almost 50 percent of Americans depend upon ground water for their drinking supplies. Ground water supplies 25 percent of all water used in the country and 40 percent of all irrigation water.

In states where water is a scarce commodity, the ownership and use of water resources is determined by the doctrine of *prior appropriation*. This includes all of the western and midwestern states. Under this doctrine, the right to water use is state-controlled rather than controlled by adjacent landowners, except for normal domestic use. If there is plenty of water in a river or stream, anyone with a permit can use the water. When the water becomes scarce, during droughts and the like, the priority of use is determined by the date of issue of each permit. The first permit-holder, chronologically, is called a *prior appropriator*. He or she is permitted to draw off all of the water he or she can reasonably use without regard for other abutters along the waterway. To obtain a state-issued permit, an owner must show a beneficial use for the water, for example farming and irrigation. The principle of prior appropriation is "first in time is first in right." Therefore, it is important that a person file for a permit as soon as possible to obtain the fullest possible water rights. Persons filing later have secondary water rights and must give way to the needs of the prior appropriator.

CHAPTER III

LAND DESCRIPTION AND SURVEY

Land ownership in the United States is controlled by such a complicated array of federal and state laws that it is practically impossible for a nonlawyer to clearly and fully understand them. Differing judicial interpretations of these laws further complicate the matter. Consequently, you must hire a lawyer to handle all your land transactions. However, hiring a lawyer shouldn't relieve you of the need to understand the basic legal aspects of land transactions, particularly in view of the fact that you may be fairly active in buying and selling land as an investor and perhaps as a developer or subdivider. Understanding the "why's" and "wherefore's" of property descriptions is as important as any of the other legal functions of land buying and selling.

LEGAL DESCRIPTION

Historically, most problems of land ownership have arisen from boundary disputes. Even in this day and age, after countless centuries of land transference, boundary disputes continue to be a significant problem.

Seven thousand years ago the Egyptians initiated surveying. Other peoples have refined the techniques, with the land system of the British Isles having the greatest influence on how the land in the United States was described and surveyed.

In order to transfer land, the law requires that a deed contain a legal description of the property. The purpose of the description is to describe the parcel in such a way that it cannot be confused with any other parcel. The legal description does not have to be precise nor technically correct, but sufficient enough to enable a competent land surveyor to locate the boundaries. The legal description is a specific identification of a parcel that is acceptable in a court of law.

The average parcel of land has been sold, resold, and sold again. It has had numerous owners, been put to various uses, and its shape and topography may have been altered several times. You can buy land without a survey, but you could have trouble actually locating it on the ground. In order to have a complete and acceptable legal description precisely distinguishing one parcel from another, it is necessary to conduct a survey that measures and delineates the parcel. I'll explain shortly the elements and requirements of a legal survey.

There are three methods of property identification used and accepted by the courts: (1) metes and bounds, (2) rectangular survey, and (3) subdivision lot and block number. As America was growing and developing in colonial days, property was described by the metes and bounds method, which located land in relation to landmarks and natural objects such as trees, rocks, ponds, and streams. This complicated system eventually gave way to the rectangular system, which is used for most of the area west of the Ohio River. The subdivision lot and block number method is used mostly in urban areas.

Metes and Bounds

Metes and bounds is the oldest method of describing land in the United States. This method is used primarily in the eastern part of the country and also in describing irregularly shaped parcels in conjunction with the rectangular survey system. Metes and bounds means measurements and boundaries. Metes are measurements of distance, or length—feet, inches, rods, and meters that determine the quantity of land. Bounds are natural and artificial monuments that serve as the edges or boundaries of a parcel. A monument is an identifiable, or tangible, landmark that serves as a corner, or turning point, of a property. Natural monuments are trees, rocks, rivers, lakes, streams, and the like. Artificial monuments are man-made landmarks such as roads, fences, houses, canals, streets, stakes, and posts. A monument may also be an intangible, such as the center line of a street or the center of a stream.

There are two variations of the metes and bounds description: (1) by monuments, and (2) by geographic reference. The first variation, by monuments, does not require exact measurements or directions. The land is actually described narratively as though you were physically walking the perimeter of the parcel. You start out at an easily identifiable point of beginning, and each corner or turning point is identified by either a natural or artificial monument. If a survey is later taken and the distances are found to be different from the narrative property description, the monuments take precedence. This often happens when a monument has been accidentally destroyed or purposely removed. I'm sure you've heard tales where an unscrupulous abutter has moved a monument to illegally increase the size of his own parcel. It is against the law to remove any type of monument. This imprecise form of description does not calculate the exact acreage of the parcel, and therefore the final sentence in the written description will read "containing x acres more or less," or some words to that effect. These words allow for clarification of any discrepancy and strengthen the description. Here is a typical description by monuments:

> A tract of land located in Wharton, Connecticut, described as follows: Beginning at the intersection of the east line of Folsom Path and the south line of Red Wing Trail; thence easterly along the south line of Folsom Path about 250 feet; thence south about 300 feet to a large oak tree; thence westerly about 250 feet to the east line of Red Wing Trail; thence northerly to the point of beginning, and containing one and three quarters acres more or less.

The more precise metes and bounds form of description, by geographic reference, is prepared by a registered surveyor. This form furnishes exact measurements and directions of the property lines. It begins by reference to a permanent marker or *bench mark*. The National Geodetic Survey has imbedded over one million bronze markers in concrete around the country to indicate latitudes, longitudes, and elevations. A surveyor then will measure from one of these bench marks to the nearest corner of the parcel to be surveyed. From this point, called the *point of beginning* (POB), all the boundary lines are identified by length and direction. The following is the written description of the parcel measured by this method and shown in Figure *3-1*.

The land in Springfield, U.S.A., bounded and described as follows:
NORTHERLY By Lot 6 on a plan hereinafter mentioned, two hundred eighty five and 93/100 (285.93) feet;
EASTERLY By land now or formerly of John Smith, one hundred eight and 00/100 (108.00) feet;
SOUTHERLY By Lot 4 as shown on said plan, two hundred seventy three and 67/100 (273.67) feet;
WESTERLY By the Easterly sideline of Main Street, one hundred twenty five and 00/100 (125.00) feet.

Containing 32,621' square feet and shown as Lot 5 on a plan entitled "Plan of land in Springfield, U.S.A., owned by James Sheerin" and recorded in Washington County Registry of Deeds Plan Book 300 Page 44.

A complete metes and bounds description prepared by a surveyor should include the date of the survey, the surveyor's name, the source of the survey data, the identity of the parcel, all dimensions and directions of property lines, reference to two or more durable monuments, and names of abutters. If it is recorded at the registry of deeds, the book and page location should also be on the plan.

Metes and bounds descriptions are still used in the six New England

Plan of land in Springfield, U.S.A. owned by James Sheerin Recorded in Plan Book 300 Page 44.

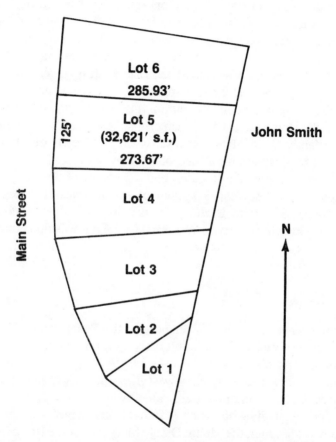

Figure 3-1. Plan of land to accompany a metes and bounds description by geographic reference

states, as well as Delaware, Georgia, Kentucky, Maryland, New Jersey, New York, North Carolina, Pennsylvania, South Carolina, Tennessee, Texas, Virginia, West Virginia, Hawaii, Washington, D.C., and parts of Ohio.

UNITED STATES GOVERNMENT SURVEY

After the Revolutionary War, pioneers, in ever-increasing numbers, moved westward establishing new frontiers. The federal government, in order to facilitate the settlement of the West, decided to sell the public lands and use the proceeds to retire the federal debt. A new system of survey was needed. The rectangular, or government, survey system was approved by Congress in 1785, providing a simple and definite means of land identification. It is used in thirty of the states that joined the Union after the thirteen original colonies. The New England and Atlantic Coast States, Texas, Hawaii, and parts of Ohio are not covered by this system; all the other states are.

The system uses the latitudes and longitudes of the earth's surface (Figure 3-2) to develop a system of square grids, forming a huge checkerboard pattern. Each square is composed of four *quadrangles* each quadrangle comprises 16 *townships* each township is made up of 32 *sections* and each section can be further broken down into any desired size.

Quadrangles

Starting where the Ohio River crosses the Pennsylvania border and moving westward at 24-mile intervals, quadrangles are formed. Each quadrangle is bounded by north--south lines (parallel to longitudes) called *meridians,* and by east--west lines (parallel to latitudes) called *base lines*. Some meridians are called *principal meridians* to identify subsequent subdivision. Each is individually named such as the San ernadino Meridian, the Mount Diablo Meridian, or the Boise Meridian. There are 36 principal meridians located at key spots around the country (Figure 3-3). Each quadrangle then is an area of land 24 miles square and made up of 16 individual townships.

Townships

There are 16 townships within each quadrangle. Each township is a square 6 miles on each side, or 36 square miles. The townships are

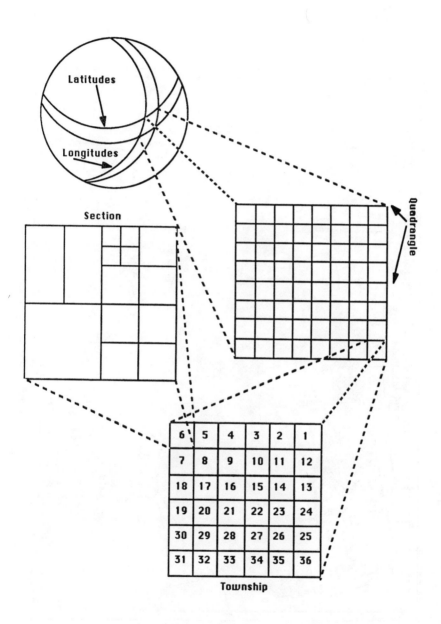

Figure 3-2. The government survey method

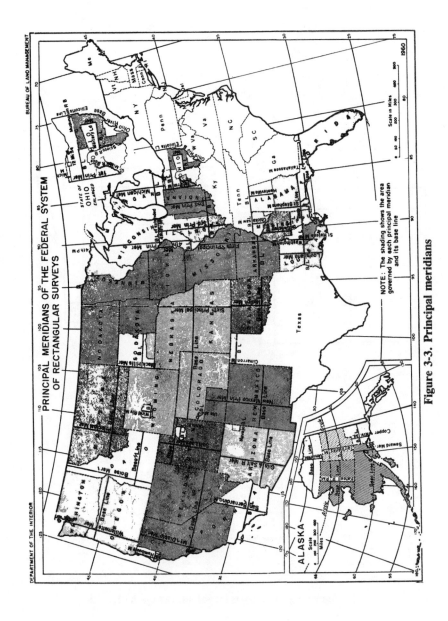

Figure 3-3. Principal meridians

identified by two coordinates. Those townships numbered in the horizontal direction (east--west) are called a tier of townships. There are 4 townships in each tier, numbered from one to four. Those townships numbered in the vertical direction (north--south) are called a range of townships. There are 4 townships in each range, numbered from one to four. The tier and range numbers together identify a specific township (Figure 3-4). Within each township there are 36 sections.

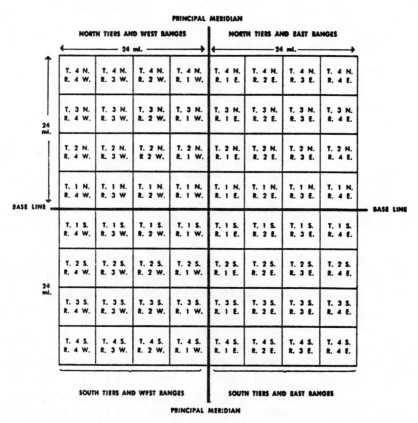

Figure 3-4. Townships by tiers and range

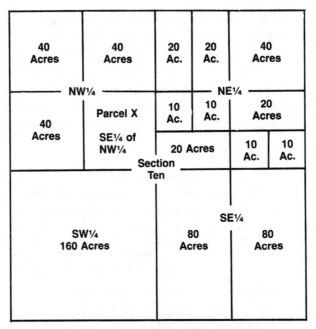

Figure 3-5. The division of a section

Sections

There are 36 sections in each township. Each section is one mile on a side, containing 640 acres. Each section within a township is numbered sequentially, 1 through 36, starting with the northeast section and moving alternately, serpentine, east to west then west to east, ending with section 36 in the southeast corner.

Each 640-acre section is then quartered into 160-acre parcels called *quarter sections* designated as the northeast, southeast, northwest, and southwest quarters. These quarter sections are then quartered into parcels of 40 acres, called *square forties*. A square forty can then be quartered into four parcels of 10 acres each, which, in turn, can be subdivided into five-acre parcels, etc. Figure 3-5 shows some possible subdivisions of a section.

In writing the description of a parcel you begin with the smallest portion and progress upward through all subdivisions to the section number, then township and range, finally identifying the principal meridian. You write the description from left to right; you read the description from right to left. The description of "parcel X" shown in Figure 3-5 would read: Southeast quarter of the Northwest quarter of Section 10. You would then read the township and range numbers and lastly the name of the principal meridian in which it is located.

Because of the curvature of the surface of the earth, the meridians converge at the North Pole; thus the north line of each section is shorter by about 50 feet than the south line. To compensate for this difference, every fourth parallel line is designated as a correction line.

Lot, Block, and Subdivision Method

This method of describing property is also called the *recorded subdivision method.* It is used in urban areas where there has been a lot of subdivisions of larger parcels into individual house lots. The rectangular survey system is too cumbersome to use in describing smaller parcels; the description tends to become too involved. It is also too awkward to describe city lots by a metes and bounds description.

This method comes about when a developer hires a surveyor to subdivide a parcel of raw acreage into several house lots. The surveyor first prepares a subdivision *plat,* showing the entire property, the proposed individual lots, their sizes and dimensions, proposed and existing streets, utility easements, and any other pertinent information such as monuments, waterways, stone walls, fences, etc. Each lot in the subdivision is assigned a number, and if there are blocks, each block is assigned a number. The plat must also include the name of the subdivision, the owner's name, the surveyor's name and registration number, the date of the survey, and spaces on the plat for the signatures of the members of the board who will approve this plan—usually the planning board. (Chapter XII goes into this process in detail). If the plan meets with all the subdivision and zoning ordinances of the community, it is approved and then can be recorded in the registry of deeds office. The registry will place the plat in the land records and assign it a book and page number for ready reference. Thereafter, any individual parcel may be identified by reference to its respective lot number and book and page number. This is also known as the title reference. When describing a parcel in a deed or other legal document, you simply refer to the title reference without having to type out the full description.

ELEMENTS OF SURVEYING

I tried to make the preceding explanation of property descriptions as lucid as possible. Still, I realize, it is confusing to the beginner. Therefore, an explanation of the elements of surveying will further help you to comprehend the three descriptive survey methods and to read a plot plan with some degree of understanding. A plot plan is a picture of the land you are buying or selling. Someone once said: "A picture is worth a thousand words." It certainly is where plot plans are concerned.

Most land buyers, even persons in the real estate business, think that a title search by an attorney is all that is needed. Actually, not many attorneys fully understand the problems inherent in property descriptions. The attorney will advise you about the completeness and legality of the title to land, but not about the true physical location of the subject parcel.

If you are buying land that has been surveyed, walk the parcel. Too few of us, even when purchasing a home, just look at the property casually and we take for granted the property lines. Assumptions are made from a distance. If a row of hedges is at the back of the property, often it's just taken for granted that this is the property line, when the true property line may be several feet in front of the hedges. Again, actually "walk" the boundaries of any and all properties you are considering buying. If you are buying unsurveyed land, as many parcels are, you will need both an attorney and a surveyor cooperating with one another to confirm, in precise terms, what you are actually buying.

Not every state has complete regulations governing land surveys.

Nor does every state require surveyors to be registered as professionals in their line of work with commensurate educational and training qualifications. A licensed surveyor is trained and authorized, by specific standards, to prepare a legal survey that sets forth the description and precise location of a parcel of land.

The first thing the surveyor does is to have a title search taken on the property. If the attorney has done this already, the surveyor will not completely rely on it; his or her own title searcher will double-check it. Once the research is complete, the surveyor will do a *field survey* by actually going onto the land and using professional equipment (transit and measuring devices) to locate the land and its boundaries. As previously mentioned, preimbedded bench marks are first located. From a bench mark, the surveyor will measure in distance and direction to the nearest corner of the subject parcel. This is termed the *point of beginning* (POB). From the POB each boundary line is identified by length and direction.

Angle Measurement

The direction of a boundary line is measured by its bearing in relation to north or south on a compass, in measurements of degrees, minutes, and seconds. A full circle around a central point consists of 360 degrees and is divided into four 90-degree quadrants identified as north, east, south, and west. For example, place a circle over your plot plan so that the exact center of the circle is directly over the point of beginning with the directional arrow pointing north. A line that runs a little north of due east would have a bearing of "North 70 East." Another line south of the first bearing might have a bearing of "South 85 East" (Figure 3-6). Bearings can be measured in either a clockwise or counterclockwise direction from north or south, but not in both directions on the same plot plan. The directional arrow points north on all plot plans. Each of the 360 degrees is made up of 60 minutes, and each minute consists of 60 seconds.

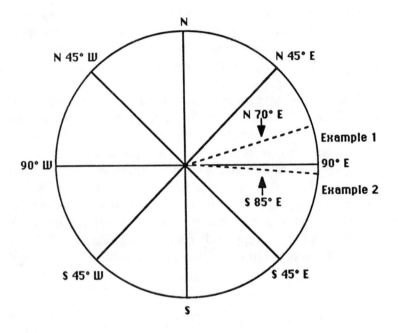

Figure 3-6. Method of angle measurement

Distance Measurement

The surveyor, in the measurement of distances, traditionally uses miles, feet, and inches. Years ago, a rod 16½ feet long was a highly used and convenient unit of measurement. Steel tapes have replaced the rod because they are longer, more accurate, and faster to use. The length of a property line is shown in feet to the nearest hundredth of a foot. For example, 89'.08 translates to eighty-nine and eight one-hundredths of a foot. Distance measurements are taken on a straight line without any consideration for height variations in the land's surface. For instance, as Figure 3-7 shows, a walking distance down a hillside of perhaps 1200 feet up and down the gradations would actually

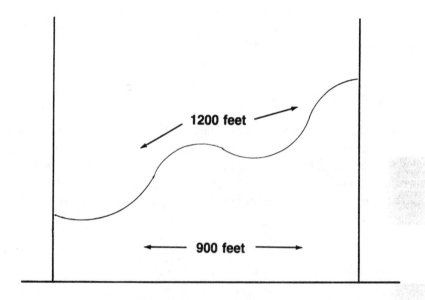

1200 feet

◄ — 900 feet — ►

Figure 3-7. Distance measurement for irregular land surface

be measured from a tape drawn taut in the air and measure perhaps only 900 feet in distance, not reflecting the rolling topography. To measure this distance in any other way than in the air would create numerous difficulties in real estate dealings.

Area Measurement

Land areas are measured in acres, square feet, and square miles. Perhaps the most commonly used number is 43,560. There are 43,560 square feet in an acre. Builders, developers, and many townships, when subdividing larger parcels, tend to round off the acre to 40,000 square feet. This is generally referred to as a "builder's acre." Thus, a

20,000-square-foot parcel would be considered a "builder's half acre."

To give you an idea of what an acre of land looks like in size: the playing area of a football field is 300 feet by 160 feet, or 48,000 square feet, which comes to 1.1 acres; that's one and one-tenth acres.

Elevation Measurement

Measurements of elevation are measured from mean sea level in New York harbor, which is the basic elevation point of reference for the United States. This is important to surveyors and developers in establishing street grades and the heights of buildings and other structures. These are measured from the bench marks preimbedded by the Geodetic Survey.

Corner Markers

Once your surveyor completes the job, you will also have the parcel physically located on the ground and set off with permanent bounds and corner markers. The type of marker used depends upon the codes of the community in which your land is located. Some typical corner markers used today are shown in Figure 3-8.

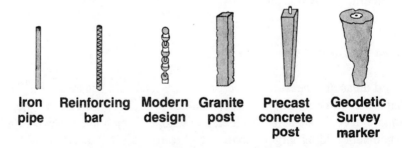

| Iron pipe | Reinforcing bar | Modern design | Granite post | Precast concrete post | Geodetic Survey marker |

Figure 3-8. Typical corner markers

Always walk the perimeter of the land with the person you are buying it from, whether it has been surveyed or not. Let the seller point out all the monuments and boundary markers that he or she knows about, even and including trees, rocks, and concrete posts—anything that is considered as a means of locating the boundaries. If the land is unsurveyed, then you, in turn, can walk the lines with your surveyor when you have a survey taken. Notify all the abutters, if possible, that you are having a survey taken and invite them to walk with you. If there are any discrepancies or disputes about property lines, then you and the abutter, along with the surveyor, could possibly work them out on the spot with a property line agreement rather than resorting to the courts for a remedy. The abutter may also have copies of old documents or deeds that may not have been recorded that will help in the survey. Your boundary line is also your abutter's boundary line, so abutters will usually be happy to work with you—especially since you will be paying for the survey.

Table 3-1
Some Basic Measure and Equivalents

Surveyor's Measures

1 link . . . . 7.92 inches	1 rood . . . . ¼ acre
25 links. . . . . 1 rod	10,890 sq. ft.
100 links. . . . . 1 chain	640 acres . . . . 1 sq. mile
1 rod . . . . 16.5 feet	1 section
4 rods . . . . 1 chain	36 sq. miles . . . . 1 township
80 chains . . . . 1 mile	36 sections

Measures of Length

1 hand. . . . . 4 inches	1 sq. yard . . . . 144 sq. inches
1 cubit . . . . 18 inches	1 sq. yard . . . . 9 sq. ft.
1 fathom . . . . 6 feet	1 sq. rod . . . . 272 ¼ sq. ft.
1 rod. . . . . 5½ yards	1 sq. rod . . . . 30"¼ sq. yards
1 furlong. . . . . 40 rods	1 sq. rood . . . . 40 sq. rods

Measures of Surface

Chapter III

Table 3-1 (Continued)
Some Basic Measure and Equivalents

Cubic Measures

1 cubic foot	1,728 cubic inches
1 cubic yard	17 cubic feet
1 standard bushel	2,150.42 cubic inches
1 standard gallon (liquid)	231 cubic inches
1 cubic foot	4/5 of a bushel
1 cord (wood)	128 cubic feet

An Acre Is:

		A Mile Is:
43,560 sq. ft.	5,280' × 8.25'	5,280 feet
4,840 sq. yds.	2,640' × 16.50'	1,760 yards
160 sq. rods	1,320' × 33'	320 rods
10 sq. chains	330' × 132'	80 chains
10 rods × 16 rods	220' × 198'	8 furlongs
5 rods × 32 rods	208.71' × 208.71'	3 mi. = 1 league
4 rods × 40 rods	165' × 264'	
4 sq. roods	110' × 396'	

Conversion to Metric Measures

1 inch = 2.540 centimeters	1 sq. inch = 6.5416 sq. cms.
1 foot = 0.3048 meter	1 sq. foot = 0.0929 sq. meter
1 yard = 0.9144 meter	1 sq. yard = 0.836 sq. meter
1 rod = 5.0292 meters	1 acre = 0.4047 hectare
1 mile = 1.609 kilometers	1 sq. mile = 2.590 sq. kms.

Circular Measures

60 seconds (") = 1 minute (')	90 degrees = 1 quadrant
60 minutes = 1 degree (°)	4 quandrants or
	360 degrees = 1 circle

52

CHAPTER IV

LAND OWNERSHIP AND LEGAL INTERESTS

Under real estate law in the United States, the rights of ownership, called the *bundle of rights,* include the right to control, possess, enjoy, and dispose of property in a legal manner. It also includes the right to use, to sell, to give as a gift, to improve, to destroy, to profit from, to remove objects from, and to will the property upon death. The courts use the terms ownership rights, property rights, and property interests interchangeably. Title also means ownership of property.

We don't actually own property; we own various rights in property. We often speak of these rights as an *estate* in real property, or simply as real estate. An estate is one or more rights with certain restrictions placed on the rights. For example, some estates cease upon the owner's demise, while others continue indefinitely. Some are owned by one person, others by multiple owners, or by spouses. Some include the right to possess for a period of time, and some have very few restrictions. These estates, or interests, are also called *tenancies.*

It's rather confusing with all of these different words having similar meanings: ownership, title, estate, rights, interests, and tenancy. You'll find this so throughout the real estate and legal professions, and most other professions for that matter. In baseball, isn't a home run also known as a homer, a grand slam, a four bagger, a round tripper, and several other names? However, as similar as they are, there are distinctions between them. A home run with one runner on base is different from a grand slam. So, too, are there distinctions in the numerous similar words of real estate law.

Estates in real estate are classified, on the basis of their duration, as either *freehold* or *nonfreehold* (also known as *leasehold*). Freehold estates exist for an indefinite length of time. That is, title may be held for the owner's lifetime and may be passed on by will unless it is sold or disposed of. The most common types of freehold estates are (1) *fee simple,* and (2) *qualified fee,* both of which continue for an indefinite period and are inheritable by the heirs of the owner, and (3) *life estate,* which ceases upon the death of the one on whose life it is based.

Leasehold estates last for a definite period of time, measured by years, months, weeks, or days. They are not ownership rights, but are considered as personal property. Where a freehold estate conveys ownership, a leasehold estate conveys only possession or use. An example would be an owner leasing land to a person to use for a specified period of time—a lease, in other words. The most common types of leasehold estates are (1) *estate for years,* (2) *periodic estate,* (3) *estate at will,* and (4) *estate at sufferance.*

FREEHOLD ESTATES

Fee Simple Estate

A *fee simple estate* is the best interest obtainable in real estate. The owner possesses all of the rights a person can have in land. The owner can do anything with the property as long as it is legal and does not interfere with the rights of others. It is subject, however, to the governmental limitations of *taxation, eminent domain,* and *police power.* I'll explain these limitations in another chapter.

The fee simple estate is of unlimited duration, and can be passed on to the owner's heirs. The terms *fee, fee simple,* and *fee simple absolute* all mean the same thing—complete ownership. All other estates are derivatives of the fee simple estate and are thus less than fee simple.

Qualified Fee Estate

A *qualified fee estate,* also known as a *determinable fee,* or a *conditional fee,* is an estate in fee simple with specified limitations. That is, it may be created upon the occurrence or nonoccurrence of a specified event, such as a man leaving his land to his daughter if she doesn't marry before she is twenty-five years old. On her twenty-fifth birthday she would inherit the land if she has not been married up to that time. It can also involve the conveyance of land upon certain conditions. For example, it may state that the land can only be used for recreational pursuits like hunting, fishing, or camping. If the specified condition ceases, that is, the land is developed for homesites, then title reverts back to the grantor or the grantor's heirs.

Life Estates

A *life estate* is a freehold in which the grantor conveys the land to the grantee for the rest of the grantee's lifetime. The life tenant is entitled to enjoy most of the rights of possession and use, including any income derived from the property. He or she is obligated to keep the property in good condition and to pay all the normal carrying costs, including taxes and mortgage interest, if any. It is an estate of indefinite duration, since it is not possible to determine how long the grantee will live. It is not an estate of inheritance—it cannot be conveyed to the life tenant's heirs. Upon the grantee's death, the life estate terminates and the grantee's interest in the land, called a *remainder,* either goes to a specified third party called a *remainderman,* or it reverts back to the original owner or his or her heirs. There are two types of life estates: *conventional life estates,* which are created by a conveyance by an owner, and *legal life estates,* which are created by operation of law without the consent of the owner. These are *dower, curtesy,* and *homestead rights.*

Legal Life Estates   The legal life estates of *dower, curtesy,* and *homestead* do not exist in every state. Where they are in effect, they vary widely in the quantity and quality of their rights.

Dower is the life estate, given by law, that a surviving wife has in her husband's land when he has died with no will (*intestate*) or when she is omitted from the will. Upon his death, her dower interest entitles her to a one-third life estate in all of his real property. The purpose of dower is to give the wife a means of support without being a burden on the community. Curtesy is a similar right that a husband has in the realty of his wife. Upon the wife's death the husband is entitled to a one-third interest in her real property.

Dower and curtesy rights have been abolished in many states and have been supplanted by statutory rights and recognition of tenancy by the entirety and community property rights. (See the discussions of these concepts under "Co-Ownership of Land," following.)

If you're buying property in any of the states that recognize dower and curtesy rights, be sure that you get both spouses to sign the conveyance documents—even if title to the property is in only one of their names. If the dower right is not released, it can create a cloud on the title. The signatures of both spouses releases these rights.

A *homestead* is a tract of land owned and occupied as the family home. Several states recognize a real property right known as the *homestead exemption law.* This law protects, to a limited degree, a family's home from attachment or forced sale by creditors for nonpayment of debts. The homestead right simply reserves an amount of money for the family in case of a foreclosure or forced sale. For example, if your state has a homestead exemption of $20,000 and a forced sale earns $35,000 for the property, then the homeowner would receive the first $20,000 with the remaining $15,000 applied to debts. Real estate taxes, mortgage liens, and mechanics' liens, however, are satisfied first; then the homestead exemption of $20,000 is applied; finally the creditors split up what's left. For an owner to gain the benefits of this law, a notice of exemption must be filed at the registry of deeds. When the owner sells the property, the exemption ends.

This homestead law is not the same as *homesteading,* which was practiced in the 1800s as our population moved westward. Homesteading in that respect was the legal acquisition of title to land by actually occupying it.

LEASEHOLD ESTATES

Although you will be dealing primarily in buying and selling land, you may periodically get involved with leases, so it would be advisable for you to have a working knowledge of them.

Leasehold estates or *less than freehold estates,* as they are also called, refer to leases that convey possession, use, and enjoyment for a limited time. They are not ownership interests, but are considered as personal property. Remember, a freehold estate conveys ownership, a leasehold estate conveys possession or use. A lease may be oral, but if it is to be for more than one year, most states require it to be in writing to be enforceable. The owner of the property is called a *lessor,* who grants permission and use to the *lessee,* or *tenant.* The lessee agrees to pay the rent and to abide by the terms of the lease. The four most common legal types of leasehold estates are the *estate for years, periodic estate, estate at will,* and *estate at sufferance.*

Estate for Years

A leasehold estate that continues for a definite period of time is known as an estate for years. It is the most common type of leasehold estate, and it automatically terminates without notice at the end of the stated period of time. The duration of this type of lease can vary from 1 week to 1 year or even to 99 years. Leases rarely extend beyond 99 years. In Massachusetts, if a leasehold exceeds 99 years, it is considered a freehold estate. As a point of interest, one of the better known 99-year leases has been in the news of late. In 1997 the 99-year lease of the British Crown Colony of Hong Kong expires and the city reverts back to China. A lease agreement may have options that can extend the leasehold for an additional specified duration.

Periodic Estate

Also known as a lease from *year to year*, or from *period to period*, a periodic estate is a tenancy of uncertain duration. It is created when the lease specifies the amount of rent for a specified period, but does not specify the duration the lease is to run. For example, if the lease specifies that $300 rent is to be paid monthly, then a month-to-month tenancy is in effect. It may be for a period of week to week, month to month, or year to year. It continues until either the lessor or lessee gives notice of termination in writing. The time of notice is usually the period in which the rent is payable. That is, a month-to-month tenancy requires one month's written notice.

Estate at Will

An estate at will is one that is indefinite in duration and is terminable at the "will" of either party. However, most states do require a reasonable notice to be given—usually thirty days. When a written lease terminates, the parties may agree to continue the tenancy until a certain event or until further notice—for example, when a lessor informs the tenant that the building is to be torn down, but the lessee has permission to remain until just before demolition begins; or when a tenant farmer is allowed to remain on the land when the written lease expires in order to harvest the crops.

Estate at Sufferance

Estate at sufferance is created when the written lease expires and the lessee remains on the land without the lessor's consent. After proper notice, the lessee must vacate the land. If the lessor accepts a rent payment from the lessee, then the estate at sufferance converts to a periodic estate.

NONPOSSESSORY INTERESTS (ENCUMBRANCES)

Nonpossessory interests are rights to use realty, but not to own (freehold estate), or possess (leasehold estate) it. *Easements, profits,* and *licenses* are the three most common types of nonpossessory interests and are encumbrances on the land.

The "bundle of rights" of ownership may be encumbered by contract or agreement. An *encumbrance* is a claim, charge, or liability against clear title and full, unhindered use of the property. It is the right held by a person other than the owner of the property. Encumbrances are classified as *liens,* which affect the title; and other encumbrances, such as easements, profits, licenses, *deed restrictions,* and *encroachments,* which affect the physical conditions and use of the property.

Liens

A lien is a legal right given to a creditor to have his or her debt or obligation satisfied from the real estate of the debtor. The creditor may initiate action to have the debtor's property sold to satisfy all, or part, of the debt. The word *lien* implies debt and adversely affects the possession and ownership of real estate. A creditor, to establish a lien against a debtor's real estate, must first record the *notice of lien* with the county clerk's office. The lien must be filed within a certain amount of time after the debt occurs, and the right to the lien has a limited period of time to run before it expires. If the debt is satisfied, then the lien is removed. If not, then foreclosure proceedings can be initiated. Liens can be voluntary or involuntary. A mortgage loan, for instance, is a *voluntary lien* that an owner willingly had placed on the property when taking out the loan. An example of an *involuntary lien* is a tax lien that is created by law (statutory) without any action by the property owner. Liens are classified into two categories: specific and general. *Specific liens* affect a certain or specific parcel of real estate, and include mortgages, taxes and special assessments, mechanics' liens, vendee's liens, vendor's liens, public utility liens, bail bond liens, and attachments. *General liens* normally affect all the property of a debtor, both personal and real. These include judgments, decedent's debts, state inheritance taxes, federal estate tax liens, and corporation franchise tax liens.

Mortgage Lien   A *mortgage lien* is the voluntary pledge of real estate as security for a mortgage loan. Under the *lien theory,* which is used in most states, the mortgage is considered as creating a lien, and possession and title remain with the mortgagor-borrower. The lien terminates when the mortgage is paid off. If the mortgagor defaults, the mortgagee-lender can acquire the property through foreclosure proceedings. In *title theory* states, the mortgagee-lender retains title until the mortgage is paid off. A few states use a combination of the lien theory and the title theory.

Mechanics' Lien   A *mechanics' lien* is a right of law granted to those who perform labor or furnish material in the improvement of real estate, such as contractors, subcontractors, laborers, engineers, architects, and materials suppliers.

The *enhancement of value theory* is the fundamental basis of a mechanics' lien. That is, due to the work performed and materials used, the real estate has been enhanced in value. The persons who performed the work and supplied the material are given the right of a lien as security for their goods and efforts. The lien can only be placed on the enhanced property. If you hire someone to clear the brush and undergrowth from your land and that person, in turn, hires someone to haul away the debris, then the lot clearer, whom you hired, is the *general contractor,* and the debris-hauler, whom the general contractor hired, is a *subcontractor.* Both the "general" and the "sub" are entitled to mechanics' liens if they are not paid for their services. If you pay the general the full amount for all services and the general contractor fails to pay the sub, then the sub can place a lien on your land. Payment to the general does not relieve the landowner from the lien rights of unknown, unpaid workers and suppliers. A claimant must record the mechanics' lien within a specific time after the work is completed, and must so notify the landowner. If the claimant does not enforce the lien, usually within two years time, then the lien will expire and be forever lost. If the landowner paid the full amount to the general and the general did not pay the sub, the general may be charged with larceny. For a mechanics' lien to be upheld, a contract must be in force between the landowner and the contractor. A third party, such as a tenant, cannot order the work done unless assigned this authority by the landowner.

There are two systems used in the United States to determine who is entitled to a mechanics' lien: the Pennsylvania System and the New York System.

States that use the Pennsylvania System require that the general contractor's right to a lien be subordinate to that of subcontractors and suppliers. If you paid the general contractor and he or she doesn't pay the subcontractors, the subcontractors can still file a mechanics' lien against you.

In the states using the New York System, only the general contractor has the right to a mechanics' lien. But, if the subcontractors give the landowner notice of the amount due them for their work beforehand, the owner can withhold payment of that amount from the general contractor and pay the subcontractors personally.

Under the New York System, any payments made by the mortgagee-lender before mechanics' liens are filed have priority over the mechanics' lien. In case of default of the mortgage, a foreclosure by the mortgagee would wipe out all mechanics' liens.

Vendee's Lien   A *vendee* is the purchaser of real estate. A *vendee's lien* is a buyer's claim against a seller's land. If a buyer puts a deposit on land and the seller defaults and fails to deliver title and refuses to return the deposit, then the vendee has a lien for the amount of money paid, including all amounts he or she may have spent to improve the land. This usually happens when land is purchased under an installment contract and the seller does not deliver title after the buyer fulfills all the terms of the contract.

Vendor's Lien   A *vendor* is the seller of real estate. A *vendor's lien* is a seller's claim against the property when it has been sold and conveyed to a buyer. This usually occurs when the seller does not receive the full purchase price. Enforcement of vendee's and vendor's liens is by foreclosure.

Bail Bond Lien   When a landowner, charged with a crime, must put up bail, he or she has three alternatives to choose from: cash, a bond placed by a bondsman, or a lien against his or her land. A *bail bond lien* is a claim on specific real estate as security for the payment of bail. The lien is recorded with the county clerk and is released when bail is discharged and recorded.

Public Utility Lien   Municipalities that supply utility services such as water to landowners may, for example, put a lien on a property owner's land for nonpayment of the water bill.

Attachment   When a law suit is pending, a creditor can place an *attachment lien* on a property to prevent a debtor from conveying title to the property until the law suit is settled. The creditor must post a *surety bond* to cover any possible loss the debtor may suffer (due to the attachment) if the creditor's suit is unsuccessful.

Judgments   A *judgment* is a court decree awarding an amount of money. It becomes a lien against all property owned by the debtor once it is recorded with the county clerk. A judgment is enforced by a *writ of execution*, issued by the court, directing the sheriff to seize and sell enough of the debtor's property that is needed to pay off the judgment, plus the expenses of the sale. A judgment lien attaches to all of the property of the debtor, both personal and real, and remains in effect for a statutory period of time, usually ten years. Once it is paid off, it is discharged. If the creditor-plaintiff wants to make known to all interested parties a possible claim against the property of the debtor before the rendering of a judgment, he or she must file and record a notice of *lis pendens*, or pendency of action. A statement of lis pendens gives notice, to all interested parties, of the pending claim against the debtor's property.

Decedent's Debts   Title to real estate passes to the heirs of the deceased, but is subject to outstanding debts left by the deceased. These are liens against the property. If you are buying land from a deceased person's estate, make sure you get proof that all debts and liens have been discharged.

Inheritance and Income Tax Liens   The federal and state governments attach liens against the real estate of a taxpayer for delinquent income and inheritance taxes. The lien is recorded with the county clerk and usually stays in effect for ten years, or until the delinquent taxes are paid.

Corporation Franchise Tax Lien   Most state governments impose a franchise tax on corporations that conduct business in their state. Delinquency of these taxes as well can result in a lien against the corporation's property.

Real Estate Tax Lien   Real estate taxes become a lien on a property when they become due. Taxes are levied by government agencies and municipalities for the general support and operation of the government. These are known as *ad valorem* taxes because they vary in relation to the value of the property being taxed. If the taxes are not paid, the property is "taken for taxes" by the town and is sold with a *tax certificate* being issued to the purchaser. The previous owner, the one that had his or her property taken, has the right to redeem the property within three years of the sale and must pay the purchaser the amount of the delinquent taxes plus interest.

Special Assessment   A *special assessment* is a special tax levied on real estate, of which the owner is required to pay a proportional share, for improvements that benefit his or her property. Such improvements may be water pipes, sewer lines, or streets and sidewalks. Special assessments are usually payable over a ten-year period in equal payments, including an interest charge.

Priority of Liens   The priority of liens, of the same type, depends upon the order in time in which they are recorded with the county clerk.

However, property tax liens, or special assessments imposed by government, have priority over all other liens regardless of when they were recorded, and certain mechanics' liens have priority over prior recorded mortgage liens.

Easements

An easement is the right one person has to use, but not possess, the real estate of another for a special purpose. The most common type of easement is a *right-of-way* over the land of another. Easements are generally classified as *easements appurtenant* and *easements in gross*.

Easement Appurtenant   Appurtenant means adjunct of, or belonging to, something else. An easement appurtenant is the right of one owner to use the land of an adjacent owner for a particular purpose. The parcel that is benefited by the easement is known as the *dominant tenement* and the parcel burdened with the easement is known as the *servient tenement*. The parcels don't necessarily have to be abutting one another, but the dominant parcel must be at the beginning, or the end, of the easement. A right-of-way easement, for example, may cross over several servient parcels to serve a dominant parcel. An easement appurtenant, in legal terms, is said to "run with the land" and is thus conveyed to subsequent owners when the parcel is sold. An easement appurtenant will have some effect upon the value of the parcels involved. An affirmative easement allows the dominant tenement owner the right to use the servient tenement owner's parcel in a particular way, such as the right to cross over it to reach a pond or highway. What is affirmative for the dominant tenement may be negative for the servient tenement if it severely limits the use of the parcel. For instance, if a right-of-way easement running through the middle of the parcel precludes the owner of the servient tenement from using the optimum location on the plot to build a home, then this would adversely affect the value of the land.

Easement in Gross   An *easement in gross* is a personal right to use the land of another. It is not necessary that the lands be adjacent to one another. Rights of ways for pipelines, sewer and power lines, or roads used by public utilities are examples of easements in gross. Other types of easements in gross are railroad rights of way and easements for billboards, signs, utility poles, and the like.

Creating an Easement

In order to create an easement the intent must be clear. Most states require that the granting of an easement be in writing in the deed or contract, but easements may also be created by *implication, prescription,* and by *estoppel.*

Implied Easement or Easement by Necessity An easement is created by implication when there is a clear intent of creating one. An example would be if an owner subdivided land into two parcels, one with an access and the other without, and sold them to two different parties. The law holds that an implied easement is created for the benefit of the landlocked dominant tenement granting an easement by necessity across the servient tenement's land.

Easement by Prescription An *easement by prescription* arises when a person uses another's land openly and continually, without the owner's permission, for a statutory period of time, usually ten to twenty years. The use must be visible and notorious enough so that the owner must know about it and be able to stop it. If the owner does not stop it during the statutory period, then an easement by prescription results. Easements by prescription cannot be obtained against state or federally owned land, or the land of minors or legally incompetent persons. An easement by prescription has similar elements to obtaining title to land by *adverse possession,* which will be explained in Chapter V.

Easement by Estoppel If a seller leads the buyer to believe there is an easement even though it is not mentioned in the deed or contract, an *easement by estoppel* is created.

Terminating Easements Easements may be terminated when the reasons for their being no longer exists, or by merger of the dominant and servient tenements (when one party becomes the owner of both parcels); also by agreement between the parties, and by abandonment or nonuse beyond the statutory period.

Profits

A profit in land is the right to remove minerals, oil, timber, or any other materials from someone else's land. A profit differs from an easement in that a profit permits removal of the resources of the land, whereas an easement simply allows use of the land.

License

A license is a privilege to enter another's land for a particular purpose. It is not an easement and can be terminated by the license grantor. Some examples of a license would be permission to park your vehicle on a neighbor's land, or to enter a ballpark or theater as a patron, or the right to hunt and fish on someone's land.

Deed Restrictions

Deed restrictions, also known as property covenants, are conditions of use placed on the property and recorded at the county recorder's office. They are most often imposed by a developer to maintain certain standards in a subdivision for the benefit of all the lot owners. Some examples of deed restrictions are

- All homes must be of a specified size and design and plans must be approved by the developer or by a committee made up of lot owners in the subdivision.
- No fences over 4 feet high are allowed.

- No trees can be cut down, except as necessary for construction purposes, without prior approval.
- Driveways must be paved.

Deed restrictions create a qualified estate. They usually have a time period that runs to about twenty-five years and may be extended by agreement of the developer or lot owners.

Encroachments

An encroachment can arise when part of a building, a driveway, or a fence illegally extends beyond the owner's land. A survey or physical inspection of the land is necessary to ascertain the existence of an encroachment. An encroachment is an encumbrance upon the property. If it is legal, it is an easement created by implication or prescription. If it is an illegal encroachment, the offended party may be able to recover damages or secure removal.

CO-OWNERSHIP OF LAND

An estate in land may be owned by one person, or by two, or more persons under several forms of co-ownership. When you purchase a parcel of land by yourself, you own an estate in *severalty*. You have complete control and responsibility for buying, developing, and selling the land. As you become more active in land investments, you may eventually join with one or more persons to buy land as co-owners, especially when you are considering larger, more expensive parcels. Often, the inclusion of a co-owner gives investors confidence in making buying and selling decisions because they can share the risks, responsibilities, and decisions.

Since there are several forms of co-ownership (also called concurrent ownership), you will have to determine which form is best for you and your co-owners to use. Considerations such as tax implications, inheritance, and responsibilities to each other must be discussed and determined. Co-ownership of property means that title to the same parcel is owned by two or more persons simultaneously. The interests of each owner do not necessarily have to be identical or equal to each other.

The two most common forms of land co-ownership are *tenancy in common* and *joint tenancy. Tenancy by the entirety* is property owned by a husband and wife. Other types of co-ownership are *community property, partnership, syndicate,* and *corporation.* Make it your responsibility to understand the following forms of co-ownership of real estate.

Tenancy in Common

Owning land in a tenancy in common form of ownership is used when two or more persons own the same land with undivided interest, whether equal or unequal. "Undivided interest" needs some explanation. An owner in common may hold a one-third interest in the land, or one half, or any fractional interest. It doesn't have to be an equal interest. Even though the owner in common has a fractional interest, it is impossible to distinguish specifically and physically which half or third he or she may own. It cannot be divided. If a deed does not state what fraction each co-owner owns, then each has an equal share. If there are two owners, then each owns an undivided one-half interest. If four owners, then each has an undivided one-quarter interest.

Actually, each owns an undivided interest in severalty. This means each owner's fractional interest is held as though he or she were a sole owner. Each owner can sell, convey, mortgage, or transfer interest without consent of the other co-owners. Upon the death of a co-owner—the law states that there are no survivor rights—the co-owner's interest passes to the heirs, not to the other co-owners (unless a co-owner is an heir of the deceased). In several states, if the property is being sold, or if a single co-owner's fractional share is being sold, the spouse must also sign the deed to release the dower or curtesy rights.

When a co-owner does sell fractional interest, the new owner becomes a tenant in common with the other co-owners. Similarly, if a co-owner mortgages his or her interest and eventually is foreclosed on, the lender becomes a tenant in common with the other co-owners.

Should a disagreement arise among the tenants in common, they may file in court an "action to partition" the land among the owners. The court will assign a referee who will attempt to divide the land into separate parcels according to each owner's fractional interest. Each owner then owns his or her land in severalty. If it is not possible to divide the land, the parcel will be sold and the proceeds equitably split up. To prevent potential problems in this regard, the co-owners can decide beforehand what each owner can, or cannot, do without the consent of all. For instance, they may prevent an owner from selling his or her interest to anyone other than an existing co-owner or at least let the co-owners have the right of first refusal.

To summarize, a tenancy in common form of ownership allows

- Unequal ownership interests
- Right of possession and use by each owner
- Freedom to convey, transfer, or mortgage one's interest

And it does not allow the right of survivorship to co-owners.

Joint Tenancy

As mentioned previously, tenants in common may own an undivided, unequal interest in land. In a joint tenancy, the owners share an undivided, equal interest in the land. In a joint tenancy, each co-owner has the right of survivorship. If one owner dies, that person's rights of ownership pass to the survivors. When there is only one surviving joint tenancy owner, he or she becomes the owner in severalty; on the last surviving owner's death, the land passes to that person's heirs alone. Because of the right of survivorship, joint tenancy is common among family members.

When a joint tenant sells his or her interest, the new owner becomes a tenant in common, not a joint tenant, with the remaining owners. This is because the law states that in a joint tenancy, the owners must have acquired title at the same time under the same instrument. The four unities of joint tenancy must exist:

- Unity of title
- Unity of time
- Unity of interest
- Unity of possession

In other words, the owners must have acquired title on a single deed, signed at the same moment of time, affording equal interest and possession to each owner. If any one of these unities is missing, then a tenancy in common exists, not a joint tenancy. Many states have abandoned the joint tenancy, and in some states the contract and deed must specify that title is to be taken in joint tenancy with right of survivorship.

Tenancy by the Entirety

A tenancy by the entirety form of ownership is a special joint tenancy between a husband and wife. Title is held by both of them as if they were one owner. Neither can sell the land without the signature of the other. In the event of divorce the estate terminates and a tenancy in common results. When one spouse dies, the surviving spouse gets full title in fee simple. If the deceased spouse had debts, his or her creditors cannot attach a lien against the land. If a married couple buys land with another married couple, or a single person, each of the married couples are tenants by the entirety and the single person a joint tenant.

Partnership

You may find it advantageous at some time to join in with one or more investors when buying larger, more expensive parcels. A partnership gives you the benefit of sharing the risks and responsibilities as well as the rewards and profits. Guided by the rules of the Uniform Partnership Act, investors may join in a tenancy in partnership.

A partnership is not a legal entity in itself—it is an association of two or more persons carrying on a business as co-owners for a profit. Title may be vested in the name of the partnership itself or in the names of any of the individual partners. If land is acquired with partnership funds, it is deemed as partnership property, regardless of whom the title is vested in. Partners share equal rights of possession and use of the partnership land. The authorized acts of one partner bind all other partners. But one partner cannot sell the partnership land, since all the partners must sign the deed. There are two kinds of partnership: general and limited.

General Partnership   In a *general partnership* form of ownership each member participates in the operation of the business. Each member also has full responsibility for all partnership debts. When any member of a partnership dies, withdraws from the partnership, or goes into bankruptcy, the partnership dissolves and must be reorganized. A deceased partner's share of the partnership goes to the surviving partners, unless stated otherwise in the partnership agreement.

Limited Partnership   Governed by the Uniform Limited Partnership Act, a limited partnership is made up of a general partner and one or more limited, or silent, partners. Under a limited partnership, the limited partners have very little, if any, involvement in the operation of the business. They play a passive, or silent, role, but are entitled to information on operative and financial details. Although title may be taken in the name of the partnership, only the general partner may sign deeds, mortgages, or contracts. The limited partners supply funds (normally in installments as they are needed) to the general partner for him or her to direct and manage the partnership interests. The general partner is usually paid a fee for services in addition to sharing in the partnership profits.

Two primary advantages of this form of ownership are the limited liability and tax benefits afforded each limited partner. Each limited partner is liable for partnership debts only up to the extent of his or her capital investment. For example, if the partnership defaults on a $200,000 mortgage, a limited partner with an investment of $50,000 in the partnership is liable only up to the $50,000 investment. This is similar to the limited liability of a corporation form of ownership, except there are no corporate taxes to pay. The tax benefits to the members of the partnership are a tax shelter. All the expenses and losses of the partnership are passed through to the partners and may be deducted on their personal tax returns. (New tax legislation may change this.) Upon the death of the general partner, the partnership is dissolved. But if one of the limited partners dies, the partnership continues, with the heirs receiving his or her partnership interests.

Corporate Ownership

If you have a large group of investors intent on buying, developing, and selling land as co-owners, you may want to consider forming a corporation. Each member of the corporation becomes a shareholder by investing an amount of capital in the corporation and each receives shares of stock. Stock is actually personal property, so each shareholder does not have direct ownership in the corporate land. A corporation is a legal entity and may own land in its corporate name as an ownership in severalty. The shareholders draw up the Articles of Incorporation and By-Laws and file them with the secretary of state in the state in which they wish to be incorporated. The state will grant a charter to the corporation recognizing it as having its own rights, privileges, and liabilities separate and distinct from its shareholders. Similar to a limited partnership, each shareholder's liability is limited to the amount of the investment. Creditors cannot come after the personal assets of a shareholder to satisfy corporate debts. The shareholders will draw up a Shareholder's Agreement outlining the rights and responsibilities of each member.

Unlike a partnership, it is not necessary for a corporation to be an income-producing business. If your corporation merely possesses and uses the land, there isn't necessarily any profit and thus no income taxes to pay. When and if the land is developed and sold, then income taxes are assessed on the profits.

If a shareholder doesn't pay his or her proportionate share of the cost of operating the corporation, then the board of directors can vote to sell his or her shares and apply the proceeds to the money owed to the corporation. The new owner simply replaces the old owner in the corporate books—a foreclosure procedure is unnecessary.

Forming a Syndicate to Buy Land

A syndicate, or joint venture, is an association of two or more persons joined together to make property investments. The form of ownership in which a syndicate holds title to land may be a corporation, a partnership, a tenancy in common, a real estate investment trust, or a limited partnership. The most common form is the limited partnership. Actually, a syndicate is not a form of ownership—it is a method of raising capital from several investors. A syndicator puts the syndicate together and manages it as a general partner. The principal reason in putting together a syndicate is to provide individual investors with the ability to buy larger properties with little personal involvement in managing the investment.

Community Property

Community property, as a form of ownership, is recognized in just eight states: Arizona, California, Idaho, Louisiana, Nevada, New Mexico, Texas, and Washington. There are several variations of the law among these eight community property states. Like a tenancy by the entirety, both spouses must agree, in writing, to the sale of their mutually owned property. Community property is any property acquired by either spouse during their marriage. Property acquired before the marriage and property inherited or received as a gift (even during the marriage) is considered as separate property and is owned solely by the spouse who has title. All property classed as separate property is free from any claims by either spouse. All property not classed as separate property is community property and the spouses are owners in common of this property. Upon divorce, the community property is equally divided.

CHAPTER V

METHODS OF TRANSFERRING TITLE

Title to land is the right, and evidence, of ownership. *Transfer* is the method in which a change of ownership occurs. The actual conveyance of ownership from one party to another is by a *deed*. The transfer of the interest and title to land is called *alienation,* and may be either involuntary or voluntary.

INVOLUNTARY ALIENATION

Title to land can be transferred without the owner's consent. These involuntary transfers are actions of law, such as the condemnation of land for the good of the public or the forced sale of land to satisfy debtors or delinquent taxes. The following sections discuss the principal methods by which an interest in real property can be transferred by involuntary alienation.

Transfer by Escheat

A fundamental law of real estate is that title must be vested in someone. When a landowner dies *intestate* (without a will) and leaves no heirs or legal claimants, the title to his or her real estate reverts to the state under the doctrine of *escheat.*

Transfer by Confiscation

In times of a national emergency or war, the government may take over property of enemy aliens, without giving compensation. This involuntary alienation of land is called *confiscation* and is executed to prevent the giving of aid and comfort to the enemy.

Transfer by Eminent Domain

The government, as well as certain corporations and public utilities, can appropriate property for public use through a *suit of condemnation.* Just and reasonable compensation, as determined by the courts, must be paid to the owner.

Transfer by Erosion

Erosion is the wearing away of land through the natural processes of nature. The action of wind and water may erode the land gradually, resulting in the involuntary loss of the land. Title may also be transferred by *accretion,* the opposite of erosion: in accretion an owner's land increases in size by the gradual, natural accumulation of deposits of soil.

Transfer by Judicial Process

The courts may order that a property be involuntarily sold to satisfy and enforce liens, judgments, unpaid mortgages, and delinquent taxes.

Transfer by Adverse Possession

A claimant without a deed may seize title to land from an owner with a deed through the involuntary method of *adverse possession*. To take title from an owner of record, the claimant's use of the owner's land must be (1) actual and hostile, (2) open and notorious, (3) exclusive, and (4) continuous and uninterrupted for a statutory period of time.

Actual and hostile. The claimant, or possessor, must use the land without the owner's permission and must deny that the true owner does, in fact, own the land. Some examples of actions that could establish actual possession are the cutting of timber and clearing the land, planting crops or grazing animals, building structures or fences, and paying taxes.

Open and notorious. The claimant must use the land in an open and notorious manner. The claimant cannot secretly use it in such a way that the owner would not notice the claimant's actions if he or she were to visit the land.

Exclusive. The claimant must be using the land alone, to the exclusion of the true owner.

Continuous and uninterrupted for a period of time. Use by the claimant must be continuous and uninterrupted from the start of the statutory time period (usually ten to twenty years). This period of time—the statute of limitations—is deemed long enough for an owner to have a reasonable opportunity to contest the claim.

If all the above conditions are met, the claimant may acquire title to the land. The purpose of adverse possession is to keep property productive for society. If you're considering buying a parcel from an owner who acquired his or her title through adverse possession, seek an attorney's advice.

Two final points: One adverse possessor may pass the right to another, keeping the uninterrupted use in effect. This is called *tacking*.

Adverse possession cannot be claimed against government lands, nor can an owner in common claim adverse possession against a co-owner.

Adverse possession is not the same as *squatters' rights,* which results in a right to use land under an easement by prescription (see Chapter IV) until death or removal. The one similarity is the fact that the owner may lose rights to land legally owned if another uses the land for some statutory period of time.

VOLUNTARY ALIENATION

To transfer title to land by *voluntary alienation* is simply what it says— with the owner's consent. The following sections discuss the various methods of voluntary title transference:

Transfer by Gift

A landowner may make a gift of property to a child or to anyone he or she chooses. The owner giving the gift is a *donor* and the receiver of the gift is the *donee.* Even though it is a gift and there is no consideration given, it is a legal transference.

Transfer by Sale

A sale "for consideration" is the normal way that title to most real property is transferred. A sales contract is prepared to arrange the transfer, and a deed actually transfers the title. *Consideration* is defined as an act or forbearance of an act, or the promise to act or to forbear from an act. In a sale of real property, the seller's consideration is the land being transferred; the buyer's consideration is usually the price of the land.

Transfer by Dedication

An owner may transfer title to his or her land by making a *dedication* of it: such as a subdivider deeding land and improvements to the town after installing streets and walkways. Once the town has title to the streets, it is responsible thereafter for maintaining them.

Transfer by Will

A will is a written instrument made by the owner to voluntarily transfer title to his or her property after death. When the owner dies, he or she is known as a *decedent*. If the owner has drawn up a will, he or she is said to have died *testate*. If the owner dies without a will, he or she is said to have died *intestate*. After a will is drawn up, the owner can still sell or transfer the property to anyone of his or her choosing and make a new will.

To be legal, a will must abide by the statutory requirements of the state where the land is located. A will cannot overlook the laws of dower and curtesy, which protect the inheritance rights of the living spouse. Nor can it overlook community property laws in those states where they are applicable, whereby the surviving spouse automatically owns one half of the community property acquired during the marriage.

A deed conveys a current interest in land, whereas a will conveys no interest until after the owner, or *testator,* dies. For a will to be valid (1) the testator must be of legal age, which is eighteen in most states, (2) he or she must be of sound mind when he or she executes the will, and (3) the act of making the will must be free. The will must be signed by two witnesses who have no interest in the estate. Upon the testator's death, his or her will must be submitted to a probate court to establish its validity.

Transfer by Descent

When an owner dies intestate, the property passes to heirs through descent in accordance with state laws. It goes to the descendants of the decedent. The surviving spouse will acquire at least a statutory share by dower-curtesy and community property rights, or the entire property if there are no other living blood relatives. The children get their share after the spouse, then the parents, brothers and sisters, aunts and uncles, all the way down to the second cousins. If there are no surviving heirs, the land reverts to the state by escheat.

PUBLIC RECORDS

A person who has an interest in land must give public notice in order to protect that interest. This notice can be actual or constructive. The possession of land—living on it or using it in some way—is termed *actual notice*. In other words, any interested party can see that an individual is using the land and may very well have an interest in it. Recording in the public records a document that shows interest in land is termed *constructive notice*.

Under the *recording acts,* all written documents affecting an interest in land must be recorded in the county where the land is located. The courts feel that the buyer of realty has the responsibility to inspect the property physically and to make an actual search of the public records to ascertain the condition of the title. A buyer cannot later plead a lack of knowledge of a defect on the title if that defect was in fact recorded—*caveat emptor.* The information is available to the buyer and he or she is responsible for learning it.

The public records are designed to protect you from fraud. Legal priority is usually given to those interests that are recorded first. Once you close on that piece of land you're buying, make sure that your attorney records the deed right away. There have been cases where a dishonest seller has sold the same parcel of land to different parties and the second buyer had his or her deed recorded first. The second buyer is the owner. The courts look on the activity as, ""First in time, first in line." The first buyer can take legal action against the seller, but had the deed been recorded right away, the first buyer would be the owner of record and would not have to go to the courts for a remedy.

To be eligible for recording, an instrument must be drawn up and executed according to specific state laws. The laws differ from state to state. Some states require that the names of all who sign any document be typed below the signatures and that a notary public witness the signing. Some states require that the attorney that prepared the instrument sign it too.

The instruments to be recorded are photocopied, the original is returned to the owner, and the copy is filed and assigned a book and page number for ready location. A recording fee is charged for each instrument filed. If the instrument is a deed, many states require revenue stamps to be affixed to it. This is, in effect, a sales tax. Once recorded, the instrument is simultaneously listed in the Grantor and Grantee Indexes.

The *Grantor Index* lists the seller alphabetically according to the date of the recording. The *Grantee Index* is a separate file of buyers, also listed alphabetically and chronologically. Deeds, mortgages, liens, judgments, assignments, as well as leases and lis pendens (pending legal action against the land), are typically filed in the Grantor and Grantee Indexes. Some states may have mortgages, wills, and lis pendens in a separate file. Get to know how they are filed at the registry that you will be working through.

When searching the title of a parcel, the index and subsequent research will yield the full *chain of title,* which will show the ownership of the land from its origin to its current owner. Any period of time in which one or more of the owners cannot be found is referred to as a *gap in the chain of title*. It must be corrected to give a good and marketable title.

Since title search is an important part of buying land, let's take a run-through of the procedure to do a title search. Let's say you want to search the title of a piece of land owned by a Giuseppe Ambessi. Since he is the owner of the parcel, his name will be in the Grantee Index because at the time of the purchase he would be the receiver, or buyer, of the property. If you know the date that he originally acquired the land, you can go right to his name. If not, you may have to look through several books to find his name, or you could get the date from the tax assessor. Look for Ambessi, Giuseppe, in alphabetical sequence and this will refer you to the book and page number in which a recorded copy of his deed is filed.

Also in the index will be reference numbers to other documents that were filed in Giuseppe Ambessi's name. Here is a representative list as you would find it in the Grantee Index:

Grantee Index

Date of Reception	Surname	Given Name	Grantor	Recorded Book—Page	Inst.	Description
1954 6 21	Albanat	Thomas B	Leon Ford	1131 542	DD	Bost. Cove St
1959 3 17		Lois G	Jon Lewis	1412 123	MTG	Bost. C St
1950 6 30	Ambessi	Guisseppe	Jos. Molina	1041 346	DD	Win. Mystic Rd
1956 9 04	Archer	George	Ken Johnson	1280 98	DD	Bost. L St

Note that the deed (shown as DD) is listed in Book 1041, Page 346. This book and page number is commonly referred to as the title reference. For instance, when you sell a lot of land, you would cite the book and page number on the purchase and sales agreement so that a prospective buyer's attorney could readily research the title. Now look up Ambessi's deed in Book 1041, Page 346. Let's assume Ambessi acquired the land in 1950 from Joseph Molina. The book and page number of Molina's deed will be cited. Write this information down so that you can also look this deed up and research it, as you are doing with Ambessi's deed. Read each document through entirely to see if there are any "clouds" (defects) and continue this somewhat tedious but necessary process, going backward in time. A cloud on the title means there is an outstanding claim or encumbrance that, if valid, would affect or impair title to the land. Examples of clouds are unpaid mortgage liens, a judgment, or dower interest.

Are there any easements listed? Any restrictions? Make notes of all the documents and their book and page locations. Look up all these documents and read them completely and write down their contents. If there is a lien on the property, such as a mortgage, you want to make sure that it is paid off, or will be paid off, before you acquire title.

After the preliminary research, look for Ambessi's name in the Grantor Index. You want to make sure that he—or any prior owner in the chain of title—hasn't sold the same parcel twice. The Grantor Index is laid out the same as the Grantee Index, except that the Grantor and Grantee columns are reversed. If you find Ambessi's name, look up the document that is listed. He may have owned other parcels that were sold and recorded, but if it's the land you are buying, there's a problem—he sold it and no longer has title to it.

After you've researched and found that he is selling you the parcel properly, your research must still continue. Check to see whether all mortgages and taxes were paid off and that any liens and judgments have been settled and cleared. In community property states, or where dower and curtesy rights still exist, make sure that both husband and wife's signatures are on the deed. This research is described in "The Title Search" later in this chapter.

If the land has been surveyed, a plan may be on file. The plan book number and page number will be written onto the margin of the deed. You can look this up and get a copy made, if needed. With a plan on file, any deeds written by a lawyer will refer to the plan in the description and this becomes part of the deed.

EVIDENCE OF TITLE

When you do buy that first parcel of land, and every parcel thereafter, you will want documentary proof that the seller is the true and legal owner of the land. You will want to acquire the best possible title to the land, *marketable title*—ownership that is readily saleable at *market value*. Market value, as you'll read in the section on appraising in Chapter VII, is the agreed-upon price between a willing seller and a willing buyer. A marketable title is deemed of sufficient quality for courts to require its acceptance by a buyer.

A landowner may not have clear and marketable title to his or her property. There may be a cloud on the property or a defect in it. If there's a mortgage on the property, there will be a lien against the title. There may be easements on the land that are not readily apparent and can only be discovered by searching the public records where all property transactions and activities are recorded. To find the clouds and defects on a title you must search the public records and remove the defects.

The Title Search

A complete search of the public records at the Registry of Deeds will yield the ownership interests and condition of the title in the form of an *abstract of title*. The abstract of title is a condensed history of all the instruments, recorded at the registry, that affect the title to the land being researched. It will include the complete history of mortgages, wills, liens, deeds, foreclosures, tax sales, and other recorded materials relating to this parcel of land.

When you buy a parcel and hire an attorney to search the title, he or she will hire an *abstractor* who specializes in title searches. The abstractor prepares the abstract, giving the condition of the title and the chain of title (prior owners), but does not render an opinion or make a judgment on the condition of the title. Your attorney will examine the entire abstract and evaluate all the facts and prepare a written report of the condition of ownership, called an *opinion of title*. An attorney's opinion of title has several limitations. If there has been an error in the public records, or a document has been overlooked by the abstractor, the attorney would not know this, and the buyer suffers. One way to decrease your risk when purchasing property is to get *title insurance* on it. Title insurance is protection against financial loss due to existing, but unknown, claims on the title at the time of the purchase. The title company will defend the title in court for defects in the public records:

forged documents, incorrect marital statements, incompetent grantors, improperly delivered deeds, and lack of a spouse's signature.

Bear in mind that all the records in the registry relating to the land are public records and are available for you to see at no charge. It is highly recommended that you hire an attorney to do your title search. But it also would be worthwhile for you to spend a day at the registry and learn the system. The personnel at the registry will show you how to use the records and how to locate specific title information so that you could do a preliminary title search of your own on any parcel of land you are considering for purchase.

The Torrens System

The *Torrens System* offers a means of settling claims in court. An owner may petition the court, and the court will search the title and give public notice that it is doing so. Any persons with claims against the property may come forward. If no claims are made, the Land Court will register the land and issue a *certificate of title*. The owner will now have clear title from any claim that may be made in the future that arises from defects before the registration was enacted. Registered land can never be lost through a claim of adverse possession. The Torrens System of registering land is in use in only a few states since it is a rather costly procedure for the petitioner.

CLOSING

The *title closing,* or *settlement* as it is also called, is the completion of the purchase of a piece of land. It is the gathering together of all the parties to the sale to see that the promises made in the real estate sales contract are kept. At the closing, all the necessary documents change hands and financial adjustments and disbursements are made. The buyer wants to be sure that the seller is delivering a clear title and that the property is in the condition promised. The seller wants to be sure that the buyer has the money to complete the sale. If everything is in order, to the satisfaction of the parties, then the documents are exchanged and recorded.

Closings may be held in various places, including the registry, the lending institution (if there is a mortgage), the broker's office, or at either attorney's office—any place that is convenient for all the parties to get together at the same time. The registry is the most preferred location because a last-minute check on the title can be made, and after the closing is completed all the pertinent documents can be recorded immediately. The interested parties in attendance are usually the buyer and seller, their attorneys, the agent for the lending institution, and the real estate broker, if one was involved in the sale. Either, or both, of the attorneys usually conduct the proceedings. When the sales contract was originally signed, a closing date was established. This date allowed the buyer enough time to have the title searched and to acquire financing if needed. From the date of the signing to the closing date, the buyer's attorney will have had the title searched and formalized his or her opinion of title and will have presented it to the buyer. The lending institution's attorney will also examine the title, to protect the bank's interests.

Closing Documents

The seller's attorney will prepare the deed and bring it to the closing properly executed and ready to be delivered to the buyer. The deed must correspond to the sales agreement and must be drawn up in suitable form for recording. If an existing mortgage is to be paid off as part of the closing, a mortgage satisfaction receipt must be signed by the old lender, acknowledging payment of the loan. This is then recorded, which removes the mortgage lien from the land. If the buyer requires financing, the attorney for the mortgagee will prepare and present the *mortgage note* to be signed by the buyer, and recorded as a new lien against the land.

Closing Statement

Besides the payment of the purchase price for the land, a typical real estate transaction involves several other expenses for both buyer and seller. The responsibility for these expenses must be allocated between the buyer and seller. The closing statement is prepared by the attorneys and presented at the closing, showing the disposition of the costs. In addition to the sales price, the proration of taxes, and interest costs, other expenses must be allocated between buyer and seller:

Seller's Fees:

Broker's commission. Any broker involved in the sale is due a commission for his or her efforts. The broker's fee should be stated in the sales agreement. If the buyer hired the broker to find land for to buy, then the buyer is responsible for the commission. Broker's fees are negotiable, ranging from 4 to 7 percent for residences and from 8 to 12 percent for land.

Revenue stamps. Most states require that a transfer tax be paid in the form of revenue stamps, which are affixed to the deed. This is usually in the amount of 55 cents for each $500 of value. The registry will not record the deed unless the stamps are affixed.

Attorney's fees. The seller's attorney prepares the deed and represents the seller at the closing. he or she may also do the title search and acquire title insurance for the seller.

Buyer's Fees:

Attorney's fees. The buyer's attorney advises and represents the buyer at the closing. The buyer's attorney examines the title and deed and looks after the buyer's interests throughout the transaction.

Mortgage fees. If the buyer has obtained financing for the purchase, there are certain charges that he or she must pay to the lending institution. Among them are loan origination fees, appraisal fee, insurance, the fee of the lender's attorney, and the charge for the credit report on the buyer that the bank had authorized.

Recording fee. Fees for recording the deed and the mortgage are paid by the buyer.

An additional expense that must be adjusted between the parties is taxes. If a residence is involved, there are also insurance and utility costs and any income or rentals that the property may be earning to be distributed fairly at the closing.

The final act of the closing procedure is the delivery of the deed from the seller to the buyer, which conveys legal title. A deed may also be delivered in *escrow*. Escrow is a method by which the parties appoint a disinterested third party to act as the escrow agent. The escrow agent will hold the deed until certain specified duties are performed by the parties. For instance, if you are buying land with a *contract for deed* (installment contract), the seller retains title until the buyer completes all the periodic payments. During this period, the escrow agent holds the deed and will present it to the buyer when payments are completed to the seller.

CHAPTER VI

GOVERNMENT LIMITATIONS TO OWNERSHIP

We have rights in the land that we own, which were fully explained in preceding chapters. We also have obligations: to our neighbors, to visitors on our land, to the community in general. Our rights are tempered by our obligations. In our form of government, someone has to protect our land rights and also see that we fulfill our land obligations.

It is the obligation of government to control land use in order to prevent actions and activities that might adversely affect the quality, character, and welfare of the community. These governmental obligations are supported by certain powers that place limitations on land ownership for the good of the community. In some instances their exercise may be unfair and unreasonable, and may even cause economic loss or hardship to landowners. Such losses may be viewed as necessary nevertheless, to facilitate an orderly development and growth, and to make periodic adjustments in response to the changing social and economic needs of the community. Public limitations and restrictions on land ownership are imposed by: (1) the right of taxation; (2) police power; (3) eminent domain; and (4) escheat. We discussed eminent domain and escheat in Chapter V, so this chapter will be devoted to the other two governmental limitations: taxation and police power.

TAXATION

One of the single most unpopular functions of the government is the right to tax real estate. This power, vested in the legislative branch of the government, is limited by the Constitution and statutory laws to safeguard against unfair or unreasonable taxation. The federal government does not tax real estate. This power is conferred only on local governments—villages, towns, cities, and counties—and other local governing agencies such as school, water, drainage, and sanitary districts. The purpose of taxes is to pay for the services provided to the community. The amount of, and method of, levying taxes varies considerably from one state to another, but the procedures involved in administering them are basically similar.

It's important for the real estate investor to have an understanding of the taxing system, because it affects the profitability of all land investments. Real estate taxes are the only true carrying costs applicable to owning and holding land. Interest expenses are a cost of borrowing the money to buy the land. Even if you own land outright, with no mortgage, you can't live on it, or use it, for free: you still have to pay taxes. Taxes are so important to local governments that the law gives them preference over all other claims by creditors of the landowner. When land is foreclosed, taxes are the first debts to be satisfied. There are two basic types of real estate taxes: (1) general real estate, or *ad valorem,* taxes, and (2) special assessments. Both taxes are levied against specific parcels and become liens on those properties.

General Taxes

General real estate taxes provide the funds for the general operation of the local government—schools, water department, town hall, building inspector, parks, town dump, and other local services. There are two theories of how taxes should be apportioned among the community residents. One theory is that taxes should be imposed in proportion to benefits received from government services. This theory is not fully practical, however, since those persons needing and receiving the services are often the least able to pay. The second theory, called *ad valorem* (Latin for "at value") taxes, is based on the value of the property, which translates to the more expensive properties paying higher taxes than less expensive properties.

Property taxes follow the ad valorem theory and are levied as a percentage of value. The first step in determining value is an assessment.

The Assessment Process The tax assessor must appraise the fair market value of each and every parcel of real estate in his or her locality, each year, for the purpose of levying taxes. This value represents the amount of money that the property would sell for if placed on the market. The assessment process uses the three approaches to value estimation: cost approach, market approach, and income approach. An explanation of these methods is covered in detail in Chapter VII. Briefly, the cost approach is a collection of information on what it would actually cost to replace the property at current prices, plus the value of the land, which is determined by comparative sales. The market approach determines a fair market value by comparing the property with recent, comparable sales. The income approach uses the income producing capacity of a property to determine its value.

In estimating the value of property, the land and structures are valued separately, then both are combined on the tax bill. Look at your own tax bill and you'll see a land valuation and a separate valuation for your home, then a total. The assessor keeps track of all real estate sold in his or her jurisdiction. If the assessor knows what a parcel is sold for, he or she knows its true market value. Those properties in the surrounding area that are not sold are compared to the properties that are sold to determine a fair market value. For example, if a three-acre parcel of land sold for $25,000, then similar unsold three-acre parcels in the surrounding area must have a market value of $25,000. If they're a little smaller, they are worth a little less. If a little larger, then they are worth a little more. Generally, what an assessor would do in areas where there are large amounts of unsold raw acreage is to arrive at an average per-acre value and apply this to all the land in the immediate area. If the assessor determines that land in the area is worth $1500 per acre, then a ten-acre parcel would be valued at $15,000 and a twenty-three acre parcel would be valued at $34,500.

State laws may require that all property in a community be physically reassessed periodically. This may be done by private evaluation firms or by the assessor. The laws may also require assessments to be a certain percentage of market value varying from 25 to 100 percent. For example, if the assessment ratio is 25 percent, then a parcel of land with a true market value of $15,000 would be taxed at 25 percent of the figure, or $3750. After the assessor appraises the property, the final tax is determined by the assessed value and the tax rate.

Whatever percentage is used, the assessor must do it on a uniform basis. That is, if one piece of property is assessed at a 25 percent assessment rate, all the property in the community must be at the same 25 percent rate so that taxation will be fair and equitable. Owners of similarly valued properties should be paying the same amount of tax.

This objective of uniformity is not always easy to achieve because of the numerous variables affecting value. Since property evaluations are almost as much a matter of opinion as of fact, there is considerable opportunity for disagreement between assessors and property owners. Disgruntled property owners can appeal their assessment to a local review board. If still dissatisfied, the property owner can appeal to the courts.

Tax Rate Each year the town government predetermines how much money it will need to perform its functions. A budget, which is the first step in the taxing process, is prepared. The budgeting needs are then compared to the estimate of moneys that will be received from sources other than real estate taxes. This revenue is subtracted from the budgetary needs, and the remaining amount needed is to be collected in the form of real estate taxes. If, for example, the budgetary needs for your town are $25 million for the year, with $5 million coming from other sources, then the shortfall of $20 million must come from real estate taxes.

Assessed Value   The next step in determining the general tax is based on the assessed value and the tax rate. If the fair market value of all your town's property is $800 million and the assessment ratio of assessed value to appraised market value is 25 percent, the total assessed value of the real estate is $200 million ($800 million × 25%). The $20 million needed for the budget is then divided by the $200 million assessed value ($20 million ÷ 200 million = .10). The tax rate then is .10, or 10 percent. The town will charge a tax of 10 percent, or $10 for every $100 of assessed value. Let's assume your home has an appraised market value of $80,000. Since the assessment ratio is 25 percent, your home's assessed value, for tax purposes, is $20,000. The $20,000 assessed value multiplied by the 10 percent rate would result in your receiving a tax bill of $2000 for the year. To ease the taxpayers' burden, taxes are usually paid in two installments per year.

Exemptions   Of significant concern to taxpayers is the number of tax-exempt properties within their community. These generally include all government property and property owned by nonprofit institutions, such as churches, hospitals, and private schools. Some of the larger metropolitan areas, Boston for instance, have up to 50 percent of its taxable property exempt because of the profusion of colleges and churches located within the city limits. These properties require the services of the community, but don't pay taxes for those services. Their fair share of the costs of services are usually absorbed by all the town's taxpayers.

Some institutions do, however, pay a sum of money to the community in lieu of taxes. For instance, in towns where there are state parks (which aren't taxed) the state will give a sum of money to the town in which the park is located. In some towns veterans and the elderly are allowed to pay reduced taxes, and tax reductions are often offered to industries if they locate a facility within the community with a promise of jobs to residents.

Special Assessments

Special assessments arc levied against specific properties to help pay
for improvements that benefit those particular properties. Street paving, curbing and sidewalks, lighting, and the extension of water lines
are typical improvements of this sort. The justification for the assessment is that the improvements enhance the value of the affected properties. The costs of any improvement are spread among the property
owners benefitted. This is a one-time tax, separate from your real estate
tax. It may be paid off over a period of several years, with interest
charged on the unpaid balance. For instance, if a town water line was
extended across the front of your land with an assessment (also called a
betterment charge) cost to you of $1500, you could pay $150 per year
for ten years with perhaps a 10 percent annual rate of interest charged
on the declining unpaid balance.

When you're researching a parcel of land that you are considering
purchasing, check with the town hall to see if there are any special
assessment taxes levied against the parcel. Also, ask if any betterment
work is planned for that immediate area in the near future.

POLICE POWER

The term *police power* sounds ominous, conjuring up images of
George Orwell's Big Brother. But this is the kind of Big Brother
stewardship that is supposed to be good for us—most of the time,
anyway. As with most of the legal aspects involved in real estate
investing, it is important to understand the usual applications of the
government's police power so that when you do encounter it you can
act quickly and responsibly. Certainly, understanding land use regulations will be difficult for the newcomer. But take solace, it is a difficulty shared by even those with a lot of experience in this arena. That's
why there are so many attorneys involved in real estate, and even they
can be confused with the inconsistencies in the law.

The government has the right—a right we've given it—to enact and exercise the necessary rules and regulations for our collective good. The exercise of this right, called police power, includes all the regulations of land consistent with the due process of law considered necessary for our welfare. State governments delegate police power authority, through enabling acts, to local governments. Actually, state governments don't often get involved with local land use matters. It's generally recognized that local governments are better situated to engage in regulating land use in their jurisdictions. These delegated powers include planning, zoning ordinances, building codes, and subdivision regulations.

Planning

Today we are so used to the idea of planning community growth—so familiar with the delicate balance between development restrictions for residents on one hand and incentives for developers on the other—that it seems unimaginable that communities could grow without a systematic plan. Yet since the discovery of our nation most communities grew just that way. Buildings were constructed, roads established, businesses formed—all in a haphazard manner.

The founding fathers of some of our cities did consider planning. In fact, in the mid seventeenth century the Dutch laid out New Amsterdam (New York City) similar to communities in their native land. Our nation's capital was patterned in 1791 after major cities in France by the French designer Charles L'Enfant. Several major colonial cities like Williamsburg, Virginia, were patterned after English communities. But even these cities, once they grew beyond the central core, tended to grow with abandon.

Theories of Growth   City planners, designers, demographers, and other students of community growth have analyzed how our major metropolitan areas have developed. From their studies four major theories on growth were formulated. Knowing these theories will help you to determine the direction of growth in the areas you plan to invest in.

These four theories are Concentric Circle Theory, Axial Theory, Sector Theory, and the Multiple Nuclei Theory.

Concentric Circle Theory. Based on studies of the development of the City of Chicago in the 1930s, this theory states that land tends to develop in a pattern of concentric circles outward from the central business and retail district. The central district is the hub, or center of activity, from which all other zones radiate. The next circle of activity is a transition zone of both commercial and industrial activities that service the central business district. Next is a low-income housing zone containing older housing. A middle-income zone follows, consisting of early suburban developments. The final circle of activity is the commuting zone of newer, higher-income suburbs and semirural properties.

Axial Theory. This theory, outlined in 1932 by Frederick M. Babcock, an appraiser studying urban growth, modifies the Concentric Circle Theory by stating that land develops outward from the central business district along the major transportation systems, or axes. This theory proposes that a distant site located on a major artery will develop faster than a site closer to the central business district that is not on a major transportation route.

Sector Theory. In 1939 Homer Hoyt, a major force in real estate development and economics, refined the Axial Theory by considering the appeal of one transportation corridor over another. Hoyt found that groups of a similar nature tended to locate together in a single sector. Members of the wholesale food business grouped together, as did the clothing business and automobile distributors, primarily because of their combined use of common sources of supply and distribution. Residential neighborhoods also expand in the same manner. Wealthy neighborhoods, as they grow, tend to attract the well-to-do, for instance. An interesting point of the development of the Sector Theory is that the more affluent neighborhoods tend to be in the western suburbs of most major municipalities. It is not known why this is so—perhaps because they are located upwind from industrial fumes and pollutants. Look at your own city and see where the wealth has congregated.

Multiple Nuclei Theory. This theory, proposed in 1945 by C. D. Harris and E. L. Ullman, takes into consideration the affect of the automobile on urban growth. The Multiple Nuclei Theory holds that there are several central business districts of various sizes in a given area and that growth expands outward from all of them.

The Need for Controls The advent of the automobile and its attendant problems further exacerbated the need for controls. Some areas grew without making provisions for utilities, transportation needs, parking, and pedestrian safety. No provision was made for off-street parking and even today downtown parking is no longer possible in many congested areas. As the cities grew, so too did the suburbs. Some suburbs have experienced very serious problems due to a lack of planning and control of their growth. Many subdivisions were approved and developed without consideration for adequate water, sewage disposal, streets, lighting, parking, and so on. In some areas lots are so small that neighboring properties are contaminating one another's soil. The growth of the unplanned suburbs has merely extended the problems of the unplanned cities. It took until this century for us to wake up and establish effective planning controls. We're now aware that planning is inextricably tied to the quality of urban development. Today, city planning is an integral part of most of our communities, small and large. Urban planners receive college degrees after being armed with the necessary studies and training to improve our communities and afford us a better quality of life.

Ideally, planning should precede development, but in most communities this just didn't happen. Instead, planning was instituted in response to already existing development and growth pressures. Many communities still react after the fact rather than planning for growth, as is the case in most of our older metropolitan areas. But they can still be salvaged. Urban renewal can be the rebirth of many ill-planned, or unplanned, layouts.

Through land planning, smaller and growing communities have learned well and are able to prevent many of the earlier problems our larger cities have experienced. Let's take a look at how land planning operates.

Planning starts at the national level and moves down to regional, state, and local levels. The federal government, for instance, has developed and maintains our interstate highway system and regulates all other transportation methods: air, water, and rail. Regional planning takes on problems of energy and water supply and economic growth. State planning takes on similar intrastate problems, and local authorities concern themselves with the safety and welfare of their neighborhoods. They coordinate their efforts and activities for their mutual good.

The Master Plan   The first step in the planning process is the creation of a planning commission. The members of the commission are appointed by the town leaders: the mayor, selectmen, or other authorities. The makeup of the commission differs from one state to another. Generally, there are five to fifteen members, often including the mayor and other town officials, along with professional planners and several lay citizens. The planning commission's function is to prepare a land use plan for the development or redevelopment of the community. This land use plan, called a *master plan* or *comprehensive plan,* is designed to prevent haphazard growth and piecemeal zoning. In preparing the master plan, the planning commission advises on the current and future use of the land in the community, tempered by the financial ability of the community to carry out the plan. For example, if a large area is to be devoted to parks and recreation, can the town reasonably afford to do so without placing a burden on the townspeople? The Standard Planning Enabling Act of 1928 describes the master plan thus:

> The plan shall be made with the general purpose of guiding and accomplishing a coordinated, adjusted, and harmonious development of the municipality and its environs which will, in accordance with present and future needs, best promote health, safety, morals, order, convenience, property, and general welfare, as well as efficiency and economy in the process of development; including among other things adequate provisions for traffic, the promotion of safety from fire and other damages, adequate provision for light and air, the promotion of the healthful and convenient distribution of the population, the promotion of good civic design and arrangement,

wise and efficient expenditure of public funds, and the adequate possession of public utilities and other public requirements.

The master plan is a statement of goals covering the physical development of the community with respect to social, economic, and political objectives. It allocates land for residential, commercial, industrial, recreational, and public uses. The plan defines what utilities are needed now and projects what will be needed in the future. It provides for recreational and educational facilities, police and fire services, and the control and routing of vehicular traffic patterns—locating major land uses in the areas that are best suited for them. It controls the density and location of the population, and the intensity of building construction.

In preparing the master plan the commission first takes an inventory of its resources. Topography, climate, population characteristics, employment, skills, transportation, taxes, current land uses, and other physical, social, and economic data are collected and analyzed, and trends are discovered and planned for. The master plan sets the stage for the other land use controls that implement it: zoning ordinances, subdivision regulations, and building codes.

Zoning Ordinances

Zoning is the tool employed to carry out the goals and objectives of the master plan. It is exercised by means of ordinances that determine and regulate the use of land. Zoning ordinances consist of (1) the formalized written and graphic text setting forth what can and cannot be done with land, and (2) the zoning map that delineates land use district boundaries. There are no national or state zoning controls, only local zoning ordinances.

Experience has shown that growth without controls results in undesirable conditions. Zoning prevents these undesirable conditions by regulating the use of land. It is concerned with the proper development of land at its highest and best use, for the purpose of promoting and safeguarding the safety, health, convenience, and welfare of the majority of the citizens.

In colonial America before the eighteenth century, zoning controlled the location of noxious or undesirable businesses. Distilleries, slaughterhouses, gunpowder mills, and tanneries were forced to locate away from the general population.

More formalized zoning practices started at the start of this century. In 1916 New York City instituted the first zoning ordinances out of a growing concern of how skyscrapers would adversely affect property values by blocking sunlight and air from existing structures. Since then, practically every part of the country has become guided and controlled by zoning. Today's zoning laws are more refined than earlier laws and they are continually being refined, revised, updated, adjusted, and strengthened in response to the growth and needs of communities.

A local zoning board, which consists of community-appointed members, is responsible for the maintenance of the zoning ordinances. Zoning ordinances must be fair and reasonable and must not violate the rights of individuals and landowners. The Fourteenth Amendment to the Constitution and statutory laws protect their rights. If a zoning ordinance proves destructive, arbitrary, or confiscatory, it may be ruled void by the courts. To be valid, a zoning ordinance must be clear and specific; be nondiscriminatory; promote public health, safety, and welfare; and be administered equitably and reasonably.

Though zoning ordinances vary from community to community, they generally include variations of the following major topics:

- Purpose and authority
- Establishment of zoning districts
- Dimensional regulations
- Nonconforming uses
- Special regulations
- Administration and enforcement
- Amendments
- Definitions

Zoning divides up a community into land use classifications. Certain areas are designated for residential use only, others for commercial or industrial use, others for public uses such as schools, municipal buildings, and libraries, and still others for recreational purposes like parks, beaches, and tennis courts. The following is a breakdown of various subclassifications included in a typical small town zoning ordinance:

R-R   Residential—Rural
R-L   Residential—Low Density
R-M   Residential—Medium Density
C-L   Commercial—Low Density
C-H   Commercial—High Density
I   Industrial
A   Agricultural

The single-family residential district is the highest (that is, the most strictly regulated) zoning district. All other districts are determined by how they affect it. Richard F. Babcock in his book *The Zoning Game* said:

> The insulation of the single-family detached dwelling was the primary objective of the early zoning ordinances and the objective is predominate today.

A major goal of zoning is to obtain a workable mix, or homogeneity, within a given zoning district. Therefore, the zoning districts are even further broken down into subclassifications. A district zoned for residential use, for example, may be classified as "A-Residential" for single family residences or "B-Residential" for two-family residences or "C-Residential" for home occupations. A home occupation is a trade that can be practiced out of your home without being disruptive to the residential nature of the neighborhood. A lawyer, doctor, tailor, real estate broker, or financial advisor—even a palm reader—may be allowed to use a restricted amount of space in his or her home to conduct business. In rapidly growing and highly developed communities the number and variety of zoning classifications is greater. But the residential districts are still provided the greatest protection from adverse conditions; industrial districts, the least. Table 6-1 illustrates the variety of subclassifications in a larger community.

Chapter VI

Table 6-1
Typical Zoning Subclassifications for a Larger Community

Zoning Designation	Code	Minimum Lot Size	Minimum Frontage	Lot Width	Minimum Set-backs Front	Minimum Set-backs Rear & Side
Residential	RA	10,000	-	100	10	10
Residential	RA-1	15,000	-	100	10	10
Residential	RA-2	15,000	120	-	15	15
Residential	RB	20,000	-	135	20	20
Residential	RB-1	20,000	135	-	20	20
Residential	RC	35,000	-	150	40	30
Residential	RC-1	35,000	150	-	40	30
Residential	RD	40,000	-	150	40	30
Residential	RD-1	40,000	150	-	40	30
Business	B	7,500	100	-	20	30
Business	B-1	20,000	120	-	20	30
Industrial	I	80,000	200	-	60	30
Industrial	I-1	100,000	250	-	60	30

Zoning is not covered in a title search. You can't rely on your lawyer or a title examiner for this information. It is up to you to find out about it. Each town you go into will differ from every other town in its use and application of zoning. Lot sizes may differ; one town may accept one-fifth of an acre as a buildable homesite, another town may require homesites to be three acres in size. A given land use may be restricted in one town and the same use may be readily accepted in another town. It's your responsibility to know the zoning laws in every town where you own land, or will own land, and how they affect your desired use of that land. Go over to your town hall and get a copy of the zoning ordinances for a dollar or two—and pick up copies of the building codes and subdivision rules and regulations also. Read them through entirely and get a feeling of what zoning is all about. Go to a neighboring town and get a copy of their zoning ordinances and compare the two. You'll see a lot of differences, but there will be one overriding similarity—their purpose. They were both created for the welfare of the citizenry.

Variations of Zoning   A frequent situation occurs when a building does not conform to the zoning use because it was built prior to the enactment of the zoning laws, or prior to a change in the law. Since it existed before the zoning law or the change in the zoning law, it is not in violation. It is called a nonconforming use and is allowed to continue, but the nonconforming use cannot be expanded. If you owned a grocery store, for example, in a district that was later rezoned to all residential, you can continue to operate the store, but you cannot enlarge it. If your store is destroyed or torn down, then any new building and its use must conform to existing zoning laws.

The typical zoning ordinance includes *permitted uses* and *special exceptions*. A permitted use needs no additional approval from authorities as long as it conforms to building codes and subdivision regulations. A special exception may be authorized if certain standards are met, such as building height, traffic flow, parking facilities, and noise control. A petition may be presented to a zoning board of appeals if you wanted to operate in exception to the zoning laws. For example, you might want to operate a country inn out of your overly large single-family home in a residential district. The board of appeals may grant a special use permit where a need exists and is not normally allowed.

A *variance,* an exception because of hardship as a result of zoning, may be approved if it doesn't create a detrimental situation to the public. A variance is an approved deviation from the existing zoning ordinances. An example would be the right to build within a restricted area, say within 100 feet of a wetland, because of the configuration of your lot. In this case you would also have to get the approval of the local environmental agency. A variance won't be granted if the landowner's hardship was self-created.

Exclusionary zoning, or "snob zoning," is indirectly designed to keep out certain types or classes of people by exaggerating or over-qualifying the zoning. Dictating extra large lot sizes would exclude moderate-income people from the community because they couldn't afford to buy the larger, more expensive lots.

Subdivision Regulations

Planning is the first step in the exercise of police power; zoning is the second; and subdivision regulations constitute the third step.

Subdivision regulations are locally developed laws controlling the conversion of raw acreage into other uses. Dividing up a parcel into any number of smaller parcels—whether into two lots or 2000—is a subdivision. Chapter XII, "Subdividing Your Land," includes an in-depth explanation of subdivision regulations.

Building Codes

Planning starts the regulatory process in directing the community's growth. Zoning takes over, controlling the use of the land. Subdivision regulations come into play next by controlling the improvement to the land. Finally, building codes pick up the responsibility in the regulatory chain where subdivision regulations leave off by controlling the construction and occupancy of buildings on the land. A building code is a series of state or local ordinances that regulate the construction, alteration, and maintenance of structures within the community. They specify the structural requirements, kinds of materials, sanitary equipment, electrical and plumbing systems, and fire prevention standards. A building permit is required when constructing a new building, and separate permits must be obtained from the fire inspector, the electrical inspector, the plumbing inspector, and the health agent.

Building codes are especially stringent for buildings that will hold several persons, such as hospitals, schools, apartments, churches, office buildings, and stores.

New Amsterdam (New York City) created the first building codes in 1625. Their purpose then was to prevent roof fires—reasonable thinking when you consider that our forefathers constructed their roofs of dried straw and reeds.

Fire prevention is as important in today's building codes as it was then. Several code requirements concern the layout of buildings for efficient and rapid evacuation in case of fire. Windows, particularly in bedrooms, must be large enough for an adult to climb through. Materials, as much as possible, must be fireproof.

Building codes also consider adequacy of ventilation, proper and sufficient lighting, structural soundness, architectural balance, electrical wiring and equipment, and plumbing needs.

Most regulations today are based on the nation-wide Uniform Building Code. Its stated purpose is to prevent people from being hurt physically of financially by providing minimum uniform standards of building construction. Most communities around the country conform to this code with adjustments necessitated by climatic and topographic conditions and regional tastes.

The enforcement of the building codes begins in the building inspector's department. Before starting construction on your new seventy-room mansion, you must submit your plans to the building inspector for approval and pay a permit fee. Through the permit application process, town authorities are able to keep track of all new construction and repairs that are made in their community. They can also verify compliance with local laws by an examination of the plans and a series of visits to inspect the work in progress. When the building inspector examines the house plans, he or she can see if you are in compliance with, not only the building codes, but also the zoning ordinances and the subdivision regulations. If, for example, you purchased your lot in a subdivision that was approved by the town planning board and recorded at the registry of deeds, the inspector will have a copy of the recorded plan in his or her office. If the streets weren't completed or other improvements were inadequate, the plan would not have been approved by the planning board and the building inspector will not issue a building permit. If you are in compliance with the zoning ordinances, subdivision regulations, and building codes, the inspector will issue a building permit. This is your authority to start construction. The law does not require you to hire a professional builder to construct your house; you can do it yourself. However, the plumbing and electrical utilities must be installed by a licensed practitioner.

Quite often persons working on their own house will not apply for a permit. Maybe they want to do something that is not allowed by the codes. Or, if they are adding several rooms, they know that their tax assessment will be increased by this increased value added to their property, and they may try to keep it secret. If found out, the penalty could be severe. The inspector can require that you rip out all the work done without a permit.

If your land is not serviced by a town sewage system, then you will have to install a permanent septic system with leach lines. Prior to applying for a building permit, you must submit plans for a sewage disposal system to the local health agent for his or her approval. The bulldozer operator usually digs the hole for a septic system at the same time as the hole for the house foundation. After the tanks are placed in the hole, the health agent will inspect and approve the system, and then it can be covered up.

It is important for you to find out before you buy your land if the land is suitable for a septic system. You can't tell by a visual scan of the land what's below the surface. The land must be permeable to readily absorb septic tank effluent. If the subsoil consists of clay or similar impervious materials, water cannot flow through them, and a septic permit will be denied for your lot. You will than have to go through the costly process of removing and replacing the impervious material with more suitable porous soils. Or you may have to dig the hole deeper to install the septic system below the clay. Either way it costs more than a routine septic system. To protect yourself in this event, include a contingency clause in your sales contract that the land must pass a *percolation test*. The percolation test will determine how quickly and effectively water will drain through the existing soil. If it's all clay, you won't want to buy the land. If you can't install a septic system on your land, it is of no value to you for residential purposes.

Construction work is inspected as it progresses. Usually, the first visit by the inspector is to examine the foundation. If you are installing a septic system, the health agent will come out at this time. The second visit by the building inspector will occur when the roof and framing are complete and all pipes, vents, and chimneys are installed. The electrical and plumbing inspectors will come by to inspect what they are responsible for at this point in the construction schedule. The next visit by the building inspector will be to inspect the walls before the plaster is applied and the siding put on. The fire inspector will come by to see if the fire laws have been complied with, in particular the installation of the burner. The final inspection comes after the building is completed and ready for occupancy. The building is now considered safe for you to live in.

Banks will not release the final draw, or payment, on a construction loan until the occupancy permit is issued. A certificate of occupancy is an official notice that all the codes have been complied with and that the structure is fit for use. In some communities certain existing buildings must be physically inspected each year to detect code violations, and some communities require an inspection whenever ownership changes.

A building permit must not be in conflict or violation of deed restrictions or subdivision restrictions. For example, if you obtain a permit to build a 1000-square-foot house in a subdivision that requires homes to have a minimum of 1500 square feet of living space, then the subdivision restrictions take precedence. Private restrictions can be more stringent than government restrictions, but not less so. For example, if the town ordinances dictate that a home must have at least 1000 square feet of living space, then a subdivision restriction allowing less would be void. Rights of adjoining owners in a subdivision prevail over government restrictions when there is a conflict and the restrictions are more limiting.

Many less-developed communities will allow you to live in a temporary dwelling on the lot while building your permanent residence. A trailer, camper, bus, van, or even a tent will do. The building inspector may enter your property at any reasonable time to inspect it. If you try to keep the building inspector out, he or she will come back with the police to enforce the right to inspect the property. If you buy land with a building on it that you plan to use right away, make sure that it meets current building and health codes. As with other government regulations, you can get a copy of your local building codes, printed in booklet form, from your town hall for a couple of dollars.

CHAPTER VII

APPRAISING AND NEGOTIATING

Appraising and negotiating seem to be strange bedfellows to include in a single chapter. When structuring this book, I had intended to separate them with each as a separate chapter. However, on analysis it became more logical to pair them together. Once you have located the land you want to buy, you need to determine what you should pay for it; that's where the appraising comes into play. You must get the seller to agree to accept this amount; that's where the negotiating takes its role: they go hand in hand. Actually, no single chapter of this book stands by itself in the land buying and selling process; they are all thoroughly dependent on and supportive of one another.

Appraising may seem more than a bit confusing and complicated to you, and understandably so. Professional appraisers spend years learning and perfecting their craft. You don't have to know it as well as they do, of course, but a basic understanding of how they go about their task will help you in selecting the right parcels to purchase, improve, and resell.

APPRAISING

Some people seem to have an inherent ability to judge the value of a parcel of land "off the top of their head." Don't fool yourself; that "top of the head" guesstimation is usually buttressed by a sound education of land values and personal knowledge of the neighborhood. Occasionally, someone with little or no formal training can make a reasonable guess as to value; the secret, however, is to be able to do it consistently and accurately. An entire career is devoted to appraising.

Let me point out that appraising is a very demanding, complicated, and exacting field. There is no rigid mathematical or scientific formula. It isn't a science, but simply a collection of facts about the subject parcel and an analysis of those facts. A little knowledge and appreciation of how an appraiser goes about his or her tasks will stand you in good stead when you start venturing out estimating the value of land that you are considering buying. Your methods won't be as technical, nor as thorough, but they'll have similar end results—an educated and reasonable estimate of value. As a land investor, you must be able to make intelligent decisions about what you are willing to pay for a parcel of land. How do you do this? How do you know when a parcel is a good deal or overpriced? This boils down to deciding how much the parcel is worth and what its value is to you.

Value

To appraise land is to estimate its value based on all available pertinent facts. Let me stress, however, that it is an estimate. A dozen trained and capable appraisers evaluating the same parcel on the same day will, more than likely, arrive at a dozen different estimates of value. Hopefully, because of their expertise, all will be within a reasonable range of one another.

Value has many "faces": insurable value, salvage value, fair rental value, and fair market value, to name just a few. It is essential to know that value is not just cost or price, but also worth. Land has a useful life extending over decades; its value, therefore, is the present worth of its future benefits. Price is the amount of money asked for the land, while cost is the amount expended in acquiring it.

People make value. For land to have value it must be wanted by someone for some purpose—the prerequisites of utility and scarcity must be present. Utility, on the demand side, is the reason you would be willing to pay a certain price—it renders a service and fills a need; scarcity, on the supply side, is the necessity of paying a certain price. The greater the supply, the lower its value, and vice versa. The finest parcel of land will have little demand and little utility if it is so remote as to make it impractical for people to use it.

Location

Land has the unique characteristics of being durable, immobile, and without substitute. Except for acts of God, and perhaps a bulldozer, land is virtually indestructible—it is durable. Unlike machinery, buildings, tools, and the like, it cannot be moved from one place to another—it is immobile. Each and every piece of land has unique physical characteristics that make it different from any other piece of land, and it has only one location—it is without substitute. The environment or setting in which we find land is the single greatest influence in determining value. Some parcels have a built-in locational value because of a favorable view, or good soil conditions, or ideal topography, or easy accessability. All land—in fact, all real estate—is judged primarily on its location. You've heard it before: the three most important factors affecting the value of land are location, location, and location. That is: the location of the land within the immediate area or neighborhood; the location of the neighborhood within the city or town, and the location of the city within the region.

Purpose of an Appraisal

Everyone uses real estate in one way or another and must pay for this use, either by rental or outright purchase. Decisions on what the payments will be involve an estimate of value, which in turn requires an appraisal of some kind. Appraisals are made for many and varied reasons: for assessing taxes, for condemnations, to settle an estate, for insurance coverage, and as a basis for a mortgage. The fundamental purpose is to estimate a specific value such as insurable value, salvage value, fair rental value, selling or purchase price, and most often, market value.

Market Value   The American Institute of Real Estate Appraisers defines market value as

> The highest price estimated in terms of money which a property will bring if exposed for sale in the open market, allowing a reasonable time to find a purchaser who buys with knowledge of all the uses to which it is adapted and for which it is capable of being used.

Or more succinctly:

> The price at which a willing seller would sell and a willing buyer would buy, neither being under abnormal pressure.

An appraiser, in arriving at a market value conclusion, must take into consideration the social, economic, physical, and governmental forces that affect the current conditions of the marketplace as it relates to both the buyer and the seller. The forces are briefly described below.

Social Forces
- Population growth, decline, and density
- Family size
- Ethnic considerations
- Births, deaths, marriages, and divorces
- Recreational, religious, educational, cultural, and aesthetic considerations

If the residents are of similar economic, social, ethnic and cultural backgrounds, this homogeneity will certainly affect the desirability of the neighborhood to prospective buyers. In time, all neighborhoods change. As they change and new people move in, the newer group is usually on a lower economic plane. When this happens, the tendency is for those of a higher economic and social status to move out.

Economic Forces
- Commercial and industrial trends
- Employment standards and trends
- Money, credit, and taxes

Commercial and industrial activities, employment trends, availability of credit, tax rates, and interest rates all have a profound affect on purchasing power. And purchasing power affects real estate values.

Physical Forces
- Climatology
- Geology
- Amenities
- Ecology

The geographical location of a neighborhood most assuredly affects desirability. It may be located near undesirable commercial and industrial developments, railroad yards, or a town disposal area. On the other hand, it may be next to the ocean or a large conservation area.

Governmental Forces
- Zoning
- Police and fire ordinances
- Building codes
- Public health restrictions

Strong, well planned zoning regulations and health and safety restrictions protect neighborhoods from adverse influences that may diminish desirability, and thus decrease value.

Neighborhood Desirability To measure the desirability of a neighborhood, several features must be considered:

Economic Stability. Changes in purchasing power affect the ability of people to purchase real estate and meet the costs of ownership, resulting in changes in property values. The economic characteristics of the current residents will influence the type and quality of future residents. Statistically, the highest and lowest income groups are the least stable, while the middle income group is the most stable.

Adverse Conditions. People want to live in the best neighborhood they can afford. The more affluent can live in a desirable neighborhood of their choosing, whereas the lower income people live in less desirable neighborhoods that afford them only the bare necessities. Zoning restrictions protect against certain environmental hazards such as poor traffic conditions, dangerous physical hazards like erosion or steep streets, poor drainage, and smoke and other offensive odors. The absence of these adverse conditions makes a neighborhood more desirable.

Social Services. A neighborhood should be adequately served by social and commercial activities. Essential considerations are the quality and proximity of schools, libraries, religious centers, shopping, hospitals, and transportation.

Amenities. Proximity to lakes, parks, beaches, mountains, and their recreational offerings affects neighborhood desirability.

Adequate fire and police protection and the existence of gas, water, electricity, and telephones, as well as equitable taxation, are additional features contributing to desirability. When acquiring a parcel of land, you must take all these into consideration; the lots that you will be developing will one day be an integral part of an active and growing neighborhood.

Economic Principles

Land, like steel or wheat or lumber, is a commodity, and its utilization and valuation is deeply rooted in the same economic principals that affect other commodities. An understanding of these economic principles is essential insofar as they relate to the evaluation process of property.

Principle of Anticipation   Value is created by the expectation of future benefits. An individual purchases a parcel with the expectation of utilizing it for a specific purpose, or eventually selling it for an anticipated profit.

Principle of Balance   Equilibrium of services creates and maintains value. Value will decrease if there are fewer services than a neighborhood needs and also when there are more services than a neighborhood can support. For example, if there are too many clothing stores in a neighborhood, some will succeed at the expense of others, or none of them will yield a satisfactory return on investment.

Principle of Change   Change is ever-present. Nothing remains the same. The future, not the past, is of primary concern in estimating value. With land, although the change is not readily discernible, the surrounding area may more readily show change.

Principle of Competition   Excess profits tend to attract competition, and competition quite often diminishes profits. This principle should warn you about nice parcels to subdivide near other nice parcels: keep your activities to yourself as much as possible and buy the other parcels when you can. Don't invite competition.

Principle of Conformity   To achieve its highest value, land must be utilized to conform to established patterns of the neighborhood. If the neighborhood is made up of half-acre lots, a two-acre lot would certainly be out of place and its true value would be diminished by its lack of conformity.

Principle of Contribution   The value of each component of the property depends on how much it increases or decreases value by its presence. For instance, if one lot out of four that you have subdivided is smaller than the other three, how much does this smaller size decrease its own value and increase the value of the other three?

Principle of Diminishing Returns   An investment will produce a certain return up to the point where it reaches a maximum return. Additional expenditures will not produce similar return or value, but less. If you buy a parcel, remove the debris, fill the holes, and put a fence around it, you've improved it to perhaps its current maximum value. Additional expenditures to improve the property will not necessarily increase its value—this is the point of diminishing returns.

Principle of Highest and Best Use   Stated simply, the highest and best use is the most profitable use to which the land can be put, or the use that will yield the highest return on investment. In evaluating the highest and best use you must take the limiting factors that govern the use of the property into consideration—such as zoning, easements, location, and demand for the particular use. You may feel that the ten-acre parcel that you are interested in buying would be a great site for a shopping mall. But if zoning precludes this use, then you have to expend your efforts on studying what is allowed and forget what is not allowed. An opinion of value is formed by analyzing all the factors that will influence your eventual use of the property. You must evaluate its value as is, and also as it will be when developed to its highest and best use.

Principle of Substitution The maximum value of a parcel tends to be determined by the cost of acquiring a substitute parcel of equal utility. When several parcels with substantially the same utility are available, the lowest-priced one will be in greater demand.

Principle of Supply and Demand Demand for land is created by scarcity and is limited by the financial ability of potential buyers to satisfy their needs. The greater the supply, the lower the value. Conversely, the lesser the supply, the higher the value. An increasing supply, or a declining demand, adversely affects market value.

Each of these principles is interdependent and have a circuitous relationship with one another. For instance, anticipation of a profit creates a demand; demand produces a profit; profits stimulate competition; competition increases supply; more supply diminishes profits; diminished profits lessen demand; less demand decreases the supply; decreased supply creates anticipation of profits, and around and around it goes.

Approaches to Value

This final segment on appraising explains the three methods that are used in the appraisal process: the *market data approach*, which estimates value by recent selling prices of similar properties; the *income approach*, which estimates value by capitalizing income; and the *cost approach*, which estimates value by determining the cost of reproducing the property.

Market Data Approach The market data approach (also known as the *sales comparison approach*) is the method most often used for appraising vacant lots, raw acreage, and single-family homes. It is primarily a comparison of the subject property with other similar parcels that have sold recently, or are currently for sale. You must make sure to analyze parcels that are as nearly comparable as possible to the subject in size, condition, location, and selling terms. When the real estate market is healthy and active, there will be many comparables available, affording you a more reliable conclusion.

The selling price alone is not sufficient. You have to look into the terms of the sales to see if there were any extraordinary circumstances that determined the selling prices. Two lots side by side and similar in every physical respect may sell for significantly different prices because of the different urgencies of the two situations. One seller may have a pressing need to sell his or her parcel and may have accepted a price less than fair market value; the owner of the abutting lot may be in no particular hurry and hold firm on his or her asking price.

You'll never find two parcels that are similar in all respects; therefore, adjustments for the differences will have to be made. If one of the comparables was sold two or three years ago, it's certainly worth more today, if only because of inflation, and its selling price must be updated to reflect current market conditions.

The Income Approach   The income approach concerns the present value of the future benefits, or income, of property ownership. It is used when evaluating income-producing properties like apartment houses, office buildings, and shopping centers. Although you may never buy a property with an income-producing structure on it, it would be of value for you to understand how this method of property evaluation is conducted.

There are several variations of the income approach. The most acceptable way is to first determine the annual gross income of the property, such as rents, and then deduct the operating expenses to arrive at the annual net income. Next, divide the net income by whatever rate of interest is necessary to attract capital to this kind of investment. The end result is the estimate of value by the income approach.

As an example, take an apartment house that yields a $75,000 net income per year. Determine what percent of return will be satisfactory to you; it's your money and you can decide on any return you want—within reason. What percent would it take to attract your money into this investment? Assume 12 percent. So, if the apartments yield a net of $75,000 and your desired rate is 12 percent, you should pay no more than $625,000 for the property because that is what its estimate of value is by the income approach.

$$\frac{\text{Net income}}{\text{Desired return}} \quad \frac{\$75,000}{.12} = \$625,000 \text{ estimated value}$$

Cost Approach This method estimates value by determining what it would cost to replace the property in its current condition, less accrued depreciation. It is principally used in appraising public buildings, schools, hospitals, churches, and railway stations. Once you've determined the value of the buildings (less depreciation), you add this cost to the value of the land, which was determined through the market data approach.

To determine the cost of the structures, you simply find out from local contractors what it would cost to replace the buildings at today's prices, and then adjust these figures by the loss of value (depreciation) that the building has incurred since it was built new. If the property includes a nine-year-old building with a useful life of 20 years, and it's going to depreciate the same amount each year, deduct one-twentieth of its replacement costs for each of the 10 years of its existence and subtract this total amount from the replacement value of the building:

$$\frac{\text{Replacement cost}}{\text{Useful life}} \quad \frac{\$80,000}{20 \text{ yrs.}} = \$4000/\text{yr. depreciation}$$

$$\$4000 \times 9 \text{ yrs. (age of bldg.)} = \$36,000 \text{ Total depreciation}$$

Replacement cost	$80,000
Total depreciation	− 36,000
Current market value	$44,000

Finally, you add the current market value of $44,000 to the previously determined value of the land, and you have your cost approach estimate.

The income approach and the cost approach can get a lot more complicated. I've kept the explanations simple here so as not to confuse you—or me. If you are going to be buying land only, you won't be using either approach. You will be using a variation of the market data approach coupled with the subdivision approach, which is explained in Chapter XII. For our purposes here, let's just state that in the subdivision method you estimate the number of lots and arrive at a selling price for each. From that you deduct the development and land improvement costs, sales and carrying charges, and your desired profit:

1. Gross selling price. Determine number of lots and selling price of each.
2. Development costs. Deduct:

> Surveying and engineering costs.
> Water and sewer lines.
> Utility deposits.
> Street grading and paving.

3. Indirect cost. Deduct:

> Interest on land purchase price.
> Interest on development costs.
> Taxes.

4. Deduct desired profit.

The final step for the appraiser is to correlate the three approaches to value. Each approach is analyzed and weighted for its reliability. The final estimate of value may or may not be any one of the three approaches, nor an average of the three. The appraiser will choose a final estimate of value that, in his or her judgment, is the most reasonable.

NEGOTIATING

In most parts of the world, bargaining is an accepted and expected way of doing business, whether you are buying a freshly killed chicken or a

Ming vase. Yet here in the United States, where most of us pride ourselves on our general economic common sense and buying know-how, we rarely, if ever, bargain for anything. Once in a great while, when purchasing a used car or an old mirror at a yard sale, we'll throw out an offer, and not surprisingly it's usually accepted, or at least the original asking price is bargained down. The fact that we're reluctant to bargain certainly costs us a great deal of potential savings over our lifetimes. The next time you go to the drug store, make an offer below the ticketed price of any item, and the druggist will think you are peculiar, since this is not the way Americans do business.

Yet in purchasing real estate you would be considered peculiar if you didn't bargain for the best deal—for this is the way Americans, and everyone else around the world, purchase real estate: they bargain for it. Bargaining and bartering are as much a part of the real estate buying process as are closing costs and title searches.

Your profit is already made at the time you purchase the land. That's right, when you buy it. If you buy it at the right price, then it's easier to make the full profit when you eventually resell it. You buy right by bargaining.

The methods and ways of bargaining are as old as civilization and are well established and proven. We all want a bargain when we purchase something. When I buy land, I want a bargain, and you will too. But you're going to have to work for that bargain by negotiating for the best deal that you can get. The sequence of negotiating goes a little like this: The seller asks a certain price, the buyer offers a lesser price. The seller reduces his or her asking price, the buyer increases his or her offer. Eventually they arrive at the point that a willing seller and a willing buyer agree, and a sale is consummated. Sounds simple—and it is if you follow the time-proven techniques of negotiating. Let's take a look at the techniques.

Sell Yourself

You must remember that in almost all of the instances in which you'll be negotiating for a satisfactory purchase price, you'll be dealing with an individual, a person like yourself—not a hard-nosed, business-minded corporation. The process won't be any simpler than dealing with a corporation, but there will be more emotion and sensitivity involved. Treat the seller with the same honesty and courtesy that you would expect in return. Don't try to "steal" the land; those days are gone. Simply approach the seller and try to buy the property at the best price you can negotiate for. The best deals are those in which both buyer and seller are satisfied.

To sell real estate to a prospect you must first let the prospect know he or she can trust you. The same holds true when buying real estate. You have to sell yourself to the landowner and make him or her want to do business with you. So start selling before you buy. You don't have to become buddies, but you must come across as being honest, sincere, and capable. With this groundwork laid out beforehand, you can then proceed in a businesslike manner.

Not every seller is willing to bargain. There will be occasions when an owner will tell you his or her price and accept nothing less. But this is the exception. You should proceed with the assumption that all sellers are willing to dicker and will reduce their asking price if you will increase your offering price. Sellers always set an asking price higher (often much higher) than what they truly expect to receive for their land. They are thus setting up a negotiating position from which to bargain. When you hear the words "asking price," you know that bargaining is expected. Even when you don't hear those words, assume that bargaining is expected, and most often welcomed. The seller certainly wants to get top dollar for his or her property, but a seller wants the buyer to be satisfied too. The seller will have set not only the highest asking price, but also, in his or her own mind, the lowest price that he or she will accept. You, as the buyer, will have to decide upon your initial offering price and your final offering price. When the seller's lowest price is at, or near, the buyer's highest offer, a sale is made.

The largest concessions are made by both the buyer and seller in the early stages of negotiations. The seller will lower his or her initial asking price more readily and more drastically, and at the same time the buyer will raise his or her offer more readily and more significantly. As time elapses during the negotiating period, both buyer and seller become more adamant in their respective positions, and less malleable. Even though the seller has a bottom-dollar amount that he or she will offer, these figures can be changed by some emotional factors that may enter into the picture.

Emotion

Emotion will most assuredly play a role in most of your negotiating transactions. During the bargaining process, something may happen to either party that may have an effect on the sale. A personal loss, an illness, or even winning a lottery may change the whole complexion of the pending sale. For instance, if the seller unexpectedly receives a windfall profit from the sale of a different parcel, he or she may be predisposed to become overly generous and reduce the asking price below what you would reasonably expect. It could work the other way too; the seller may not feel compelled to take any offer and may hold out for his or her initial asking price.

The more anxious a landowner is to sell his or her property, the more compromising and amenable to bargaining he or she will be. The less anxious, the less amenable. If the land has been on the market for a short period of time, the owner will more than likely keep the asking price firm, even if it's overpriced. It's a natural tendency to overprice your own property because of your personal knowledge and attachment to it. You always feel that tomorrow you will find a buyer willing to pay what you are asking. All you need is one buyer. However, the longer the parcel remains unsold, the more willing the owner becomes to bargain and the more realistic and true to current market value the price becomes. The owner may feel that would-be purchasers will think something is wrong with the land the longer it remains unsold.

Find out how long the property has been for sale, and if there have been any price reductions while it has been on the market. If it has been for sale for quite some time, and there have been price reductions, perhaps there *is* something wrong with it. The parcel may be too remote, too barren, or too precipitous, all of which contribute to limiting the market. Perhaps there are easements or encumbrances on the property that have dissuaded others from buying it. In any event, if you know the reason it hasn't sold, and you aren't yourself dissuaded, then you are in a good position to start your bargaining.

Why Is the Owner Selling?

What does the owner say his or her reason for selling is? What do you think the reason is? A seller's stated reason and true reason may be worlds apart. Not everybody sells his or her property for the purpose of making a killing. Sellers often have several reasons, and some of them could be more important than money. If the owner had previously purchased the land as an investment to resell some day for a profit, you may find his or her price inflexible, particularly if the seller doesn't have any pressing reason, other than the profit motive, for selling. If the seller bought the land for another purpose—to build on, to farm, to subdivide, or some similar reason—and his or her plans have changed, you can be relatively assured that he or she will compromise on the price and terms of the sale. It's quite possible that an elderly landowner may have priorities relative to his or her age and health that determine the reasons for selling. Also, if the owner has lived on the land for a long time, he or she may be very concerned with what you're going to do with his or her land and how it's going to affect the community and the neighbors. An owner's emotional attachment to the land and what your plans for it are will significantly affect the bargaining process.

If the property owner lives on the land that is for sale, or has recently moved from it, he or she will probably want to sell as fast as possible. The owner may need the money to purchase property elsewhere or may simply want to settle personal and financial affairs; an owner in this situation may be willing to accept any reasonable offer.

The more pressures on the owner to sell, the more anxious and willing he or she will be to bargain. Find out why the owner is selling and work this knowledge to your advantage. If you can be fairly sure of the owner's primary reason for selling, you can approach the negotiating table with greater confidence. If you're buying land that has some personal attachment to it, such as land that has been in the family for generations, then you should proceed with some understanding and consideration of the owner's emotional state. A tactful and friendly approach will make it easier for you to buy the land, and for the owner to sell. You've got to convince the owner that you are the person he or she should deal with.

Use an Intermediary

Try to go through an intermediary if possible. If you and the seller have a mutual, trustworthy friend, perhaps he or she can arrange the initial meeting. This could be a neighbor, a fellow club member, banker, attorney—anyone you and the owner trust that will pave the way for you.

Real Estate Broker

If you are working through a real estate broker, utilize his or her talents. The broker can tell you the facts of the listing, how long it has been on the market, any offers, price decreases, comparable properties, and their prices. Don't forget that the broker represents the seller, and all the broker's efforts will be for the seller's benefit. Yet, the broker doesn't get paid until a sale is made, so the broker will become a mediator and do his or her best to bring buyer and seller together. Many times all your contacts will be with the broker, and you may not meet the seller in person until the day of the closing, if then.

Reference Points

Once the meeting is set and underway, utilize any available points of reference. If you and the seller have attended the same school, or follow the same sports team or hobby, bring these into play to help bring down the invisible "shield" that the buyer maintains to protect himself or herself from the onslaught of the "invader" buyer. The seller is wary of you. He or she thinks you want to steal the property, and his or her attitude toward you will be apprehensive at first. Points of reference are good ways of breaking the ice and getting to know one another a little better personally.

However, don't wander too far from the reason you're at the meeting—to buy the land. Get the pleasantries out of the way and then tactfully get down to business.

Be Businesslike

Let the seller know that you are capable and honest and that you share his or her hopes for a smooth transaction. Don't lose sight of the fact that this is a business transaction. Demonstrate that you will do your utmost to make things agreeable and that you expect that both of you will proceed in an expeditious manner to complete this sale. In real estate sales, time is of the essence and it is expected that neither of the parties will drag their feet. If you're buying land to have it subdivided into a given amount of lots and the sale is predicated upon this, then both parties must expect that the closing will be delayed while the buyer or seller has the required plan drawn up, submitted to the planning board, and approved. This all takes a long time, and a provision for the delay must appear in the purchase and sales contract.

Be Low-Key

Although you want to impart the fact that you are a capable developer and know what you are doing, you certainly don't want to boast about how much money you are going to make from the property once you develop it. You may not even want the seller to know what you're going to do with the property because the profit potential for you may dissuade him or her from selling you the land. If you can, keep your intentions to yourself. Also, don't brag about your other land successes if you have any. People are funny about others' successes. The seller could become immediately jealous and decide to break off any negotiations. Or the seller may increase the selling price substantially, since your "big mouth" indicated that you can afford to pay more. There's nothing wrong with your making a profit, which is why you're dealing with the seller, but in his or her eyes your profit may seem unreasonable.

Watch Your Language

There are certain words and phrases you may not want to use if you know that the seller has an emotional attachment to the land. Avoid using developers' terminology such as "clearing the land," "subdividing the parcel," or "leveling the land." Such phrases may evoke a shudder in the seller and alter his or her feelings in dealing with you. You can refer to your plan vaguely as "my plans" and let it go at that. Truthfully, it isn't very often that you can avoid telling the seller your plans, but you can try to when it serves your purpose. "Don't let your right hand know what your left hand is doing," serves a manifold purpose in real estate.

Accentuate the Negative

Each and every parcel of land has a deficiency of some kind. No matter how desirable it is presented to be by the owner, it will have some undesirable feature in the eyes of the buyer. The seller, to get a top-dollar price, is going to stress the positive features only. For each bad point that you bring up, the seller will counter with a corresponding good point. Once in a while you may run across a seller who voluntarily points out the negatives, but his or her naiveté will most assuredly change if the negatives continually dissuade potential buyers. The seller cannot, knowingly, cover up or avoid mentioning any serious or detrimental defects or adverse conditions in the property and its chain of title. But he or she can be evasive and not volunteer any information on lesser negatives, such as an abundance of similar, slow-selling properties in the area, or overly restrictive building and zoning ordinances.

You, as the buyer, have to maintain the aggressive stance in the bargaining process. You have to stay on the offensive and put the limiting and negative features to work at reducing the asking price. You have to find the land's deficiencies and point them out to the seller. The seller knows about them, of course, but your intention is to let him or her know that you know about them. Don't be overly critical and negative, however, because you may raise the seller's defenses too high and he or she may break off negotiations.

Stressing the negative has to be done tactfully and honestly. Don't create any negatives that aren't truly there. The less anxious the seller is to sell the property, the less will he or she accept your criticism of it. You have to get the seller to agree, at least in his or her mind, that there are indeed deficiencies and that compromise may be necessary because of them.

Your greatest bargaining edge is the seller's need to sell. The seller's greatest edge is a lack of pressure to sell. Some defects and deficiencies will be more costly than others to correct and these must be stressed. Don't "nit-pick" if it's really an inconsequential defect—forget it, it's not worth antagonizing the seller over. And you don't have to counteract all of his or her positives with negatives. If you find you have to, then why buy the land?

Buyer's Fever

Sooner or later you're going to catch it. Some day, some parcel will so excite you, for one reason or another, that you know you must own it. Once you make an offer or start to bargain with the owner, he or she knows how badly you want the property.

There is nothing wrong with the seller's knowing that you want the land, but as a wise negotiator you must keep a rein on your enthusiasm and not let it be overly apparent. A show of "buyer's fever" on your part will swing the bargaining edge to the seller and cause him or her to remain steadfast on his or her price and terms, knowing that you are willing to pay top dollar to get it.

Too many times buyer's fever has caused an overanxious buyer to pay too much for the land, thus affecting potential profit when he or she resells. Buyer's fever can be caused by your spotting a hidden potential in the land that is not apparent to others. Or you could just be anxious to buy something soon because you've been looking for a long time and haven't even come close to buying anything yet. You may love the location of the land and its amenities and lose your good judgment of its value to you.

Don't fall in love with any piece of land that you are buying for an investment. Let your mind rule your heart. If you cannot make a reasonable profit on it, no matter how much you like it, don't buy it.

Often an owner can create buyer's fever simply by stating that several other people are interested in purchasing the land. You don't know if this is true or not. The seller may be just trying to create an urgency to make you act quickly. It also sometimes happens that the owner truly believes that another party has buyer's fever for the land when the party has only been placating the seller. You've got to keep cool and proceed intelligently.

Brokers, too, try to create buyer's fever to consummate a sale. If they don't have an exclusive listing on the property, then other brokers could very well sell the land from under them and all of their efforts and costs will have been for naught. They will quite often have you believing a sales agreement with another buyer is in the works and you should act now to preserve this land for yourself. Is it true? Maybe so, but proceed intelligently. If it is true and you lose your chance, there'll be other chances. Don't despair over this property—it isn't the last piece of land on earth.

In short, don't reveal your anxiety to buy; you may lose your bargaining leverage. The seller is more anxious than you are.

First Offer

After the preliminaries, it's time to do battle. You are at the point of making your first offer, and rest assured there will be a second offer, and perhaps a third. All the spadework has been done. You know what the value of the land is to you. You have determined projected costs of improvements and legal and carrying costs until you resell the land. You know what you can resell the land for, and you've established a profit that you expect for your efforts. From this information you've reached a conclusion about the range of your offer: a bottom-dollar to a top-dollar offer.

You have to start somewhere; even after you have purchased several parcels, you will find that there is no true place to start, no right first offer. This fact is due primarily to the variables involved; most specifically the changeable human variables, the buyer and the seller. An offer to one seller 10 percent less than the asking price may be vehemently rejected, whereas an offer of 40 percent less than the asking price to another seller may be eagerly accepted.

You are playing a game of strategy and wits and you must use all the tools and information that you have at your disposal. The market condition is one bit of information that you definitely have to consider. If real estate sales are normal, in your opinion, and the asking price of the property is fairly reasonable, you can make your initial bid your bottom dollar-offer. This offer can range anywhere from 10 percent to 25 percent—even up to 30 percent below the seller's asking price. If market conditions have been slow and it's a buyer's market, you could even make your first offer as much as 50 percent less than the asking price.

Many investors choose to use their bottom-dollar offer first. This strategy serves several purposes. The seller may completely take you by surprise and accept your seemingly ridiculous low offer. It could be that many people have looked at the land and nobody has gone as far as putting it on paper and making a firm offer. Maybe this is one of the seller's "feeling good" days or some happy event has put him or her in a charitable frame of mind—or he or she may simply have taken a liking to you. Don't rely upon this welcome event happening very often though. I've been lucky to be the beneficiary of a pleasantly changed seller on two occasions, not to any great extent where I was overwhelmed with a drastic price decrease, but with a modest decrease and a satisfactory arrangement of the financial terms.

Occasionally, the shrewder investors will throw out their bottom-dollar offer first with the intention of staggering the owner into believing that perhaps the property isn't really as great as he or she imagines it to be and perhaps it is overpriced. You must be able to read the seller pretty well to be able to do this. Not in a personal sense, but at least you need to know what his or her reactions might be.

In fact, from your very first meeting start analyzing the seller. Size up your adversary. What type of character is the seller? Is he or she the nervous type? Is he or she open and honest? Does he or she appear anxious to sell? Knowledge of any of these facts are bargaining tools. Plant seeds in the seller's mind. Drop little hints or facts about the property, market conditions, lack of satisfactory financing, or any other relative facts that you can bring up and use as bargaining leverage in later meetings. Be subtle and tactful enough to let him or her hear what you're saying (and what you're not saying), but don't startle the seller—just plant the seeds. Each time you meet, watch his or her reactions to your comments (the seller is watching you too) on his or her property and try to read his or her body language. When you suggested that land like this is not in high demand in the current marketplace, how did the seller react? What were his or her comments? facial expression? When you presented your bottom-dollar offer, what was the seller's body language? More importantly, what did the seller mean by what he or she said? We don't always say what we mean, nor mean what we say.

Armed with some answers about the seller's character and supplemented by a buyer's market (if there is one at the time), you can go forward and present your bottom-dollar offer. You may, however, risk the chance of insulting the seller, and he or she may call off the negotiations completely. Take the risk. Present your lowest offer. Even if it's not a buyer's market, take the risk. Most properties are sold at about 15 percent less than the asking price. Unless there are extenuating circumstances, always take the risk and offer at least 25 to 30 percent below the asking price on your first offer. If it is rejected, you've at least left yourself plenty of room to maneuver with subsequent offers.

CHAPTER VIII

FINANCING

Of the numerous and varied phases of the land buying process, nothing confuses or seems more mysterious to the land investor than the financing phase. The numbers are complex and the language seemingly secretive. Yet to succeed in this field, you must learn the secret language of the lenders and know how to decode their cryptic numbers.

Financing is the heart of most real estate transactions and will prove to be the key ingredient to the success of most of your land investment ventures. An old real estate adage says it perfectly: "If you can't finance it, you can't buy it."

Many people think that a cash payment is the best way to buy property. This may have been true when inflation was only 2 or 3 percent per year and interest rates were below 5 percent, but in today's high-interest and high-inflation economy, cash purchases are downright foolhardy. Using O.P.M. (other people's money) through borrowing is the only way to buy property. If you have an aversion towards borrowing, you had better change this attitude because borrowing is the principal profit method of land investing.

It is important for you to understand some of the basic financing methods and have a working knowledge of the instruments of financing. Besides a cash payment, there are three common ways to buy land: *purchase money mortgage, a contract for deed* and *assuming an existing mortgage.*

PURCHASE MONEY MORTGAGE

Some of your land purchases will be financed by the seller. A purchase money mortgage is used when the seller is handling the financing. The seller doesn't actually loan you money to buy the property. You simply make an agreed-upon down payment, the seller gives you a deed, and you make periodic payments until the total amount is paid off. For instance, you buy a ten-acre tract of land for $50,000. You pay the seller a down payment of $10,000 and receive a deed and the seller takes back a mortgage for $40,000 to be paid, over a stated period of time, at a specified percentage.

Why would a seller agree to finance his or her own land? First of all, you may not be able to get a bank loan on land with only a 20 percent down payment. Second, if the seller is in a high tax bracket, the spreading out of payments may place him or her in a more favorable tax position. Third, the seller may ask a higher selling price and charge a higher interest rate if he or she is financing the sale. On the other hand, if the seller has had the land on the market for a long time, he or she may feel that financing is necessary to sell it, and the terms may be better for you than ordinary bank financing.

The periodic payments that you'll be making to the seller to pay off the purchase money mortgage must, of course, be within your ability to pay. If they aren't, you may be able to reduce the periodic payment by getting the seller to agree to an "interest only" purchase money mortgage. You may have to sweeten the pot by agreeing to a little higher interest rate, but it reduces your payments—and the interest is a deductible expense anyway.

CONTRACT FOR DEED

This method of financing is also called a *land contract*, or an *install-ment sales contract*. It is another way for a seller to personally finance the sale of his or her land. The buyer generally makes a small cash down payment and then makes periodic installment payments until the purchase price and interest are paid off.

A seller feels more secure with a contract for deed method of financing than with a purchase money mortgage. When you buy land using a purchase money mortgage, the seller transfers title to you and only retains a lien against the land. With a contract for deed, you make a cash down payment and agree to pay the balance of the purchase price, plus interest, over a specified period of time—you get delivery of the deed only after you've paid off the entire mortgage. The seller retains title to the land during the payoff period. If you are unable to make your installment payments, then the seller can simply ask you to vacate the land. Since the seller has retained title, he or she does not have to go through a court foreclosure. The seller would end up with all the monies that you have paid and the land as well.

A land contract is not the wisest way to buy land. If you must use this method, then insist that the contract be recorded immediately with the county clerk. The recording gives public notice that you are buying the land, and if the seller tries to sell the same parcel to someone else, then you are protected by the recording. A dishonest seller could actually encumber the land with additional mortgages, easements, and liens that will negatively affect the title you will receive. Include in your contract a clause that specifically forbids the seller from encumbering the property.

Land contract sales are very often placed in escrow in the hands of a third party. The seller will make the deed out in the name of the buyer and turn it over to an escrow agent. The escrow agent collects the periodic payments for the seller; when the final payment is received, the escrow agent delivers the deed to the buyer.

Don't allow the seller to put a *prepayment penalty clause* into the land contract, which would penalize you if you were to pay the balance off sooner than scheduled. If your payments are $200 per month, you should be allowed to pay $200 or more per month. Suppose you bought a piece of land and arranged for a payoff in 48 months. If you found a buyer for your land after you've owned it for just 12 months, you certainly want to pay off the existing land contract so that you could transfer title to your new buyer. Make sure that you are allowed to pay off the mortgage as fast as you want to.

ASSUMING AN EXISTING MORTGAGE

A mortgage is a lien against property. You borrow money to buy the land and promise to pay it back, with interest, using the land as collateral. If you want to buy a piece of land that the seller still owes money on under a mortgage, you can "assume" the seller's mortgage. For example, you want to buy a parcel with a selling price of $50,000 with an existing mortgage on the property of $40,000. You will pay the seller $10,000 cash and take over, or assume, an existing mortgage of $40,000. You replace the seller and become the mortgagor responsible for paying off the $40,000. In periods of high interest rates and limited financing, mortgage assumptions are quite common. Most mortgages have a clause that prevents transferring the mortgage without written approval from the lender. If the lender does approve the transfer, it will probably be for a higher interest rate.

BONDS AND MORTGAGES

When you finance the purchase of an automobile, you pledge the vehicle itself as security (collateral) for the loan. If you fail to make the periodic payments, the financial institution that lent you the money will repossess the vehicle. They will own your down payment, the vehicle, and whatever periodic payments you have made. Most real estate transactions are financed in basically the same way, with the involved property being pledged as security for the loan. This is known as a mortgage loan.

The mortgage loan is the traditional method of financing real estate. The first, or *primary* mortgage, is the most common form of financing. It has priority over all subsequent liens such as second mortgages and other *junior,* mortgages, which are mortgages on property that is already financed. Only tax liens have priority over first mortgages.

There are two instruments involved when land is pledged as security for a loan. These are the *bond* and the *mortgage*. The bond is the written instrument in which the borrower promises to repay the loan under certain conditions. The mortgage is the written instrument that pledges the real estate as security for the loan.

The Bond

For a mortgage to be valid, there must be a debt and there must be evidence of this debt. In most states the bond is the evidence of the debt. Some states use a *promissory note*, which is similar to a bond, but lacks a seal. The bond is a sealed, written agreement executed by the borrower, acknowledging that he is legally indebted to the lender for the sum of money borrowed. The borrower promises to repay the debt to the lender under certain conditions, usually in periodic installments of principal and interest.

The debt is a personal obligation of the borrower. If only a mortgage was executed, the borrower could abandon the property and forget the debt. The note is enforceable against the borrower wherever he or she may go. Under the Uniform Commercial Code, a negotiable instrument must be in writing with a signed promise by the maker to pay a sum of money under specified terms. The bond, or note, is delivered, with the mortgage, to the lender at the closing. The bond is not recorded, since it represents a personal obligation and not real property.

The Mortgage

The purpose of a mortgage is to create a lien against real estate that can be recorded. If there is a default in the repayment of the debt, the property may be sold to satisfy the debt. Each state has its own mortgage laws, but they generally include certain common requirements to be enforceable:

- It must be in writing
- Legally competent parties
- Must include a mortgaging clause pledging the real estate as security
- The debt must be described along with the payment terms
- The real estate must be legally described
- The mortgage must be witnessed, delivered, and accepted

The two parties to a mortgage are the *mortgagor* (borrower) and the *mortgagee* (lender). The *principal* is the amount of money that you borrow. *Interest* is the consideration given for the use of the money. *Simple interest* is the interest paid on the principal at a stated rate. *Compound interest* is the interest on the unpaid interest.

The method of making periodic payments to reduce the principal is called *amortization*. The two primary types of amortized loans are the *fully amortized* and *unamortized*. A fully amortized loan is the most common payment method. It combines the payment of both principal and interest in each identical installment. In the early years of the loan, most of the payment is applied to the interest. The amount paid is the same every month, but the amount paid for interest decreases because the amount of the principal gets less after each installment. With an unamortized loan, only interest is paid, with the principal paid in a lump sum at the end of the loan period. (This final payment is called a balloon payment.)

There are two basic theories of mortgage law used in the United States: the *title theory* and the *lien theory*. In states that use the title theory, the basic concept is that upon the making of a mortgage, the mortgagor passes title to the property to the mortgagee subject to the payment of the debt. The mortgagor retains possession and use of the property during the mortgage period. In the lien theory states, the making of a mortgage creates a lien on the land and does not convey title; title remains with the mortgagor.

Deed of Trust

Some states use the *deed of trust* in place of a mortgage. In a typical mortgage transaction there are two parties, the mortgagor and the mortgagee. With a deed of trust, there are three parties to the transaction: the mortgagor, known in this case as the *trustor*; the lender, known as the *beneficiary*; and the third party, the *trustee*. The trustor (mortgagor) pledges the land as security for the loan, transferring title to the trustee.

Lenders prefer to use the deed of trust because of time and convenience in moving upon the borrower in case of default. The mortgage is a lien on the property and foreclosure proceedings can take as long as three years to complete. A deed of trust is not a lien; instead title is conveyed to a trustee to be held as security. If the borrower defaults, the trustee has the right to sell the property to satisfy the terms of the debt without having to go through the long foreclosure procedure as with a standard mortgage. Usually, the third party trustee is a public trustee such as the county clerk, who will handle all of the trust deeds recorded in his county.

Types of Mortgages

The following are the primary types of mortgages and several variations of these types.

FHA Insured Mortgage   The Federal Housing Administration, a government agency instituted under the National Housing Act of 1934, is under the jurisdiction of the Department of Housing and Urban Development. For a fee of .05 percent of the unpaid balance, paid by the borrower, it will insure the lender against any losses suffered on mortgage loans. FHA loans may be made on up to 97 percent of the value of newly constructed low-cost homes. Keep this in mind if you plan to build and sell houses in your subdivision—not to finance the construction of the homes themselves, but rather to finance the customers who will be buying your homes.

VA Guaranteed Mortgage　The Veterans Administration, under the Serviceman's Readjustment Act of 1944, will guarantee a certain percentage of a mortgage loan, made by a lender, to a qualified veteran. The maximum amount of the guarantee is $20,000, or 60 percent of the purchase price of the home.

Conventional Mortgage　A *conventional mortgage* is neither insured nor guaranteed by the government. It is insured by private mortgage insurance companies such as Mortgage Guaranty Insurance Corporation (MGIC) and Investors Mortgage Insurance Corporation (IMIC). Conventional mortgages are normally made at lower loan-to-value ratios than VA or FHA loans. (The loan-to-value ratio is the percentage of the appraised value of the property that will be given as a loan.) The majority of homes in the United States are financed by conventional mortgage loans.

Construction Loan　A *construction loan* is a special-purpose mortgage given to finance new building construction. It is a short-term loan, usually running six to twelve months or until completion of the construction. A construction loan granted to a builder extends to the sale of the house. The entire loan is not fully paid out to the builder at one time. Instead, funds are disbursed in installments called "draws" at certain stages of construction. For instance, a certain amount is paid out for the excavation and foundation, and after they are completed the lender's agent will inspect the work performed and then authorize the next payout, or draw. When the home is "framed in," it is inspected and the next payout is authorized. This continues until all the money borrowed is drawn from the bank. When the home is completed and sold, then a permanent mortgage must be arranged for the buyer.

Second and Junior Mortgage　The traditional mortgage that we have been discussing is a *first mortgage* that is a lien on the involved property and has priority over all subsequent mortgages. The next mortgage in priority is a *second mortgage*; after that a *third mortgage*. Sometimes mortgages are stacked up one after another up to six or seven deep in priority. Mortgages after the first mortgage are known as junior mortgages.

There are two important clauses in a junior mortgage that you should be aware of: the *default-in-prior-mortgage clause,* and the *subordination clause.* A default-in-prior-mortgage clause states that if the borrower defaults on the payment of principal, interest, or taxes on any prior mortgage, such payments may be made by the junior mortgagee. This clause protects the junior mortgagee. If a prior mortgage is foreclosed, the junior mortgagee may purchase the property to protect the loan. The subordination clause protects the borrower. It states that if a prior mortgage is removed, the junior mortgage will not automatically become a first mortgage, but will be fixed in position in the event that the mortgagor seeks a new first mortgage.

Participation Mortgage A *participation mortgage* is one in which two or more lenders are involved. For example, a lender may be willing to lend say 60 percent of the amount to be borrowed, and a second lender makes up the difference. A *participation agreement* is made between the lenders: the first lender becomes the mortgage owner of a certain amount of the principal and interest, and the second lender owns the balance. Participation mortgages are made on very large developments, such as a large office building, where a single lender is unwilling to take the risk of financing the entire project. A participation mortgage is not to be confused with a lender's participation in a mortgage, in which the lender will share in the revenues of the project in addition to the interest charged.

Wraparound Mortgage A *wraparound mortgage* is a second mortgage that includes an existing mortgage. It is used when the existing mortgage cannot be repaid and a second lender assumes the payment by giving a new and larger mortgage at a higher interest rate. The existing mortgage is not paid off. The second lender simply makes the payments on the first loan and collects a premium from the borrower by wrapping the higher interest rate second mortgage around the lower-interest-rate first mortgage.

Blanket Mortgage   A blanket mortgage covers more than one parcel of real estate, for example one mortgage with two houses pledged as security for the debt. A *partial release clause* is typically incorporated into a blanket mortgage: the mortgagee agrees to release part of the property upon payment of part of the loan. Blanket mortgages are often used in the sale of a subdivision, and the lender receives a percentage of each lot that is sold. As each lot is sold, the lender will release the lot from the mortgage so that title can be passed to the new lot owner. The blanket mortgage continues to be a lien on the remaining unsold lots until the full amount of the loan is satisfied.

Package Mortgage   A mortgage that includes personal property is termed a package mortgage. With a residence this could include an air conditioner, washing machine and dryer, refrigerator, stove, or dishwasher. The personal property becomes security for the loan along with the realty, and cannot be sold or disposed of without the consent of the mortgagee.

Open-End Mortgage   An open-end mortgage allows additional funds to be borrowed after the loan balance has been reduced to a predetermined amount. For example, you may borrow additional funds on an existing open-end mortgage to remodel your home. The new funds are normally loaned on the terms of the original agreement; however, in some instances, they may be subject to renegotiation.

FORECLOSURE

If the borrower fails to make the payments, or breaches any of the terms of the mortgage, a *default* exists and the mortgagee may foreclose on the mortgage. Mortgages usually are in default because of death, divorce, or some other temporary difficulty that the mortgagor is experiencing. Lenders realize that borrowers can get into temporary difficulties and given a little extra time will make good on the default. If the default extends beyond a reasonable amount of time, the lender will begin foreclosure proceedings.

An *acceleration clause* is written into the mortgage to assist the lender in a foreclosure. Upon default, the lender has the legal right to accelerate the maturity of the mortgage by declaring the full principal immediately due for payment. Without this clause, a lender could demand only the defaulted payment, since the balance of the debt is not immediately due. The lender would have to start foreclosure suits for each monthly payment as it became overdue.

Foreclosure is the legal process initiated by the lender to force immediate payment of the debt. The foreclosure process can take up to three years to complete. Each state has its own laws governing foreclosure, with the end result being the borrower losing the land pledged as security. The procedure begins with a summons and a copy of the complaint being served on the borrower with a *lis pendens* (notice of pendency of action) being filed with the county clerk. The lis pendens is a notice to any concerned party that there is an action pending on the pledged land.

The borrower is allowed a period of time, called the *equitable right of redemption,* to correct the default. Through this right, the borrower may pay off the debt and all foreclosure costs incurred by the lender and retain the land. If the borrower fails to do so, then after the foreclosure sale he or she still has the *statutory right of redemption.* This is the right by which the borrower may recover the foreclosed land by paying the foreclosure sales price and all related costs within a certain period of time after the foreclosure sale.

Both borrowers and lenders try to avoid foreclosure. For the borrower, it is an unfortunate event because he or she will lose the land, and for the lender it is a drawn-out, and costly process. The lender must declare a default, begin foreclosure action, go through the sale, and finally have to wait up to a year after the sale to allow the borrower his statutory redemption rights. When you take out a mortgage to buy land, make certain that a right of redemption clause is in your agreement. Even though your state laws may provide for this right, it is a good double protection for you. You never know what misfortune may befall you, putting you into default and eventual foreclosure. This right gives you the chance to bail yourself out and redeem your land.

There are four general types of foreclosure proceedings:*strict fore-closure, foreclosure by entry and possession, judicial foreclosure*, and *nonjudicial foreclosure*.

Strict foreclosure is where the court provides that the lender take over the land and the borrower loses all rights of redemption and does not share in the proceeds if the land is sold for more than the debt.

Foreclosure by entry and possession, used in some of the New England states, allows the lender to take peaceful possession of the land for a period of time. After a period of redemption, the lender acquires title to the land.

Judicial foreclosure provides that the pledged land may be sold by court order. A public sale will be advertised and held, and the land sold to the highest bidder.

Nonjudicial foreclosure is used when a *power of sale clause* is contained in the loan agreement. With this procedure, the lender doesn't have to go to court, but merely gives notice, allows for a redemption period, and advertises the amount due and the date of the sale. If the selling price of the land exceeds the amount of the debt, plus foreclosure costs, the surplus money usually goes to the borrower. If the selling price is less than the debt, plus costs, then the lender may obtain a *deficiency judgment* against the borrower to collect the difference.

The foreclosure proceedings are time-consuming, costly, and embarrassing to the involved parties, particularly the borrower. If you find yourself running into financial difficulties and you may default on the payments for your land, don't just let the payments go by without approaching the lender and trying to work out an equitable payment arrangement. One alternative is *friendly foreclosure*, in which you sell or give a deed to the lender before an anticipated foreclosure. The lender now becomes the owner of the property (which remains subject to all junior liens that would have been removed by foreclosure). Friendly foreclosure, because it is by agreement and not by civil action, is much faster than a normal foreclosure. It also avoids the stigma of a forced foreclosure on the borrower's credit history and assures junior lien holders that they will be paid.

LENDERS IN THE MORTGAGE MARKET

Most real estate loans are obtained from the primary and secondary lenders that make up the mortgage money market. *Primary lenders* are banks and insurance companies. They supply funds directly to borrowers. *Secondary lenders* are pension funds, federally supported agencies, and some insurance companies that buy loans or originate loans through other sources.

Primary Lenders

The majority of real estate loans are obtained from financial institutions created to store people's savings. To cover their operating overhead and earn income, they lend out the savings and charge interest. Mortgage loans are a primary interest-earning vehicle for savings and loan associations, commercial banks, mutual savings banks, life insurance companies, mortgage banking companies, and a few other lenders.

Savings and Loan Associations   Better than half of all home mortgages come from federally chartered savings and loan associations. (In Louisiana they are called *homestead associations,* in Massachusetts *cooperative banks.*) They are members of the Federal Home Loan Bank system (FHLB) and the Federal Savings and Loan Insurance Corporation (FSLIC). FHLB supervises the lending activities of all of its members and allows them to borrow funds on short notice to pay off withdrawal accounts and to finance mortgages. The FSLIC insures depositor's funds against possible bank failures.

Real estate mortgages are the primary outlet of their investments; over 85 percent of their assets are placed into the mortgage market. Savings and loan associations are the most flexible of all the financial institutions. You may approach them for a land mortgage, but without a house on the land as security, they may lend only a small percentage of the appraised value of the land. If you do buy a large parcel with a house on it, the savings and loans will finance second homes that are within a 100-mile radius of their home office.

Savings and loans are privately owned by stockholders and were established to promote sound savings and investment of their members' deposits. Over the years their policies have changed and they now accept deposits from, and lend money to, nonmembers.

Commercial Banks   Commercial banks are rather conservative in loaning money on real estate because they are not specifically set up to finance long-term loans. They must, by law, maintain greater liquidity in their assets than other financial institutions. Most of their assets are in demand (checking) accounts rather than long-term savings accounts, so they are more subject to immediate withdrawal of deposits. They invest their funds in corporate bonds, government securities, consumer installment loans, and short-term business loans to finance inventories, payrolls, and working capital. They are a prime source of funds for commercial and industrial real estate and will lend money for land development up to two thirds of the appraised value of the land.

Mutual Savings Banks   Concentrated in the northeastern and mid-Atlantic states, mutual savings banks are the oldest type of savings institution in the country and are similar in function to savings and loan associations. They are very active in mortgage financing, making loans that are secured by income property or single-family residences; to a lesser degree will lend funds on land.

Life Insurance Companies   Many major projects being developed in large cities across the country are funded by insurance companies. Insurance companies handle large amounts of money that they receive in insurance premiums, and they are constantly searching for high-yield investments in which to place their funds. In recent years, they have paid particular attention to their investment profits because claims have been offsetting much of the premium payments. Today, many insurance companies want a participation arrangement in which they not only lend the money at interest, but also share in the equity of the project.

Unless you are a large developer and need huge sums of capital, then insurance companies aren't for you as a source of funds.

Mortgage Companies A mortgage company is any person, firm, or corporation engaged in the business of lending money on the security of real estate. They serve secondary lenders such as life insurance companies and governmental agencies that want to invest in mortgages.

There is a distinction between a mortgage company and a *mortgage broker.* Mortgage brokers bring borrowers and lenders together and will service the loans for a fee. Servicing a loan includes billing, collecting payments, paying taxes on the property, and handling defaults.

Pension and Trust Funds Pension fund monies are accumulated to provide income for retirement years. The funds do not invest heavily in the mortgage market because their expertise in the mortgage market is not strong. Trust funds are administered by a *trustee* who watches over the investments of the *trustor.* They do invest, in a limited way, in specialized real estate activities.

Farmers Home Administration The Farmers Home Administration (FHA), an agency of the Department of Agriculture, makes loans to farmers and others in rural areas who are unable to obtain reasonable loans from other sources. The property must be located in a rural area with a population of less than 10,000 persons. The goal is to provide funding for a modestly priced home on a minimal sized lot. The down payment is small, and interest rates are very low, usually ranging from 1 to 9 percent, and depend on the financial ability of the borrower.

The Federal Land Bank The Federal Land Bank, created in 1917, gives mortgages to individuals to buy land and build structures for agricultural use. It obtains funds by selling bonds to the public secured by first mortgages on farms and ranches. It is organized into twelve regional banks that grant loans up to 85 percent of value, with interest rates below the average.

Real Estate Investment Trusts Real Estate Investment Trusts (REIT) are corporations, usually formed by large banks and insurance companies, that sell shares to the public and invest in various real estate projects. They give small investors the chance to invest in large, diversified properties that are out of financial reach of most individuals. They are exempt from corporate income taxes on income distributed to their shareholders. REITs invest primarily in short-term, high-yield construction loans, long-term mortgages, and real estate activities of all kinds.

The Secondary Mortgage Market

The purchase and sale of mortgages between lenders and public or private agencies is referred to as the secondary mortgage market. The borrower has no direct participation in this market, but does benefit from the funds that are directed into the mortgage market by the secondary lenders. Loans are bought and sold in the secondary market after they have been originated. A primary lender (a savings bank, for example) may need additional money to satisfy the mortgage demands in its area and will sell a quantity of its existing loans to the secondary market to raise the needed funds. When a loan is sold, the original lender continues to service the loan and passes the payments on to the agency that has purchased the loan.

An agency that buys a quantity of loans is termed a *warehousing agency*. The warehousing agency sells the loans to investors and charges a fee for servicing the loan. The major warehousing agencies involved in the secondary market are the Federal National Mortgage Association, and the Federal Home Loan Mortgage Corporation, and private mortgage corporations.

Federal National Mortgage Association Popularly called "Fannie Mae," the Federal National Mortgage Association (FNMA) was created by Congress in 1938 to provide a secondary market for residential loans. In 1968, Fannie Mae became a privately owned corporation without changing its public purpose. It deals in conventional, FHA-insured, and VA guaranteed loans.

Fannie Mae raises funds to purchase loans by selling its own government-backed FNMA bonds at prevailing interest rates. Mortgages purchased by FNMA are made available for resale to private investors. Bids to purchase FNMA bonds are made by telephone with a minimum purchase of $200,000 and a maximum of $3 million.

Government National Mortgage Association   The Government National Mortgage Association (GNMA), popularly called "Ginnie Mae," a federal agency under the Department of Housing and Urban Development (HUD), was created by Congress in 1968 when Fannie Mae became a privately owned corporation. Ginnie Mae has three primary functions: it provides assistance for disadvantaged residential borrowers, for example, low-cost housing; it raises funds for lending, thereby stabilizing mortgage lending and home building activities; and it manages its own large portfolio of mortgages. In times of high interest rates and tight money, Fannie Mae and Ginnie Mae will join together in a *tandem plan* in which FNMA purchases high-risk, low-yield loans at full market rates, with GNMA guaranteeing payment and absorbing, at a loss, the difference between the low yield and current prices.

Federal Home Loan Mortgage Corporation   Known as "Freddie Mac," the Federal Home Loan Mortgage Corporation was created by Congress in 1970 to provide a secondary mortgage market for conventional loans. It does for conventional mortgages what Fannie Mae does for VA and FHA mortgages.

Real Estate Loans and Investment   Now that you know about some of the sources of financing to buy your property, you must take care that the type of financing you choose does not trap you into something you didn't intend. Keep in mind that vacant land does not, in and of itself, make money for you. There are no rents to collect, no buildings to depreciate. You're not going to be farming it or leasing it out to a tenant farmer, nor will you be cutting its timber for resale. If you are doing any of these, then your strategies and tactics will be quite different, but I'm assuming you're buying the land for fairly quick resale or you're planning on subdividing it and reselling the lots. Therefore, the money you have invested in the land and any taxes, development costs, and legal and selling fees are all part of the carrying costs of this particular parcel. The carrying costs, if they weren't tied up in the land, would be earning interest in any other number of investment vehicles such as certificates of deposit or stocks and bonds. Your goal will be to improve the property and resell it in a very short time.

The financing that you will be seeking will be temporary and will have to be flexible enough to allow for readjustment as you progress. If someone wanted to buy your newly purchased land, you certainly want to be able to sell it to him. Many lenders include *prepayment clauses* in their agreement of sale that precludes the alternative of paying off the loan early. They do this because it guarantees that you will continue to pay interest to them. Also, some lenders realize that the land may be resold in a short time and therefore the borrower will have to pay the penalty in order to resell the land. If you can avoid it, keep the prepayment clause out of your sales agreements.

OPTIONS

An option is a contract in which the seller (*optionor*), for consideration, gives a prospective buyer (*optionee*) the exclusive right, for a period of time, to purchase a parcel of land for a fixed price subject to agreed terms and conditions.

To be legally binding, an option, like any real estate contract, must be in writing and must include the names and signatures of both the optionor and optionee, the period of time the option is for, the price and terms of the sale, and the amount of consideration given by the optionee. The purpose of an option is to take the land off the market until the optionee decides whether to buy the property. The optionor, for consideration, promises not to sell the land to anyone else during the option period. If the seller breaks the option contract, then the optionee can sue for damages. If the optionee decides not to exercise the option, then the consideration is forfeited and kept by the optionor and the property is put back on the market. If the optionee does exercise the option, then the consideration is credited toward the purchase price. Unless it is stated otherwise in the terms, option rights are transferable.

You may sell or assign your option rights to whomever you choose.

During the option period, the optionee can utilize the time to make a feasibility study of the highest and best use of the land and not have to pay the normal landowner carrying costs. An option allows you to buy more land than you could otherwise afford to buy outright. If you find additional parcels that you are interested in at the same time, you can tie them up with options so that you can decide which is best for you to buy first. If you are inclined to buy more than one parcel, the option period will give you time to shop for financing.

Perhaps you will find an owner with several parcels that you would be interested in buying. You could write an option that gives you the right to buy the parcels individually over a period of time. This way you can develop and resell one parcel and use the proceeds to buy and develop each successive parcel.

You receive no legal rights, nor title in the land, during the option period—other than those written into the agreement. The agreement must allow you time to research the property and its potential uses. A right of extension beyond the initial option period should be a standard inclusion in any of your options in case you do not complete your research on time. Don't get too all-inclusive; include only the truly necessary contingencies. The seller wants to sell the land, not option it.

You may lose some of a buyer's usual negotiating leverage with an option, and the more all-inclusive it is the more leverage you may lose. Don't tie the property up for an undue length of time. It isn't fair to the owner and you may adversely affect your reputation as an optionor of property. Generally, a ninety-day option will give you sufficient time to complete your research. If your goal is to sell the option for a quick profit, you may need more time to develop prospects; a six-month option may be more advantageous for this purpose. If you've researched the land and decided not to exercise your option, it would be good business sense, and enhance your reputation as well, to turn over the results of your research to the landowner. The data is no longer of any use to you, but it may help the landowner sell the property.

CHAPTER IX

REAL ESTATE CONTRACTS AND DEEDS

The real estate business uses many special instruments and documents that have been created specifically for conveying real property interests. Most of the instruments are preprinted contracts and agreements. It's not necessary that they be printed (they are still legal even if written out completely by hand)—it just saves time and makes for a standardized and systematic procedure. In your land-buying activities, you'll be using several of these contracts and agreements. Make it your responsibility to know them and their characteristics.

CONTRACTS

A contract is a voluntary and legally binding agreement between competent parties who, for consideration, agree to do or refrain from doing some legal act. In creating a contract, the parties must perform in accordance with the *law of contracts,* which are rules and customs concerning the creation, transfer, and disposition of rights through mutual agreement.

Some of the more common contracts and agreements involved in the transfer of ownership interests in land are the contract of sale between buyer and seller, options, listing agreements, and escrow agreements. Later in this chapter we'll discuss them all in detail.

A real estate contract may be created by *express* or *implied* intent. Most real estate contracts are express contracts in that the parties express the terms, conditions, and intentions by oral or written statements. In an implied contract the parties imply their intentions by their acts and conduct.

Contracts are also classified as either *bilateral* or *unilateral*. In a bilateral contract a promise is given in exchange for another promise; both parties promise to do something. A real estate sales contract is a bilateral contract, since the owner promises to sell the land and the buyer promises to pay a consideration for the land. In a unilateral (one-sided) contract, one party promises to make a payment in return for an act by a second party. The performance of the act is the acceptance of the offer. For example, a landowner agrees to pay a commission to a broker if the broker sells his land. The promise to pay the commission is binding only if the broker sells the land.

Essentials of a Valid Contract

A valid and enforceable real estate contract must contain the elements of any legal contract: (1) a written and signed instrument; (2) competent parties; (3) an offer and acceptance; (4) consideration; (5) for a legal object, and (6) a legal description. If any of these elements is missing, there is no contract.

Written and Signed Under the Statute of Frauds, contracts conveying an interest in real estate must be in writing to be enforceable. The statute's purpose is to prevent fraudulent claims that may arise from alleged oral agreements. The written terms may not be changed by oral agreement. The contract must also be signed by all parties to it; the seller's spouse must also sign to relinquish any marital rights of dower, curtesy, or homestead.

Competent Parties To be valid, the parties to a contract must be of legal age and mentally competent to act for themselves to enter into a contract. Minors may enter into a contract, but they may disaffirm it at their option. A minor can bind an adult to a contract, but an adult cannot bind a minor. Most states accept 18 years as the legal age for minors to reach majority, or legal age. Contracts signed by a mentally incompetent person are void.

Offer and Acceptance A valid contract requires a "meeting of the minds," or mutual assent, by the parties involved regarding the agreement. They should understand the terms and conditions of the contract and enter into it voluntarily. Once the contract is accepted, it is enforceable. Up to that time it may be withdrawn or modified by either party. A mutual mistake voids the contract.

Consideration Anything of value given in return for a promise is consideration. It is also what each party gives, or receives, from one another. The amount of money given in a sale is consideration to the seller. The deed conveying title is consideration for the buyer. For an agreement to be binding, both parties must give consideration.

Unless there is evidence of fraud, the courts will normally not inquire into the adequacy of the consideration. For instance, if you paid $10,000 for a parcel of land and a week later resold it for $40,000, the first seller cannot come to you and say that the $10,000 consideration was insufficient and seek the court's help.

Legal Object A contract is enforceable only if its intent and purpose is legal. A contract made for an illegal purpose is void and unenforceable. It cannot be in violation of any federal, state, or local statutes, or against public policy.

Legal Description An acceptable legal description of the property being sold is required in the contract. If an honest mistake is made in the description, the contract is still valid.

Technical and Legal Effects

There are certain technical and legal ramifications of a contract, including certain definitions, that you must know to understand the contract and agreement process.

Valid   A *valid* contract contains all the essential elements required by law and is binding and enforceable on the parties.

Void   A *void* contract is no contract at all, because it does not meet all the essential elements of a contract; since it is not a contract, it cannot be ratified, nor enforced.

Voidable   A *voidable* contract may be cancelled by one of the parties. As we mentioned earlier, a minor, at his or her option, may void a contract with an adult, but the adult cannot void it.

Unenforceable   An *unenforceable* contract may be cancelled if one, or more, parties chooses not to perform his or her end of the deal, and the other party cannot force it to be honored. For instance, in states that require a listing agreement to be in writing, if it isn't in writing, nor signed by the parties, it is unenforceable.

Discharge of Contract

A contract may be discharged in three ways. It may be legally performed. It may be breached if one of the parties defaults. Or it may be discharged by operation of law.

Performance   Performance occurs when the contract is carried out, by both parties, to the full extent of the terms and conditions.

A contract may be legally assigned to another party. For instance, if you decided that you did not want to, or couldn't, buy a parcel of land that you had signed a contract to purchase, then you may substitute another person in your place. This person is known as an *assignee* and acquires all the rights that you had under the terms of the contract.

A contract may also be performed by *novation,* which is the mutually agreed upon substitution of the contract with a new contract.

Default   If the seller defaults on the contract, then the buyer may either terminate the contract and recover his earnest money; file a suit for specific performance to make the seller perform; or sue for damages. If the buyer defaults, the seller has basically the same remedies: he may terminate the contract and keep the earnest money; file a suit for specific performance; or sue for damages.

By Operation of Law When a contract is discharged by operation of law, it usually means it was illegally altered or assigned. A contract is destroyed legally if there is an alteration or erasure without the consent of both parties. Bankruptcy of one of the parties may discharge a contract: if a person becomes bankrupt, he or she is released from all contracts. Misrepresentation, fraud, undue influence, or duress placed on either party renders the contract voidable by the injured party.

Types of Real Estate Contracts

Contract of Sale The *contract of sale* (Figure 9-1) is also called *a sales contract, a purchase and sales agreement, an agreement of sale,* and several other descriptive names. It is the key instrument drawn up when land is bought and sold. Its purpose is to hold the sale together until the details are worked out. The buyer needs time to arrange financing and to have the title searched. The buyer may also want to conduct soil tests and perhaps have a survey taken, among other things. Time is needed too, to work out the mechanics of the closing.

Regardless of what the contract of sale is called, when it is signed by the prospective buyer, it is an offer; when it is signed by the seller as well, it becomes a contract.

The sales contract is the single most important document in the sale of real estate, since it details the terms and conditions between the parties. The contract for the sale of real estate is divided into several parts. The first part of the sales contract usually includes the name and address of the prospective buyer, the description of the land, the earnest money amount, the financial arrangements, title evidence, and closing details.

Earnest money is a sum of money used as a down payment to evidence good faith on the part of the prospective buyer. The earnest money deposit, usually 10 percent of the purchase price, binds the prospective buyer to the terms of the offer. If it is given to a real estate broker, acting as an agent for the seller, the broker must place the

AGREEMENT MADE AT   ON

(Seller)   AGREES TO SELL

(Buyer)   AGREES TO BUY

PROPERTY: The land and buildings thereon located at No.
in
consisting of approximately   square feet.

PRICE IS   DOLLARS,
PAID AS FOLLOWS:
    Deposit – Receipt acknowledged (To Be Held By Broker).. $ ....
    Cash on passing of papers (Including Mortgage Funds, if Any) .... $ ....
                                              TOTAL PRICE .... $ ....

Said premises are to be conveyed at   M. on or before   at the Registry of
Deeds in which the deed should by law be recorded, or at the office of
if requested, by a good and sufficient deed conveying a good and clear record and marketable title
thereto free from encumbrances except the provisions of the local zoning laws, taxes for the current
year and except also: *(Note: Restrictions, easements, liens for municipal betterments, and other
encumbrances, etc., if any, should be set forth here.)*

The seller may use the purchase money or any portion thereof to clear or perfect his title; all
instruments procured therefor to be recorded simultaneously with said deed. Either party may have
thirty days extension to cure any defect found in title. Time is of the essence of this contract.
TENANTS

If the seller shall be unable to give title or to make conveyance as above stipulated, any payments
made under this agreement shall be refunded, and all other obligations of either party hereunto shall
cease. The acceptance of a deed by the Buyer shall be deemed to be a full performance and discharge
hereof.

ADJUSTMENTS – Interest, taxes, collected rents, and water rates, shall be apportioned to date of
conveyance. Seller shall pay betterments attaching prior to this agreement. The buildings on said
premises shall, until the performance of this agreement, be kept insured in the sum of
                              Dollars by the Seller and, in case of any loss all sums recovered
or recoverable on account of said insurance shall be paid over or assigned, on conveyance to the buyer,
unless the premises shall previously have been restored to their former condition by the Seller.

FIXTURES, shades, screens, awnings, storm doors, and windows, stoves, heaters, oil burners, heating
equipment, walks, and hardy shrubs attached to or used with the property are included in this sale.

A fee for professional services of   is due from the Seller to

SPECIAL PROVISIONS – *(Note: Insert any agreements in addition to or contradicting the above.)*

Husbands or Wives signing below agree in consideration of the foregoing to join in said deed and to
release all Statutory and other rights and interests in said premises. If buyer defaults he waives claim to
the deposit above which becomes the property of the seller and broker, equally as liquidated damages.

....
                                                          (Seller)
....
    (Husbands and Wives)   (Buyer)

        From the office of ....
FORM 1223 S Conv. (REV.) 8-73

Figure 9.1. A Contract of Sale Form

deposit into an escrow account until the final settlement and closing of the sale.

The next part of the sales contract will include the buyer's agreement to purchase, followed by the seller's agreement to sell. This part provides for the acceptance, by the seller, of the buyer's price, terms, and conditions as stated in the contract.

If a real estate broker is involved in the transaction, his identity and commission arrangements would be in the next part, and perhaps also the disposition instructions of any forfeited earnest money. If the buyer defaults, the seller and broker will have predetermined how each would share the earnest money that the buyer forfeited by not consummating the sale.

Finally, the parties to the sale sign the contract.

The principal function of the sales contract is to reduce the agreement to writing under the terms of the Statute of Frauds. Preprinted form contracts are used in most real estate transactions because most of the transactions themselves are very similar in nature. The form contract is designed as a sort of plan or schedule of the flow of the sale through to its completion.

As mentioned above, the contract is divided into several parts. A typical form contract will include

Parties. The name and address of the buyer and the seller.

Legal Description. The correct legal description of the property should be written in the contract. Description is usually by one of the following methods: lot and block number, metes and bounds, government survey, or monuments.

Financial Arrangements. The terms of payment should be stated in full detail: the purchase price, the down payment, and the term of payments.

Subject To. A "subject to" clause shows the limits and restrictions to the title, such as mortgages, covenants, and restrictions, or any other limitations that should be included.

Closing. The time and place of the proposed closing and the apportionment of monies due from buyer and seller.

Title. Evidence of title—documentary proof that the seller is in fact the owner and that the title is clear and marketable, such as an abstract of title or a title insurance policy.

Destruction and Default. Provisions must be included in the event of damage to the property. Remedies in case of default should also be noted.

Signatures. All parties to the contract must sign.

Broker's Clause. If a real estate broker is involved with the transaction, his or her identity and commission arrangement should be stated.

Installment Land Contract An *installment land contract* has a variety of names: *a real estate contract, a contract for deed,* and a *land contract* are some of them. They all mean, and do, the same thing; that is, the buyer makes periodic payments, with interest, over a period of years. Title remains with the seller until the final installment payment is made. The term of payment is usually two to five years.

Although it can be used to finance any kind of real estate, the installment land contract is normally used for the sale of farm land, raw acreage, or vacant homesites. It's used most often when a buyer does not have enough cash to make a sufficient down payment. A benefit to the seller is that the payments are received over a number of years, thereby spreading out, and minimizing, income tax responsibilities. Additionally, for the seller's benefit and protection, the land contract provides that in the event of default by the buyer, the contract may be cancelled, with the seller retaining all the monies paid to date.

Binder A binder is a brief written agreement between buyer and seller prior to entering into a longer and more formal contract. If the binder includes all the terms of the agreement and is written and signed, then it meets the requirements under the Statute of Frauds and it is a valid contract despite its simple form. If it lacks some of the essential elements, it would serve simply as a receipt of a sum of money in anticipation of the execution of a legal sales contract.

Options An option is a contract in which the owner (optionor) gives to another (optionee) the exclusive right, for a period of time, to buy his or her land at a specified price. For this right to have the land held off the market during the option period, the optionee must usually pay a fee to the optionor. Time is of the essence with an option; if it is not exercised within the allotted time, it automatically expires and the fee is kept by the optionor.

The primary purpose of an option is to allow the optionee a period of time to decide whether to buy the land. The optionee may be interested in buying abutting properties and plans to consummate the option once the owners of the abutting properties agree to sell. Or the optionee may be looking into the development possibilities of the optioned property; if the numbers don't come out in his or her favor, then he or she would let the option lapse.

Escrow Agreement   *Escrow* is the deposit of something of value, such as money, or legal documents, with a third party to be held until certain acts or conditions are accomplished. In some states it is common for the transaction to be closed through an escrow agent. The escrow agent could be a real estate broker, an attorney, a lender, or an escrow company, who is not a party to the contract and will not benefit in any way from it. The parties to the contract enter into an escrow agreement, separate from the sales contract, that sets forth instructions for the escrow agent. The closing in escrow was discussed fully in Chapter V.

Listing Agreement   A listing agreement is a contract of employment of a real estate broker, by an owner, to buy, sell, or lease real estate. You will most assuredly be dealing with real estate brokers in your land buying and selling efforts, so it is important for you to know and understand the contractual obligations of the various types of listing agreements. A deeper explanation of listing agreements is included in Chapter XV.

DEEDS

Prior to the development of written instruments, the transfer of title to land was simply done verbally or symbolically. The buyer and seller would go onto the land and the seller would hand a clod of dirt, or a branch from a tree, to the buyer and verbally announce that he was passing title to him. Needless to say, many disputes arose because of the lack of evidence of a sale. Buyers started having neighbors stand by as witnesses to the sale, but witnesses die, or move away, and evidence vanishes. Eventually, written documents showing land transfers were developed into what are now known as deeds.

A deed is a legal, written instrument by which title to land is conveyed by the owner (the grantor) to a buyer (the grantee). A deed is not the title to the land; it is the instrument used to transfer the title. Remember, title is ownership.

There are several types of deeds, with the primary distinction between them being the responsibilities and guarantees that the grantor makes concerning the title. These guarantees are termed *warranties*. The grantor warrants that he or she owns the land and that there are no clouds on the title beyond what he or she says there are. The owner is personally guaranteeing his or her statements and may be held responsible for them in case they are later proven false.

Of the many types of deeds, several are used for special purposes. For our intent, we'll only discuss the more common types.

Types of Deeds

General Warranty Deed　Of all the deeds, a general warranty deed provides the greatest protection to the buyer. The seller warrants good title, free of liens and encumbrances except those written in the deed, which the seller will defend against all claimants. The advantage of a general warranty deed is that the seller gives five specific warranties, called covenants, which must be written into the deed:

Covenant of Seizin. The seller warrants that he or she holds, or is seized with, full fee simple title to the land. In addition, the seller warrants that he or she has the right to sell the land and has not previously sold it to anyone else. If this covenant is broken, the buyer may recover the full purchase price.

Covenant against Encumbrances. The seller warrants that the land is free from any liens and encumbrances, other than those specifically written in the deed. Liens and encumbrances would include mortgages, easements, deed restrictions, tax and assessment liens, mechanics' liens, and rights of spouses. If the covenant is broken, then the buyer may sue for expenses to remove the lien and encumbrance.

Covenant of Quiet Enjoyment. The seller warrants that the buyer will be able to quietly enjoy the land and not be disturbed by the actions of third parties claiming superior title. The buyer may sue for damages if this covenant is broken.

Covenant of Further Assurance. The seller promises to obtain any additional documents necessary to give good title as stated in the deed. If a mistake was made in the deed, the seller must rewrite and correct the error.

Covenant of Warranty of Title. The seller guarantees the title forever and will defend it against the claims of other persons.

These five covenants cover not only the period that the seller owned the land, but extend back through the chain of title to its origin. They give the same protection as a title insurance policy, but the covenants make the seller responsible for defending the title, whereas with a title insurance policy, the title insurance company is liable.

Special Warranty Deed   This deed carries only one covenant. The seller only warrants the title against the lawful claims arising during his or her period of ownership.

Bargain and Sale Deed   This deed is similar to a special warranty deed. The seller warrants that he or she has title and has not encumbered the land in any way. The words "grant, bargain, and sell," or "grant and release" are typically used in the granting clause.

Quitclaim Deed   A quitclaim deed is the simplest form of deed and provides the buyer with the least protection. It conveys only the interest that the seller has in the land. The seller warrants only that at the time of the delivery of the deed, the land was free of all encumbrances made by him or her. Quitclaim deeds are used to correct defects and to clear up clouds upon the title such as a case where a property with a weak title claim is inherited.

Requirements for a Valid Deed

The conveying of an interest in real estate must be in writing. The deed fulfills this requirement, and since it is a contract it must be executed with the same formality that is required for an enforceable contract. In addition to being in writing, it is essential that a valid deed include a legally competent grantor, a legally competent grantee, consideration, a granting and habendum clause, a legal description, proper execution, and delivery and acceptance.

A Legally Competent Grantor   A grantor must be of legal age and mentally competent to act for himself. The rules covering contracts usually apply in determining the competence of the grantor. The legal age in most states is 18. A deed executed by a minor is considered voidable at the option of the minor until legal age is reached. If the grantor is married, the marital status should be noted in the deed and both married persons should sign the deed as grantors in order to waive any marital rights. The grantor's name must be correctly spelled, followed by his or her address to aid in identification. If the title was acquired in one name and sold in another, both names should be shown. This is common when a single woman buys land and later marries. The conveyance must show both her maiden and married names. A deed that conveys corporation land must be signed by a corporate officer empowered with the right to sell the land, and the corporate seal must be affixed.

Grantee   The grantee is the person receiving the land being conveyed. The grantee must be identifiable and capable of owning title. A deed that names a fictitious person as a grantee is considered void.

Consideration   To be valid, a deed must have good and valuable consideration. Consideration is something of value given in a contractual agreement. You'll notice in many deeds, when the land is conveyed as a gift from one relative to another, the amount of consideration is stated as "love and appreciation." This is referred to as *good consideration. Valuable consideration* is money or its equivalent. Normally, it is customary to mention some financial amount in addition to "love and appreciation," such as "$5 and other good and valuable consideration." A $1 consideration will legally support the conveyance of land worth $1 million. It is not necessary that the amount of consideration be specified in the deed for it to be enforceable. Only in deeds executed by a guardian or executor must the actual price be stated.

A Granting Clause and Habendum Clause   The *granting clause* contains words that indicate the intentions of the grantor to convey interest. Words like "convey and warrant," "grant," "grant and re-lease," "grant, bargain, and sell," are typical granting words. Only a present interest can be conveyed; that is, a deed conveying title at a future date, or upon the grantor's death, is invalid.

The granting clause should also indicate the interest that is being conveyed, such as a fee simple estate, a life estate, or any limitations on the grantee's interest.

The habendum clause begins with the words "to have and to hold," and it describes the ownership to be enjoyed by the grantee. Deed restrictions and other limitations and encumbrances are stated after the habendum clause.

Legal Description   A description that sufficiently identifies the land to be conveyed must be included in the deed for it to be enforce-able. A street address is usually not satisfactory. A description that would allow a qualified surveyor to locate the boundaries is considered adequate.

Proper Execution   The deed must be signed by the grantor with appropriate witnesses and acknowledged by a notary public. It is only necessary for the grantor to sign the deed, not the grantee. If the grantor is unable to write, he or she may sign with an "X," witnessed by two persons. The registry of deeds will not record the deed unless it is acknowledged by a notary. This is to prevent the recording of forged or fraudulent documents. A deed executed by an owner in debt, to a relative, with the intent to defraud creditors, is void.

Delivery and Acceptance   The final step in the conveyance of title procedure is the delivery of the deed by the grantor and the acceptance of it by the grantee. The actual or implied intent is necessary by both the grantor and the grantee. Delivery must occur while the grantor is living. If the grantor signed a deed conveying title and died before making delivery, then the deed is not enforceable. The acceptance is implied if the grantee either records the deed, takes possession of the land, mortgages it, gives consideration, or reconveys it.

CHAPTER X

LAND—WHERE TO FIND IT

Before we discuss where to buy land, let's talk a little about what kinds of land you will be buying. Like people, land comes in all shapes, sizes, and descriptions. The three categories of land of primary concern to you for investment will be raw land, farmland, and vacant lots.

RAW LAND

Simply put, raw land is any acreage that is undeveloped, not in use, and has no specific use determined for it as yet. Also called rural land by some, it is acreage in its natural, unimproved state. It is the primary source of land for builders, developers, and subdividers, as well as investors. It may be forest, desert, mountain, swamp, or prairie. It may be high or low, wet or dry, accessible or inaccessible.

The greatest opportunities for land investors and speculators are in raw land. The noted economist Adam Smith said of raw land:

> The purchase and improvement of uncultivated land is the most profitable employment of the smallest, as well as greatest capitals

and the road of all the fortune which can be acquired in that country, America.

Be aware of the several risks involved in speculating in land. If you don't improve the value of the land and sell it quickly, then you'll have to bear the carrying costs. Remember, raw land doesn't produce income for you, and if you borrowed money to buy the land, the interest costs coupled with the taxes may be an unacceptable burden to you. The land may also have some physical or legal deficiencies that could interfere with your future plans for it. Make sure you are up on the latest zoning and building restrictions in your area. You don't want to be surprised. This is why raw land holds such good potential for you. The knowledgeable person searches for the hidden value in raw land and works with, and around, the deficiencies. Gullies and depressions can be filled, hills can be leveled out, unwanted vegetation can be removed, trees can be cut down, pruned, or planted. Use your imagination and seek out the passed-over parcel with the hidden potential and earn yourself a handsome profit from it. Much of the arid and seemingly worthless desert land of our southwestern states has been converted into flourishing retirement havens complete with replicas of Old World landmarks and other equally impressive amenities. The wetlands of south Florida are now covered with luxurious resorts and expensive residential subdivisions. Many a remote and heretofore inaccessible mountain has become a thriving ski mecca.

Buying raw land can be akin to gambling. You're betting that there will be a demand for this land. You're guessing on the direction of growth outward from a metropolitan area. You certainly want to buy in the direction of growth because demand will ultimately increase for your land, thereby increasing its value. If you buy on the opposite side of town, away from the direction of growth, it could be a long time for you to find buyers. As a rule, the farther you are from the metropolitan area, the cheaper the land.

There are regional and locational determinants that alter this fact. For instance, land fifty miles from the center of Cody, Wyoming, will be cheaper by far than land fifty miles from the center of San Francisco.

Topographical characteristics will be another determinant of value.

Whether it is flat or rolling countryside, well-treed or barren will determine demand and value. Are there any utilities—water and electricity—nearby? Are any rivers, ponds, or scenic vistas available? Is the land easily accessible over well-paved highways, or do you have to travel by llama to get to it?

One problem with land investing is having to find or develop meaningful statistics to help decide the feasibility of each purchase. However, most statistics are based on averages, and averages don't tell you a lot about a specific parcel that you may be interested in. Besides, you're not interested in averages I trust; you certainly don't want an average profit—you want more. Armed with the information you're learning from this book, you will be aware of the risks and deficiencies inherent in raw land investing and be able to minimize their effects.

Fast-growing areas certainly reduce your land buying risks, because eventually an end user will buy the land from you. The state of Florida is by far the fastest-growing area in the country and is projected to continue growing rapidly for the rest of this century. Prognosticators predict that the population of Florida will increase from 50 percent to 75 percent within the 1980s alone. California and Texas and several other Sun Belt states are not too far behind Florida in growth predictions. These are facts well known to everyone, so many investors and speculators are investing in these states. Money will still be made here, but often you'll be dealing with speculative land that has passed through the ownership of one, two, three, or more prior speculators, and the land's value may be at peak. You'll also be competing with many other investors for the same parcels. If you live in these fast-growing states, by all means continue buying land there. But if you live elsewhere, buy in your own backyard. Stay within a reasonable geographic area, an area that you can easily learn all there is to learn about land and values and the political and social issues that affect land values.

Let's get back to buying in the path of growth. How do you determine the path of growth? Most communities expand horizontally except in the core section of large cities, where the skyscraper is the norm. They grow horizontally not only because the land is cheaper as you get away from the center of the community, but also because zoning ordinances put restrictions on height, forcing horizontal growth. Go to the library and town hall and study the demographics for your county for the past couple of decades. Most libraries have available a master plan and growth history of the county. Draw a map of the county and plot out where the growth has been. Has growth been sparse and well distributed, or has it been concentrated in certain areas? As you plot on the map, you'll see the trend developing—the direction of growth. This is where new homes are being built and population growing. Now it is your task to seek out parcels just in front of this growth: in areas where growth can be expected to catch up shortly.

FARMLAND

Today's Farm Economy

Farmers today are under a multi-pronged economic onslaught. Particularly the small farmer, who is locked in by crop restrictions and can't keep up with increasing costs. To improve productivity the small farmer must use a wide variety of mechanical devices and equipment all of which are quite expensive to buy and to maintain. For most of the year, due to weather conditions, this expensive machinery lies idle. Whenever the weather is favorable, land holdings must be increased to spread costs over a broader area. To acquire additional land and purchase more machinery money must be borrowed at exceedingly high interest rates; if it is available at all. Unite these problems with the decreasing prices a farmer receives from farm products and you can readily understand why so many farms are falling into foreclosure. Many farmers are getting out of the business either through involuntary bankruptcy or simply because the value of their land has gone beyond the practicality of using it for farming. As growing communities spread out toward nearby farmlands, the highest and best use principle takes over, resulting in an increase in the value of the farmland for other purposes. Much of today's suburbia was yesterday's farmland. Commercial and industrial uses have also been applied to much of the changing rural landscape. Manufacturing companies like the cheaper farmland where they can build efficient facilities on one level rather than on several floors. Increasingly, farmland will be changed to urban use as population pressures move against a fixed supply of land. During the 1970s, rural areas grew faster than metropolitan areas, reversing the trend of the previous century and a half. The proportion of farmers in our society today is 1 of every 60 Americans compared to 1 in 6 in 1900 and 1 in 4 in 1790. You'll hear this many times: "Buy in the direction of growth." In Chapter I I quoted Will Rogers: "It's easy to make money. Just figure out where people are going, and then buy the land before they get there." After reading this far into this book, doesn't his statement make a lot more sense? By the way, he did have a follow-up sentence: "If they don't go there, then don't buy the land."

Farmland is very similar to raw land in that it is quite close to being in its natural state. Although it's being used for agricultural purposes, there have been very little improvements done to the land itself, other than the farm structures, which can be subdivided from the land. If roads must be installed, the task will be relatively easy; the land is already cleared of forests, and more often than not the land will be fairly flat or gently rolling, providing few obstacles for the cost-conscious developer.

There is no shortage of farmland in any part of this great country. Unfortunately a lot of it has become available because of the economic restraints placed on farmers, particularly in the Corn Belt states. Many farmers paid too much for their land during their overeager expansion efforts. Some of this land is now selling for one half of its original purchase price. It won't take too long, however, for this land to be absorbed by profitable farm operations, and the prices will start climbing again.

For our purposes as investors we're not interested in the crop-producing aspects of farmland. We're more interested in the current highest and best use, and in most cases that would be for residential subdivisions. Most farmland sold today is purchased by nonfarmers.

Some individuals keep the farm functioning by leasing to tenant farmers or run the operation themselves as a gentleman farmer. Some even make a profit at it.

Farms are income-producing properties, and depreciation may be taken by the investor on the farm buildings and equipment used in producing the income. If you do keep the farm functioning as it was intended, you can collect what revenues it does earn, but more importantly the land will be appreciating in value while you own it. When you resell it as a farm you'll collect your profit.

Often, capital-starved farmers will sell a portion of their acreage. If you could buy into a situation like this with road frontage, it would be a good way for you to start your land-investing career.

If you don't intend to be a farmer, but rather intend to subdivide for vacation or second-home lots, make sure you buy land as close to a metropolitan area as you can. Your market is in the city. Your future prospects live there and most of them will be averse to travelling more than 100 to 150 miles from their primary residence.

USDA Land Classification

While land is a scarce commodity, it is also true that it may be modified considerably. It is this modification that allows various uses of land as situations and economic conditions change. The United States Department of Agriculture (USDA) has developed a system of classifying land that you can use as a rough measurement in evaluating farmland and raw acreage. This system was established for grading the land primarily for agricultural purposes, but it's an additional bit of information that the speculator can use. The first four classifications outline land that can be cultivated without doing significant or permanent damage to the land. The last four classifications list less desirable land classes:

Class I This is highly cultivable land and is adaptable to a variety of crop types. It retains water and has good drainage. The soil is level and deep and does not suffer from the effects of wind or water erosion.

Class II   This type of soil is almost as cultivable as the above Class I type. The terrain is gently rolling with deep soil. Contour planting and strip cropping may be necessary to deter erosion.

Class III   Sloping terrain, poor drainage, and erosion are common difficulties. The soil is shallow and moderately cultivable.

Class IV   Shallow and wet soils. Limited cultivation possibilities. More ideally suited to orchards and vineyards.

Class V   Not cultivable. Suited for grazing and forestry.

Class VI   Steep slopes, shallow soil, high alkali content and susceptible to erosion. Suited to grazing and forestry.

Class VII   More severe condition than Class VI. Suitable for grazing and forestry.

Class VIII   Not good for cultivation, grazing or forestry. Best use is for hunting or preservation.

VACANT LOTS

If you're urban-oriented, know it well, and prefer to invest there, you should consider investing in vacant lots.

As cities expand horizontally, they generally do so in leaps and bounds. Abutting parcels are not necessarily developed in sequence. For instance, a developer or investor may purchase a parcel on Main Street at the fringe of the community and the next several parcels of land may be skipped over and left idle for several years, with more outlying parcels being improved first. Builders often buy a tract of land and develop it, ignoring smaller abutting parcels. Maybe they weren't interested in it, maybe they couldn't afford to purchase any more land, or maybe they simply overlooked it. The skipped-over parcels are the ones you should look into. Improvements to the surrounding land will increase the value of the skipped-over parcels.

Inner-city lots too may have hidden value for you. Downtown land is expensive, but often there are vacant lots just on the fringes of the downtown area. These lots could serve as supplementary parking lots for the usually traffic-snarled and congested downtown. If you could buy up several abutting vacant lots and seek a zoning change for a commercial venture, your fortune could be made overnight. Vacant and deteriorating houses or other types of buildings with several abutting lots could be an investor's gold mine. Many industrial and high-technology firms are moving into inner-city locations to help alleviate unemployment and to seek large labor pools. You could be "Johnny on the spot" for them if you have an inner-city location for them to build a new facility on.

The urban renewal and redevelopment authorities of many cities, as well as the Department of Housing and Urban Development (HUD), own many city parcels, both vacant and developed. They periodically put them up for auction. Attend any of these auctions and you'll see imaginative people seeking hidden values. Most vacant lots are the result of damage to a building by fire or similar circumstances, which led to demolition of the building. A lot of HUD's foreclosed properties result in empty tenements, which are vandalized and eventually razed. I recently saw a bit of ironic graffiti on the wall of a building that was scheduled for demolition: "On this site the redevelopment authority will erect another vacant lot." Some of these lots can be purchased very cheaply; as low as a couple of hundred dollars in many cases. Quite often lots of this type have a lot of debris on them and need only to be cleaned up to make them more attractive to potential buyers. You could haul away the trash, rake the plot smooth, patch up the cracked sidewalk in front of it, put a fence around it, and place it on the market. This alone may be enough to sell it. Once it's in its improved condition even abutters will see it in a different light and perhaps be interested in buying it from you.

I subdivided a parcel of land and ended up with a seemingly useless, small, odd-shaped lot with utility lines running through the middle of it. It wouldn't have much value to most people, but the abutting parcel contained a small apartment house, and I approached the absentee owner about it. He purchased it as a parking area for his tenants. Before title passed, the abutter at the rear of the lot made an offer for it. He wanted to build a tennis court on it for his condominium complex, which had no room to expand. The apartment house owner won out because he was first with a down payment, but both of them used their imaginations, as did I.

A vacant lot in a deteriorating neighborhood should be avoided. You can tell a deteriorating neighborhood by the way the homes and streets are maintained. Most neighborhoods go through cycles. They grow and develop, then deteriorate, then start improving again.

The "baby-boomers" and "Yuppies" are moving back into the central city, buying up tenements and brownstones and fixing them up to live there. This is the type of neighborhood where you want to buy vacant lots. Their improvements to their properties will increase the value of your lot.

Lots in proximity to the wants and needs of people, such as churches, schools, stores, and medical services, are good investments. Always check the building and zoning codes to see what uses are permitted for the lot. You don't want to own a lot that you can use only as a victory garden.

On occasion heirs will simply continue paying taxes on their inherited properties without taking a second thought about them. The properties may be scattered, a house in one section, a vacant lot here, a vacant lot there. They may not have been considering selling, and they may not have even seen any of the property. If you approach them with a reasonable offer, you might be able to shake a "gem" loose.

Out-of-state owners are also good sources of vacant lots to purchase. They may have moved away from the area years ago and have practically forgotten about the lot except when they pay taxes on it. They may welcome the chance to get rid of it.

Even in suburbia vacant lots are available. Many early buyers in a new subdivision purchase their lots cheaply, don't build on them, and later move from the area; often they are willing to part with the lot for a reasonable profit to them.

Chapter X

THE SELLERS OF LAND

The Federal Government

The government—federal, state, county, city, and town—is second only to individuals as the largest landowners in the country. Of the almost 2 billion acres of terra firma in the United States our various governments own better than 25 percent of it.

Most of the government-owned lands are in the western states. Up to 75 percent of the land west of the Mississippi River is owned by the federal government, and the individual states own as much as 10 percent of the land within their borders. Much of the western land is not of high value—deserts, prairies, wetlands, badlands, mountains, canyons, and the like. A great deal of land is rented out to farmers and ranchers for grazing livestock.

Certainly not all the land is low-value land. The entire Pacific coastline, for instance, and land in and around every municipality and community. But most of the available government lands between the Pacific and the Mississippi is of minimal value to the land investor.

East of the Mississippi is another story. Most of our populated areas are located there, and most of the land is usable. The government doesn't own nearly as much land in the East, but it still has title to a lot of land.

Again, however, it is important for you to concentrate your land buying efforts within reasonable geographic limits. If you live in North Carolina, it would be unrealistic for you to buy and sell land in North Dakota, or vice versa. Yes, land may be very cheap in North Dakota compared to your burgeoning community in North Carolina, but you just don't know the region and the logistics will trip you up. Stay within as small a geographic area as is feasible for you from a profit standpoint. There may be enough available federal lands within your own county to keep you busy for years.

The Bureau of Land Management   Your starting point to find out about federally owned lands is to write to

United States Department of the Interior
Bureau of Land Management
Washington, DC 20240

The Bureau of Land Management (BLM) will send you a pamphlet on the sale of public lands. The BLM is divided into regional and district offices, each of which handles the disposition and sale of surplus federal lands within their jurisdiction.

Each office has its own procedure for the sale of lands. The sale may be at auction or be sealed bids, and the deposit amount and payment schedules may differ. Once the land is determined to be excess to the government's needs, a sale date is determined. The bids may have to be submitted either by mail or by an oral auction. The BLM may decide to have competitive bids with preference given to abutting or neighboring property owners. All bids must include a "good faith" deposit, which is generally 10 percent of the bid amount. The highest bidder wins and must be prepared to pay for the land in full. The BLM does not offer terms. Deposits of the losing bidders are returned to them.

Keep in mind when buying land from the federal government that they often retain title to all mineral rights. If you find gold, it's not yours to keep.

Most BLM land is not of much use to the average investor. It's usually isolated, desolate, and barren. Here's a list of the various regional offices of the BLM that you can contact if you are interested in this kind of land:

ALASKA
Bureau of Land Management
701 C Street
Box 13
Anchorage, AK 99513

ARIZONA
Bureau of Land Management
2400 Valley Bank Center
Phoenix, AZ 85073

Chapter X

CALIFORNIA
Bureau of Land Management
2800 Cottage Way
Sacramento, CA 95825

COLORADO and KANSAS
Bureau of Land Management
1037 20th Street
Denver, CO 80202

IDAHO
Bureau of Land Management
3380 Americana Terrace
Boise, ID 83706

MONTANA and NORTH & SOUTH DAKOTA
Bureau of Land Management
222 N. 32nd Street
Billings, MT 59107

NEW MEXICO, OKLAHOMA, and TEXAS
Bureau of Land Management
Montoya Federal Bldg.
P.O. Box 1449
Santa Fe, NM 87501

OREGON and WASHINGTON
Bureau of Land Management
825 N.E. Multnomah Street
P.O. Box 2965
Portland, OR 97208

UTAH
Bureau of Land Management
136 E. South Temple
Salt Lake City, UT 84111

WYOMING and NEBRASKA
Bureau of Land Management
2515 Warren Ave.
Cheyenne, WY 82003

EASTERN STATES
Bureau of Land Management
350 S. Pickett St.
Alexandria, VA 22304

The General Services Administration   The General Services Administration (GSA), that stalwart purchasing arm of the federal government, is another source of federal property. It's not too often that they have undeveloped land for sale; it's generally real estate with buildings or other structures on it—old federal office buildings, post offices, warehouses, army barracks, and sometimes entire military bases are typical GSA properties.

All federal departments and agencies must notify the GSA when they have surplus real estate. The GSA will then contact all other government departments to see if they have an authorized need for the surplus property. If there is a need, then the property is transferred. If no agency wants it, then it is placed on a bimonthly listing of all the properties that the GSA has available for sale or auction. You can get a free, updated version of this listing, called the "U.S. Real Property Sales List," by writing to

The Consumer Information Center
Pueblo, CO 81009

For descriptions and prices of properties specifically located within your geographic area you will have to write to the regional or district GSA offices. You can request to be placed on the mailing list of the regional office—a list of these offices is below. As with the BLM lands, sales are by competitive sealed bid. There are no terms, you must mail in a deposit equal to 10 percent of your bid amount, and be prepared to pay cash if your bid is the highest.

General Services Administration Regional Offices

NEW ENGLAND
McCormack Post Office and Courthouse
Boston, MA 02109

NEW YORK and NEW JERSEY
26 Federal Plaza
New York, N.Y. 10007

WASHINGTON, D.C., PENNSYLVANIA, VIRGINIA, MARYLAND, WEST VIRGINIA, and DELAWARE
7th and D Streets SW
Washington, DC 20407

ALABAMA, FLORIDA, GEORGIA, KENTUCKY, MISSISSIPPI, NORTH
CAROLINA, SOUTH CAROLINA, TENNESSEE, PUERTO RICO, and
VIRGIN ISLANDS
Russell Federal Building
75 Spring Street
Atlanta, GA 30303

ILLINOIS, INDIANA, MICHIGAN, MINNESOTA, OHIO, and WISCON-
SIN
230 South Dearborn Street
Chicago, IL 60604

ARKANSAS, IOWA, KANSAS, LOUISIANA, MISSOURI, NEBRASKA,
NEW MEXICO, OKLAHOMA, and TEXAS
819 Taylor Street
Fort Worth, TX 76102

COLORADO, MONTANA, NORTH DAKOTA, SOUTH DAKOTA, UTAH,
and WYOMING
Building 41, Denver Federal Center
Denver, CO 80225

AMERICAN SAMOA, ARIZONA, CALIFORNIA, GUAM, HAWAII, NE-
VADA, and PACIFIC TERRITORIES
525 Market Street
San Francisco, CA 94105

ALASKA, IDAHO, OREGON, and WASHINGTON
GSA Center
Auburn, WA 98002

Other Government Agencies Besides the BLM and GSA there
are several other government agencies that periodically have property
for sale. The Farmer's Home Administration (FHA), a division of the
United States Department of Agriculture (USDA), makes loans to
farmers and individuals building farm structures or homes in rural and
semi-rural communities of less than 10,000 inhabitants. The Farmer's
Home Administration lends money to persons of minimal resources to
buy an existing house, to buy a piece of land to build a house, or to
build a house on land a person already owns. They will also lend funds
to farmers for agricultural pursuits and to individuals buying land for
commercial or recreational enterprises. When a borrower defaults, the
FHA will foreclose on the property and add it to its inventory. You may

contact the FHA regional office in your sphere of operations to get a listing of the available properties they have for sale.

Do not confuse the Farmer's Home Administration with the other government agency called the FHA—the Federal Housing Administration, a division within the Department of Housing and Urban Development—which does not lend money, but insures loans made by approved lenders under regulated conditions and terms.

The Department of Health and Human Services and the Department of Education occasionally have surplus properties that you can inquire about. Also, the Department of Justice's Drug Enforcement Administration occasionally sells off confiscated properties.

Let's not forget our most cherished agency, the Internal Revenue Service. When a person doesn't pay his or her taxes, the IRS can, and will, seize the person's property and sell it off to cover the indebtedness. Usually, you can acquire real bargains at IRS auctions because they want to dispose of the property as rapidly as possible. They'll estimate a property's true market value and then discount it by estimating its *forced sale value*. From the forced sale value all mortgages and other liens are deducted to arrive at a minimum acceptable bid. You can go to your local IRS office and get a fact sheet on each property that is coming up for auction. A suitable cash deposit with your bid and a full cash payment if you are the winning bidder are requisites. As with most foreclosures, the prior owner has a right of redemption period of 180 days in which to buy back the property from you with a 20 percent interest on your money. Take heed when buying through the IRS; they don't do a title search on the properties that they foreclose on—you get only what they have acquired. Do a title search yourself before acquiring property through the IRS.

Local Governments

As I mentioned, most state-owned lands are west of the Mississippi River. Much of the state-owned land was originally given to the states by the federal government. The states manage the lands for the highest profit and are quite active in buying and selling land. Some agencies have mailing lists for notifying potential buyers of upcoming land sales and auctions. State universities too occasionally sell off surplus lands. You can write to the following agencies, in the capital of the state you are concentrating on, to find out about available properties:

State Land Commissioner
State Highway Commissioner
Department of Transportation
Department of Natural Resources
Department of Parks and Recreation
Department of Forestry
Department of Fisheries and Wildlife
Department of Water
Department of Bridges

When you read the chapter on taxation, I told you that there are no federal or state real estate taxes—only local real estate taxes assessed by counties, cities, and towns. They don't want to be landowners, so when they do acquire title through real estate delinquencies they want to put it back on the tax rolls as soon as possible to produce tax revenues. You can write to or visit the county and local treasurers, tax assessors, and town clerks to find out what lands are available and the procedure to purchase them.

Builders and Developers

When you have land for sale, some of your better prospects may be local builders. They have to put their houses somewhere, and your subdivided lots may be just the place. Builders will also be a very good source of land to buy from. When sales are strong, a builder can keep a crew busy building on the lots in his or her land inventory. If sales remain strong, the builder will be looking for additional lots to add to inventory or undeveloped land that will eventually be improved and subdivided into homesites.

Like most enterprises, building activity is cyclical. When sales turn downward, the builder has to build fewer homes and needs less workers to do so. Cutting back on overhead costs may not be enough. Although the builder may be building fewer houses with fewer workers, capital is still needed to pay for the materials and labor that are being used and for the other expenses of the operation. If revenues are decreasing, and limited to begin with, the banks who normally lend funds will hesitate to continue to do so. A routine way for builders to raise working capital is to sell off some of their land inventory. Land is as necessary to a builder as are nails and lumber, but the builder may need the cash now—replacement lots can always be purchased later. Don't feel bad for the builder, this is a commonplace and periodic course of action; besides, the price you pay for the land will be more than the builder paid for it.

The land may simply be raw acreage with good potential for you. It may also be a "paper subdivision." A paper subdivision is a subdivision plan that has been laid out by a surveyor, submitted to the town planning board and approved by it, with no physical work done to the land as yet—no trees cleared, no roads cut in, no utilities installed— just undeveloped land for now.

The normal time to get a small and uncomplicated subdivision filed and approved can take two or three years from the time you first hire the surveyor to the final approval of the plan. You're ahead of the game with a paper subdivision because you've saved one of your most valuable commodities—your time.

The builder will charge you for the approved plans, but they'll be worth every cent. You may get a good price on the land if the builder needs cash in a hurry, but the builder is not apt to be interested in financing your purchase. You'll have to find financing elsewhere.

Banks

A source of land that has proved extremely fruitful for me is banks. Nine out of the first ten properties that I was involved with were bank-owned properties.

Most banks have some type of real estate for sale. They may have acquired it through mortgage defaults or they may handle trusts and estates for individuals. They don't want to own foreclosed properties because it is a sad reminder of a poor loan, either by the borrower or the lender. Land that they have foreclosed on they add to their real estate owned (REO) list. Banks don't usually advertise the lands they have for sale, particularly foreclosed properties. Often, what the land will bring on the open market is less than the original loan's principal plus accrued interest. Rather than taking a beating on the sale of the land, they'll keep it on their books at full value.

During the early 1970s when the real estate market was in the pits, banks foreclosed on hundreds and thousands of properties. During the rest of the decade, real estate sales and prices skyrocketed and the banks divested themselves of most of their REO. Again during the early 1980s, banks have been foreclosing on properties, most often farmland.

Make an appointment and go visit all the banks in your area. The senior mortgage officer or an assistant is normally the person to see, but always ask to see the president of the bank first. If the president tells you to see a subordinate, fine, because you are recommended by and through the president now. If the president decides to handle the matter, you'll find it to be easier and more productive. Ask the bank to give you the particulars on what is in their REO account and to keep you apprised as new properties are added.

Talk also with the person in charge of handling trusts and estates. Many times land that hasn't been on the market suddenly becomes available when someone inquires. Again, if that person knows you came to the trust and estate department through the president's office, the going will be smoother. Not that working with the "lesser lights" of a bank will prove difficult, it's just that better results come about when you deal with the president.

In both cases, with the REO land and the trust and estates land, the bank may be willing to offer you good financing terms. After all, they already own some of this land. If they sell it to you and you default, they'll keep your deposit and all your payments and own the land again—not a bad deal for the bank.

Utility Companies

Recently an associate of mine purchased a choice parcel of land from the telephone company at a "steal" of a price. I've driven by that parcel a million times and paid it no heed—often we see but do not perceive. Not only have I driven by it countless times, but I had purchased a large vacant parcel directly (and I mean 50 feet away) across the street from it. I still own this parcel and will be seeking approvals to subdivide it soon.

The parcel even had a small brick building on it that the telephone company used for who knows what. Apparently they had no further use for it. The building hadn't been used for years and it just sat there. My friend approached them with an offer and after several meetings a deal was worked out. He's going to raze the building and subdivide the land into homesites. Exactly what I'm going to do across the street. Why didn't I see that land before him?

Utility companies need a lot of real estate to deliver their services to the public. Most services are delivered over easements and other rights of way over or under private property. For instance, if you live in a typical suburban neighborhood, the telephone, electric, and gas companies have installed their wires and pipelines across the front of your property either underground or strung along utility poles. The water company too, whether private or municipal, has an easement to install their services, and perhaps the cable television company. They don't own the land that their equipment is on, you do. They simply have the legal right—an easement—to use it.

The utilities also, however, own some pieces of property outright, some of which they may no longer need. It may be land that had been purchased for expansion that never materialized, or it may be properties that have become obsolete or exceeds their current needs. They don't normally decide to divest themselves of such properties, but simply leave them on the books as assets. They will, nevertheless, consider selling if they are tactfully approached. If you are aware of a particular idle parcel owned by a utility company, approach them and make an offer for it. Don't be discouraged in your dealings with them.

Chapter X

As with the government, there is a lot of red tape to cut through. Unlike many private landowners who seek a more than reasonable profit, the utilities simply want to get what the land is worth. You can expect to pay something around the appraised market value. If you persevere, deal with the hierarchy, and cut through the red tape, you may indeed end up owning a potentially profitable parcel.

Real Estate Agencies

Real estate brokers and salespersons are, of course, as knowledgeable as anyone of what is for sale within their sales area. That is their business. They have to know what is for sale and what is coming up for sale. Land and housing are their product line, it's their inventory. Without an inventory there is no payday.

I'm sure you know that the real estate broker represents the seller. It is the seller who will pay the broker if his or her efforts produce a sale. Don't be overly concerned that the broker's legal allegiance is to the seller; real estate brokers are equally cooperative and valuable to the prospective buyer as to the seller. Go into any reputable agency in your area and tell the broker that you are looking for land to invest in. The agency probably has several parcels for you to look at. And don't worry about wasting the broker's time—the broker is there to help you and is fully aware that there are more lookers than buyers. It's a numbers game to the broker. A certain percentage of the people he or she shows around will be buyers.

I'll explain in detail for you in a later chapter the advantages of working with a real estate broker. For now, however, I'll tell you about a very obvious, but often overlooked, source to start your land investing education. There are two large national real estate agencies that specialize in farmland and rural raw acreage:

United Farm Agency
612 West 47th St.
Kansas City, MO 64112

Strout Realty, Inc.
Plaza Towers
Springfield, MO 65804

Both of these firms have hundreds of agents and offices around the country and each puts out a large quarterly catalog that is a compilation of all the listings from all of their offices and agents. The catalogs are jam-packed with hundreds of properties, listed in alphabetic order by states. The catalogs are free and the agents are cooperative. When they send you a catalog, you'll also get the name and address of their local affiliate who will send you a follow-up note shortly after you receive the material. You'll also get a "want list," or questionnaire asking you what type of property you are looking for, location, and price range. The catalogs don't just whet your appetite, they give you the description of the land, the location, and the price and terms. As I said, this is a good place to start your education and find out what type of land investments are out there for you. You can look in the telephone directory to get the number of the local affiliate and ask them to send you a catalog, or you could write directly to the corporate offices above.

There are two other national agencies that will also send you information on land investments:

American Farm and Investment Digest
3546 Watson Rd.
St. Louis, MO 63139

Rural Property Bulletin
P.O. Box 2042
Sandpoint, ID 83864

Companies and Corporations

From time to time private companies and corporations will have land for sale. They may have purchased it in anticipation of expanding their existing operations or building a satellite operation. In recent years, a large high-technology firm has purchased hundreds of acres in a community near my home with plans to consolidate their far-flung enterprises. However, they are having second thoughts now. First of all, there isn't as large a labor supply in this area to satisfy their needs. The town officials are giving them a real workout on their plans besides. I expect that they will be placing much of this land back on the market in the not-too-distant future and keep only what is practical for them to use.

I know of several other local firms who own large parcels of undeveloped land and make it available to their employees for camping, hunting, fishing, and hiking. A couple of them have built cabins and recreational facilities for use by their employees. On numerous occasions I've seen companies put some of this land on the market because of a dip in sales and profits on their business operations.

Check out the ownership of larger parcels on the outskirts of your community. If some are owned by private concerns, let them know that you would be interested should they decide to sell. If you find a particularly attractive parcel, be aggressive and make an offer for it.

Through the Newspapers

When you eventually have your own land for sale, what steps will you take to sell it? Chapter XIV goes into this in depth, explaining the various marketing efforts and tools you'll use. But let me tell you here that you definitely will place an ad in the classified section of your newspaper. Practically every land seller does. For that reason, wouldn't the classifieds also be a source of land to buy? It'll probably be one of your best sources.

Look in the classifieds of your local papers and keep looking. You may not find anything right away, but keep at it. Persistence will pay for you. You should look in all the newspapers in your area. You don't have to buy them all; you could go to the library once a week and cull the classifieds.

Don't just look under "Land for Sale"; look through the general real estate ads too—houses, businesses and commercial, and opportunities.

Sometimes landowners will place their land ad under the houses for sale section. If there are ads with a home on several acres, look into it. You can always subdivide the home away from the land and sell it separately. Look also under the legal section of the classifieds for sheriff's sales, foreclosures, and land auctions. While at it, read the "Land Wanted" columns and keep a record of these names; they may one day be prospects for your land. You can also write a "Land Wanted" ad for yourself and put it in the classifieds.

Clip out all the promising ads, have a pad of paper handy, and get on the telephone. You'll generally obtain enough information over the phone to determine if you should investigate further. If the property is too expensive for you and the owner doesn't seem flexible, thank the owner and don't waste any more of your time—get on to the next possibility. The owners want to sell their land—that's why they placed the ad in the first place, so you shouldn't have any difficulty finding out everything you want to know about the land. But you'll be surprised at how little some people actually know about their own real estate. If the owner lives a distance away from the land, he or she may not be aware of any changes in zoning or in the relative growth and development of the community in general. Some specific questions to ask are

- Price and terms
- Location
- Whether the land has been surveyed
- Size, dimensions, and frontage
- Whether the title is clear
- Whether there are liens, easements, encumbrances, or restrictions
- Kinds of utilities available
- Zoning
- Terrain characteristics
- Skeletons in the closet: anything detrimental about the land you should know about

There'll be other questions that you'll develop that will be important to you as a land investor. If you get burned on any single factor in buying land, you'll forever after be wary of it. I purchased some unsurveyed land and paid the consequences. From that point forward I always ask about a survey. If the information supplied by the seller interests you, say so. Don't start to negotiate on the telephone, however. How can you truly decide the value of a piece of land without seeing it and walking on it? Gather your facts and tell the owner you'll be in touch. If you can determine right away that the land may be good for you, make an appointment to go see it, or visit it by yourself.

Through the Tax Rolls

The tax assessor's department keeps detailed records of every parcel of real estate in the community. These are working records for the assessor so that it can be determined what taxes are to be paid by property owners. These are public records and are at your disposal. Go to your own town hall and ask to see them. They may be under the care of the assessor, the town clerk, or any one of several responsible town departments. Usually, they are on a counter and readily available for public inspection. If you don't understand how to use them, ask the person in charge to help you. The records will include a map book showing the location of every parcel with a cross-reference file that shows you the owner and his or her mailing address. (The owner may not live on the parcel he or she owns, so the address may be different.) It will also show the size of the land, the zoning classification, its location, and the amount of taxes assessed. If there is a building on the land, the taxes for the land and the structure will be listed separately, then totaled. On some tax rolls a title reference may be given (book and page number) so that you can readily research the title. Betterment charges, if any, will also be listed. If you want a history of what the land has sold for in the past, the tax assessor's office keeps a separate file on this and will show you it if you ask for it.

If you drive by a parcel (make sure you *perceive* it) that you find interesting, you can go to the town hall and get all this information. Take a day or two and spend it at town hall going through the tax books.

You can simply run down the column that lists the size of the tracts of land, write down the facts, and contact the owners.

I've found and purchased several parcels this way. I've looked in the tax records, written down the information on all the parcels over a minimum size (I wanted subdividable acreage), and then contacted the owners. In some cases the land had once been on the market, but had been removed for one reason or another. In other cases the owners hadn't considered selling their land, but since I asked. . . .

CHAPTER XI

BUYING TIPS

THE RIGHT TIME TO BUY

There really isn't any right season to buy, but rather a combination of factors that determine the right time to buy. There are, however, certain bits of advice I can offer that will make the buying easier. Perhaps the simplest answer is "When the price is right." It could also be when an opportunity presents itself.

The winter has traditionally been a good time for me. I've found prices were generally a little cheaper. This may be because most prospects are not out walking in the winter wonderland, but instead are sitting by their warm hearths. Fewer prospects naturally leads to less sales activity thus cheaper prices.

Winter land shopping has some other side benefits to offer the investor. If the land you're looking at is well-treed, it can be difficult to expertly examine the land. With the leaves off the trees you can look deeply into the woods examining not only the lay of the land, but also areas suitable to site housing or to cut in roads. Boundary markers are also easier to find in the winter, unless they are under a snow cover.

When considering a parcel to buy, you should try to see it under adverse weather conditions. Sunny days make everything look good. Inclement weather will bring out the less desirable features of a parcel.

When you are ready to walk the land, dress properly. Wear good walking shoes, and clothes that you don't mind getting torn or soiled.

During your inspection, you're going to be checking on a number of things. The type of neighborhood or environment the parcel is in is important because it will affect demand. You would want to avoid a deteriorating community or an area with undesirable features like a nearby landfill or a noxious wetland. Walk the entire perimeter first, observing the land from the outside in. While you're at it, observe the condition of the abutting properties. If a neighbor has a penchant for collecting old, unregistered vehicles, rusted boilers, and similar Americana, you certainly want to know about it.

Many parcels look level when viewed from the front or one of the sidelines, but there may be a severe drop-off at the rear or one of the other sidelines. Walk into the interior of the land; there may be deep depressions not visible from the perimeter that could cause development problems. Too often I've seen secluded parcels that have become dumping grounds for inconsiderate litterers. One parcel that I examined had so much junk on it I truly wondered if I had stumbled into the town refuse area. A few old boilers or truck tires shouldn't be too much bother—they're easily removable.

What kind of frontage and access to the property is there? Is the land served by a well-maintained road? Is it a speedway, or a truck route, or on the way to the dump? You have to know these things. The amount of frontage you have is important, but if it's all several feet below the grade of the road this could cost a lot to correct.

Do you see any telephone or electric poles or hydrants nearby? The availability of utilities is a major consideration. To extend them up to the parcel from a substantial distance away would knock the profitability around a bit.

While walking the land and along the frontage, you'll be picturing how you are going to improve it. If you're buying a large parcel, the length of the roadways is critical to profitability. Of course, you're not a surveyor, so you can only estimate, at this time, where the roads will go. Your surveyor will make the final and proper decision for you when the time comes.

Is there any part of the land suitable for building? You can't tell this solely from a visual inspection. Later you will have to have a percolation test taken to see what the soil consists of and if it can support an on-site septic system. For now though, you can see if water puddles up after a heavy rainfall. This could indicate that there are unwanted materials present below the surface like clay or hardpan (a densely packed soil).

What is the soil like? Is it rocky, sandy, or heavily clayed? Each of these types can cause headaches for you economically. As you walk the land, do you sink into the soft loamy soil? Are there a lot of rock outcroppings, bogs, tidal pools, or low-water areas? All of these affect the use and value of the land. If there is no vegetation in certain areas, find out why and how to correct it. Dig a hole in the ground at least a foot deep and see how deep the topsoil may be and how far down the surface moisture extends. Rub the soil in your hand. Does it crumble, as you hope it will, which indicates good soil, or is it gritty or puttylike? Soil condition is a very important, and often overlooked, factor in smart land buying. Analyze it properly. Often, steps necessary to correct adverse soil conditions can make or break the profitability of a parcel.

Topsoil is the dark, rich, loose upper layer of the soil usually a foot or so in depth. It is rich in nutrients and highly fertile. In some areas of the country it is illegal to remove topsoil from a parcel and transfer it to another town. It is valuable, but not critical unless you plan on doing some farming. Steep slopes and deep depressions with little or no vegetation are susceptible to erosion and will have to be corrected.

The next level is the subsoil, which may run down as deep as four feet. It can consist of rock, which can pose percolation problems, or any of several other soil types like loam, clay, gravel, or sand.

The most preferred soil is loam. It is black and crumbly and consists of equal parts of clay and sand. Gravel and sand are large, loose particles that rapidly lose nutrients as water flows through them. They are gray or yellow and gritty when you rub them between your fingers. They gain and lose heat rapidly, resulting in quick freezing and thawing. Clay is made up of tiny particles that become like putty when wet and are impenetrable by water and plant roots. If you have a lot of clay on your land, you may have to remove it and replace it with more permeable soil to make the land buildable. If it is very deep, the land could be unusable. Clay is gray and sometimes blue and is heavy and solid. If the topsoil or subsoil consists of less permeable materials like clay or rock, it can cause drainage problems.

A look at the vegetation growing on the land will tell you how fertile the soil is. Look at the trees and foliage. Green trees should be green. If they're brown, find out why. Do the trees and bushes look healthy? Are they the right color for the terrain and the time of year? The leafy trees should be fully foliaged, and the pine trees should be wearing thick green needles. A live animal, bird, and insect population should be evident. Look in the trees, lift up rocks, or look in stream beds—you should find some trace. If there's no life, maybe there's something drastically wrong.

If there's water on the property, a stream, or river, or lake, check the quality of the water; it may contain pollutants from upstream or local factories. Smell the water; if it has a foul odor find out where it's coming from. If the land is on the seashore, check for excessive erosion. Is the air, in general, sweet-smelling or is there a nearby paper mill emitting sulfur smells? Check the noise level; there may be an auto racing track or an airport further down the road. In this day of toxicity and environmental problems you have to be on the alert for anything offensive to the senses. If there's something that offends you, it's going to offend a future prospect.

You're not only checking for negatives, check too for positive features that when exploited will increase the land's value. If the land is heavily wooded, lumber removal may have a value. A scenic view may be developed if certain trees were felled or hills leveled. A stone wall surrounding the land adds flavor.

Don't stop here; talk with the neighbors. Ask about the quality of life here, the tax rate, the type and cooperation of the local government, fire and police protection. Go to the nearest town hall and make some inquiries. There are several people that you could talk to in town hall such as the town clerk, the assessor, the building inspector and the health agent. The town clerk can give you a general overview of the living conditions of the community and the general attitude of the residents towards growth and development. The assessor will give you a breakdown of how land is assessed and taxed before, during, and after subdividing it.

The building inspector is an important person for you to talk to even if you're not planning on putting up any structures—the persons who will be buying lots from you will. Tell the inspector your plans and ask for advice; you may save some time and trouble when applying for a subdivision approval. Buy a copy of the building codes from the inspector and ask for an explanation of them so that you'll do the job right. The building inspector is a good person to have on your team.

The health inspector will also be involved if and when you apply for a subdivision approval. He or she may be aware of some critical or detrimental aspects of the property that may alter your decision to buy it. The health inspector knows what parts of the community have good or poor soil conditions. If there is a soil percolation problem in the general vicinity of your land, he or she will let you know about it and perhaps how to correct it. If there are underground springs or old wells on the property, he or she can assist you in locating them. If you can arrange it, take the building inspector and the health inspector to the property. Get them involved. The health inspector can take soil and water samplings and give you a report on their condition.

Go to any bank in town and ask to see the loan manager. Say that you are considering buying a parcel of land and you would like to find out about the area in general. Let the loan manager talk; he or she may tell you all you need to know. Ask some specific questions about the bank's lending practices, down payments and interest rate. Ask about the path of growth of the community. In what part of town are most loans being made? You may also want to visit another bank, or two, and ask the same questions.

Go to a local church and ask about the community. You'll get an unbiased opinion from the clergy. Drop in at the local utility companies and tell them of your plans for the land. The availability of necessary utilities is critical to the success of your investment. Without power and water what good is the land to you? If utilities are already in place at your land, you're in a good situation. If not, find out where they are and how to get them to your land and at what price.

NUMBER OF LOTS

Before you buy a piece of land you have to know, or at least have an idea of, the development costs and potential revenues and profits. In Chapter XII, on subdividing, you'll find out how to arrive at these figures, but for now I'm going to give you a technique to enable you to make "on the spot" decisions on the suitability of a parcel of land for investment. When you go to look at a parcel for the first time, you can make some tentative decisions right away about the property's potential. If the figures don't appeal to you, then walk away from the land and find another one. There'll be plenty of parcels for you to look at, so don't waste your time on marginal ones.

When you look at a parcel of raw acreage for subdivision, you'll want to be able to determine the number of lots that you can get from it—the *yield*. Knowing the yield makes it easy for you to determine the profit. If you're considering a 20-acre parcel located in an area zoned for 1-acre lots, your mental computer may tell you that the yield will be 20 1-acre lots. This would be the ideal yield; but there are some facts that will reduce the yield.

First of all, a 20-acre tract will probably require the installation of a substantial amount of paved roadway, which will use up acreage—unless you have a couple of thousand feet of existing, paved frontage and you don't have to put in roads.

Besides the land needed for the roadways, the shape and topography of the parcel will also be determining factors of the yield. A rugged terrain—high hills, deep valleys, and wetlands like bogs or marshes will also reduce the yield. Irregularly shaped parcels of land make it difficult for a surveyor to plot out the lots efficiently for the highest yield.

Zoning is another determinant. If the area is zoned for half acre lots, naturally you'll get almost twice as many lots as in 1-acre zoning. Some communities require 1-acre lots to be 43,560 square feet in size, which is a true acre. Other communities require acre lots to be 40,000 square feet in size. This is often referred to as a "builder's acre."

The difference of 3560 square feet between a true acre and a builder's acre will affect the yield whether it is a small or large parcel that you are subdividing. With a small parcel, the larger requirement of 43,560 square feet may cost you a lot or two. For example, say you have a 4.7 acre parcel with sufficient frontage so that you need only subdivide without installing a road. The 4.7 acres works out to 204,732 square feet (4.7 x 43,560). If the zoning calls for builder's acres, then your yield will be 5 house lots (204,732 ÷ 40,000 = 5). However, if the zoning calls for true 1-acre lots, then your land will yield only 4 house lots (204,732 ÷ 43,560 = 4.7). Since you can't have a seven-tenths acre lot, you'll get only 4 lots. You'll be three tenths of an acre shy of the necessary square footage for the fifth lot. With a larger parcel, say 40 or 50 acres, the additional requirement of 3560 square feet could cost you several lots.

Assume your yield were 37 lots from a 50-acre parcel. Multiplied by 37 lots, the additional requirement of 3560 square feet results in a total of 131,720 square feet, which by itself is enough footage for 3 house lots. That's 3 house lots that you won't get, and if your lots are selling for $25,000 apiece, this can be costly and may be enough to make the parcel a marginal investment.

Lot frontage requirements as dictated by zoning can also affect the yield. Each 300 feet of frontage will create 3 lots with 100 foot frontages, but only 2 lots with 150 foot frontage requirements (Figure 11-1). Not only does your yield suffer, but the cost of developing an additional 50 feet of paved roads per lot increases the average per lot cost.

When standing on a parcel of land or looking at it on a plot plan, you can use the following as a rule of thumb to make a tentative assessment

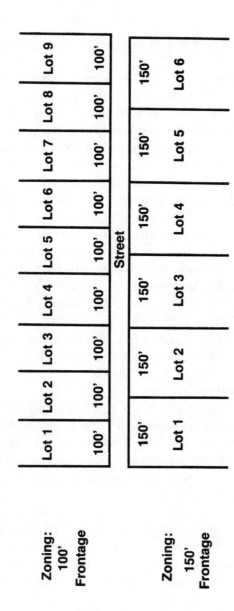

Figure 11-1. Frontage requirements and yield

of the yield. If the zoning requires all house lots to be at least 15,000 square feet, then you can expect a yield of about 2.5 lots per acre. Simply multiply the total acreage by 2.5 and you'll get the yield. If zoning requires lots to be 20,000 square feet (a builder's half acre), you can expect 1.5 lots per acre. Multiply the acreage by 1.5 to get the yield. Expect to get three quarters (0.75) of a lot for 1-acre zoning. Multiply the acreage by .75 in this case. For example, if you have 24 acres, you would get yields as follows:

ZONING REQUIREMENT	EXPECTED YIELD
15,000 sq. ft.	24 acres × 2.5 = 60 lots
20,000 sq. ft.	24 acres × 1.5 = 36 lots
40,000 sq. ft.	24 acres × .75 = 18 lots

The above is the normal expected yield assuming the parcel isn't too irregularly shaped and there are no wetlands to contend with. This isn't a scientific method, just a good rule-of-thumb measurement to make a preliminary assessment of the potential number of lots the parcel may yield.

USING USEFUL MAPS

Besides investing a good amount of time and a lot of shoe leather in searching for the right parcel to buy, there are other aids you can use. Maps help you to "see" where you are going. They help you to see how a parcel graphically and geographically fits into the scheme of a community and how it relates to and affects neighboring properties. Tax maps, aerial photographs, and road and street maps are a few of these aids. Most of them are inexpensive and easily obtainable at town offices or selected retail outlets. They all help you to get a feel for the land, and they are vital in helping you to determine the value and ultimate use of your land. You may not use more than one or two types of maps, but for your edification I've listed several that could be of use to you.

Chapter XI

Tax Maps

For taxation purposes the tax assessor's office maintains a map file of all the parcels in the community. These are not actual surveys, but are sufficient for finding land to buy. There's usually a copy machine nearby for you to make duplicates of any map. Different people use these maps for various reasons. The assessor has his or her reasons, of course, and town officials such as the building inspector, the health inspector, and the fire department use them. The planning department makes great use of them. Often you'll see real estate appraisers availing themselves of them and professional site selectors too (fast-food representatives, etc.). And of course you'll see people like you and me using them. When you study the availability of subdividable parcels of land in a community, you'll always use these maps.

Topographical Maps

A topographic, or "topo," map is usually drawn up by a surveyor or a land planner. It shows, in detail, the descriptive features of an area, such as drainage patterns and differences in land formations and contours. The map also shows pertinent artificial and natural features of the land, including major highways and even lesser roads and trails of all types, water bodies, vegetation, railroads, airports, fences, land depressions, gullies, valleys, hills and dales—the entire character of the surface of the subject land and its immediate surrounding area.

Knowledge of the topography of a parcel is important to the investor-developer in determining the physical restrictions and restraints that the "lay of the land" may impose upon development. Using the topo map in your land planning will help you to utilize and preserve the natural features such as views, trees, hills, rock groupings, wetlands, and solar heating possibilities more effectively. If you have hilly land, you want to take advantage of the hills and use them rather than bulldoze them away. You can wrap roads and driveways around small wetlands, clusters of trees, or large boulders. Houses can be sited to take advantage of the sun's rays and scenic vistas.

The Geodetic Survey has created a series of topographic maps covering the entire country. They're not as defined as a topo specific to your tract of land, since they cover larger geographic areas. The maps are printed in five colors. Man-made features and names are printed in black; water features and names are blue; road classifications, urban areas, and U.S. land lines are red; woodland areas are shown in green, and contour lines and values are tinted in brown. Geodetic Survey maps cost just over a dollar and can be bought in local stores. To get a list of the available maps and where to order them, write to the Virginia office below for areas east of the Mississippi River and to the Denver office for areas west of the Mississippi.

Branch of Distribution
U.S. Geological Survey
1200 South Eads Street
Arlington, VA 22202

Branch of Distribution
U.S. Geological Survey
Box 25286 Federal Center
Denver, CO 80225

Highway Construction Maps

The type of access to your land has an impact on its value and marketability. Well-paved, safe roads are better, of course, than rutted dirt lanes. The engineer's office of the state highway department maintains current maps of existing and proposed roadways. Your local highway department may also have copies of these maps. If you own a rural parcel soon to be linked up with a major roadway, how do you think this will affect the value of your land? Study this map and see where future roadways are going and then find out what land is available in that area. Use this knowledge to your advantage. Find out where the roads are going and get there before they do.

Soil Survey Maps

A soil survey map is necessary if you are looking at agricultural land or land with a known history of unstable soils and wetlands. Prepared by the United States Soil Conservation Office, soil survey maps deal with the types and classes of soils found in an area. If you're buying land in a populous, built-up area, you won't have much need for them. But in more isolated spots you will want to know what is below the top layer of soil. If the whole area consists of clay, you will be running into a lot of difficulty. Sandy and rocky soils, too, can cause you problems. The soil conservation office will prepare a written report for you with an accompanying color-coded map showing the soil's chemical content, density, texture, and permeability, and any flood control or water-course problems. In addition to the written soil report and map you should have a percolation test taken to see if the land can support an on-site septic system.

Traffic Count Maps

If you plan on subdividing your land for business purposes, perhaps for individual stores or a small shopping mall, the number of vehicles passing your property is an important statistic. The engineering depart-ment in your community keeps records of vehicular traffic in key areas and selected roadways. You can get copies of the map and traffic count if you need them.

Zoning Maps

A zoning map is one land-hunting tool that you can't do without. It delineates the zoning districts within the community. A zoning map generally accompanies the zoning ordinances booklet and can be ob-tained from the town hall for a couple of dollars. Zoning regulates the use of land within the community, and the map shows you what district your land is located in and what uses of the land are permitted. Zoning ordinances and maps are periodically changed and adjusted in keeping with the proper growth of the community. If you have an old zoning map, discard it and get a new one.

Utility Locator Maps

The Department of Public Works has maps that show existing and proposed locations and routes of water, sewer, and power transmission lines. When buying land in rural areas, you will want to know what services are available and where they are located. If they're already in place in front of your land, great. But if any of them are a good distance away, you will want to know where they are and the cost of getting them to your land.

The availability of utility services has a large impact on the value and marketability of land. Unless you plan on being or selling to a hermit, a pioneer, or a woodsman, make sure you have, or can easily acquire, necessary utility services. Water lines you may not have to worry about if you can sink a well. Sewage can be handled by an on-site septic system. Electricity, however, you cannot do without, nor telephone services if you plan on living in this location and have a teenage daughter.

Aerial Photographs

Aerial photography is becoming an integral part of the land planning and development process. Land planners are increasingly using state-of-the-art technology and high-definition aerial photographic equipment and measuring devices to define land terrain accurately. As a small investor, you shouldn't need such sophistication, but at times a few sample aerial photos will better allow you to picture how your parcel fits into the geographic scenario. I've used aerial photos more for marketing and advertising programs than for planning. People like to look at aerial photographs: A picture is worth a thousand words, someone once said. Potential buyers of your lots can see the proximity of your land to all the amenities and services that the area has to offer. You won't necessarily have to pay an aerial photographer to go up to take shots of your land. There are probably file drawers full of stock photos that you can choose from. Black and whites can be had for $10 and up.

Road and Street Maps

Road and street maps are not only tools to help you to scout an area looking for land to buy, but when you start selling lots the maps will serve as directions to the land for your prospects. Some road maps show entire regions, states, and counties. Other, more detailed maps depict a single community, pinpointing streets, historical sites, town offices, recreational facilities and all pertinent amenities and resources.

CONCENTRATE YOUR EFFORTS

Once you've purchased your first parcel of land and embarked on your exciting land investing career, you'll have to find a follow-up parcel. After you buy, improve, and sell the second parcel, you'll need a third. Whether or not you've bought that first parcel as yet, the process is ongoing. The hunt continues. There are literally thousands of opportunities around the country, enough for everybody that reads this book and makes a serious attempt at what they've learned.

But I want to caution you again to limit your range of activity to a manageable geographic area. You can't help getting excited about every opportunity you hear about, whether it's in your own neighborhood or several states away. Don't stretch yourself too thin. It takes time to find profitable opportunities—time and analysis. Concentrate your land-buying efforts. If you chase after opportunities all over the country, the sheer volume of opportunities will overwhelm you.

There'll be so many parcels for you to consider you may delay making decisions. You have to make sound and rapid buying decisions or someone else will buy the land right from under you. Too much analysis leads to paralysis. That's not to say that you have to be rash and make decisions without proper analysis, but don't dwell too long on your analysis. It's the "doers," not the "thinkers," that make money in land investing.

Contain your efforts within an area you feel comfortable handling. This may include your entire state, or just your county, or your own city or town. You can become expert on all of the potentially available parcels in your area of concentration and be able to keep abreast of the political and social situations that may affect your land investing activities. Trends will be more readily apparent to you and you can move with confidence. You live there: it's your home and you can keep on top of things. You'll be able to cultivate a land-hunting team for yourself— sellers and real estate brokers. Word will get around that you are a serious buyer and opportunities will seek you out.

It's easy to keep aware of happenings in your own backyard. If you're considering a local parcel, you can visit it daily. Not so with opportunities several states away. This doesn't mean that you can't spread out your area of searching. You alone know what you can handle, but be realistic. Most of us live in communities of average size and can easily handle our whole town and even the whole county. Once you've learned all you have to about land opportunities in your own backyard, then expand to nearby locales, but don't forsake your own backyard because situations change, neighborhoods grow and decline, new people move in, zoning changes. Parcels that were not for sale may now be available. One benefit of concentration is that it makes your work area manageable so that you don't overlook promising parcels.

CHAPTER XII

SUBDIVIDING YOUR LAND

Every chapter in this book is important in explaining the social, legal and economic ramifications of land investing. However, this chapter takes a paramount position. You're buying land to make money, of course, and the most typical way is to subdivide and sell off the parts of the whole. That's what this chapter is about—it explains the regulatory process of subdividing land.

To the average American the word *subdivision* has become a generic term that identifies a large, planned residential development. Actually, the division of a tract of land into two or more lots of any size is a subdivision. If you have a one-acre parcel and zoning allows you to split it up into two lots a half acre each, you have created a subdivision. If you have a thousand acres and split it up into two thousand lots, you have created a subdivision.

Most states are concerned with the proper splitting up of land and have enacted laws called *subdivision rules and regulations*. Naturally, the rules and regulations differ from state to state (did you expect otherwise?) and from community to community. It would be beneficial to you to also read the subdivision rules and regulations for your own town in conjunction with this chapter.

THE WAYS TO MAKE A PROFIT FROM REAL ESTATE

Up to this point you've been reading and learning about the legal aspects of real estate—the pros and cons of buying it and where to find it. Now that you've acquired at least a limited legal grasp of the process and have been advised of why and where to buy land, you now have to learn how to make a profit doing it.

Land, whether it be raw acreage, farmland, or vacant lots, must produce a reasonable margin of profit to warrant its purchase, development, and resale. The most difficult aspect of the land buying--selling spectrum is knowing how to make a profit. Not just a modest profit, but an ample profit. During the period of time that you own the land, from purchase to sale, you will have to improve the land in some way to increase its value and marketability.

If you don't improve the land, but just hold it for a period of time, let inflation's magic take effect, and then resell it, you would be a *speculator*. If you have a surveyor draw up a plan and get it approved to sell in its predeveloped condition, then you are a *promoter*. If you divide the land into lots, you are a *subdivider*. If you build homes on the lots, you are a *developer*. Progressing by steps—from speculator to promoter to subdivider and then to developer—is fraught with risks and requires a specific knowledge of the development process as well as a willingness to accept responsibility. However, this added challenge is amply rewarded with additional profits.

I've been involved in each of the steps, and as I acquired experience and capital I moved on up from speculator to developer and back again to speculator or subdivider or promoter. Some properties lend themselves more to speculating than to developing and vice versa. If I see that I can earn a good and rapid profit without investing a lot of money in roads and utilities, then I'll simply buy the land and turn it over quickly. On other parcels I may find it more worthwhile to stay in longer and to do some degree of improvement. You will have to decide what's best for you and the particular property you are considering, and you have to make this decision with each and every piece of land that you buy.

It may prove beneficial for you to follow a similar learning process. Resell the first piece of land you buy quickly without adding improvements. In doing so, you'll learn first hand all about what I have explained in the previous chapters—on-the-job training more or less. Become a promoter with your second land investment. Buy it, get approvals, and resell it as a paper subdivision. A paper subdivision is a subdivision approved by the planning authorities of the community, with no actual development or physical changes having been done to the land.

Going from a promoter to subdivider on your third property could be a big leap for you. If your third parcel has a lot of road frontage, then you need only divide up the lots without installing improvements. This will save you a lot of time and money. But if you have to install roads and utilities, the cost factor leaps tremendously. More often than not, the cost of developing land is more than the purchase price of the land itself.

There are two methods, as dictated by state law, for laying out subdivided land. They are known as Form A and Form C. Form A is the ideal situation; it's simple and inexpensive. If you have sufficient existing street frontage to gain access to all the potential lots, you simply have a plan drawn up, submit it for approval, and sell the lots. If you don't have enough frontage and you require roads to gain access to all the lots, then a Form C subdivision is called for: with costly engineering, public hearings, and expensive development costs.

Being a developer is the most costly, the most time consuming, and the riskiest. The developer not only buys and develops the land, but also builds houses on the land. For each house funds must be borrowed from the bank to buy the building materials and to pay for the construction labor. To build even an inexpensive house today costs over $60,000 and takes several months to complete. You can see how significant the builder's risks are.

Chapter XII

HISTORICAL OVERVIEW OF SUBDIVIDING

All areas of the country are experiencing population increases. Even with the construction of up to two million new homes annually, there is still a drastic shortage. More homes must be built to house our growing population. As a land developer, whether small or large, you will be a necessary cog in the machinery to supply this housing. Builders need lots on which to construct their houses and you will be filling this need for lots with each subdivision of land that you become involved in.

After World War I, the country experienced several boom periods in which the growing American population sought the "American Dream" of owning their own home. Land speculators, many of them unscrupulous in heart and deed, took advantage of the public's desires and naivete. They also took advantage of the uncaring attitudes of community leaders as evidenced, during those early years, by the complete lack of safeguards like planning, zoning, and subdivision controls to protect the public.

Many speculators, unhindered by legal control, built housing developments and subdivisions where and when they wanted and with whatever minimal quality they could. Subdivisions sprang up everywhere, most often in outlying areas where land was cheap—and very often out of reach of connecting utility services. In many cases, a fancy entry to the subdivision was created, extravagant advertising campaigns and promotional literature brought in prospects, and lots of houses were sold on a grand scale.

Local governments were then trapped into extending services to these outlying and remote subdivisions. Water, electricity, sewage, transportation, fire and police protection, new streets, lighting, and schools were all services that these subdivisions required. To finance these services, municipalities took on long-term debt, burdening their citizenry for decades to come. Many communities supplied the services to thousands of empty lots hoping for the exodus to suburbia that the growing use of the automobile promised to bring. The exodus didn't happen in many communities and ready-to-build lots with all services at hand stood vacant for years on end.

After World War II, several other real estate booms created additional demands for housing. Returning from the war, servicemen again sought the American Dream for their families. Entire cities sprang up practically overnight. Many subdivisions were hastily and haphazardly developed. Homes were constructed with the cheapest of materials with no concern for the safety of the buyers. Homes that were built on wetlands began to settle and foundations cracked. Roofs leaked. Septic systems backed up. Plumbing and electricity were inadequate. Roads crumbled, requiring extensive repair. There were some well-planned and well-built subdivisions, but too many were not.

Somebody woke up to the abuses prevalent in land development. "Wildcat" subdividing and development practices common in the 1920s through 1940s have for the most part ceased. Community officials were simply not knowledgeable about sound planning methods; today they are, and today subdividers and developers must abide by stringent regulations and controls for the good of the public—for the good of everybody actually, subdividers included.

THE PRELIMINARY WORK OF SUBDIVIDING

There are no uniform land development controls that apply to the entire country. Land developing ordinances are controlled by the state and local governments where the land to be developed is located. We've discussed the planning, zoning, and building process in some detail in Chapter VI. My purpose here is to introduce you to the subdividing process to show you what you can do with a piece of land to make it profitable for you and to explain the rules you must follow.

Perhaps the best procedure for developing vacant land profitably is to make a checklist so that no consideration or issue of importance is overlooked. In his book *How to Buy and Sell Land* (Institute for Business Planning, 1962), William J. Casey outlined a useful checklist of items (Figure 12-1). You will use most and maybe all of the items on this checklist both as a speculator and as a developer. The checklist is extensive, but you don't have to be an expert. You hire experts where and when needed.

Figure 12-1. A Checklist for Evaluating Potential Residential Land

A. Protection against inharmonious land uses
1. Zoning
2. Protective covenants
3. Geographic position of neighborhood in relation to other functional areas of the city
4. Character of neighboring structures
B. Physical and social attractiveness
1. Special hazards and nuisances
2. Natural physical features and landscaping
3. Neighborhood design
4. Architectural appearance of neighboring buildings
5. Compatibility among neighborhood occupants
6. Prestige
7. Friendship location pattern
C. Adequacy of civic, social, and commercial centers
1. Quality and access of schools
2. Quality and access of shopping centers
3. Churches, recreational centers, and theaters
4. Local government
D. Adequacy of transportation
1. Diversity and cost
2. Quality and frequency
3. Distance from site to boarding point
4. Time required to destination
5. Convenience
6. Private transportation
7. Roads
E. Sufficiency of utilities and services
1. Quantity
2. Quality
3. Cost

F. Level of taxes and special assessments
   1. Taxes
   2. Special assessments
G. Relative marketability
   1. Location of competing sites
   2. Finished home costs
   3. Financing
   4. Market situation for site and ripeness
   5. Housing and location to suit market demand
H. Land acquisition and development costs
   1. Land availability
   2. Land cost per area or lot
   3. Physical suitability
   4. Extent of clearing
   5. Financing
   6. Sites for community facilities
   7. Total estimated development costs
I. Local regulations
   1. Zoning
   2. Rehabilitation of previously platted land
   3. Building regulations
J. Utilities
   1. Extent of installations existing and required
   2. Water and sewerage
   3. Electricity, gas and telephone

Hiring Experts

Once you've found that parcel of land that you plan on buying, improving, and reselling, the next important action for you to take is to hire a surveyor to draw up a *subdivision plat*. A plat is a drawing, or map, that shows the land as it is, and how it will be after improvement.

The surveyor will handle most of the duties and tasks from the date you hire him or her until the date the subdivision plan is approved by the town authorities. Even after the plan is approved, the surveyor, if you choose, may be involved in the actual improvement and development of the land.

From then on the selling effort is on your shoulders. Again, however, you can hire an expert in the field—a real estate broker. The more experts you hire, the more it's going to cost you. You can't do the surveying (the law won't allow that) but you certainly can do the selling. All states require a license to sell real estate, but not if it's your own property.

A surveyor is trained to advise you of the most feasible and profitable layout of your land. Surveyors are licensed by the state as being qualified to conduct surveys and to design efficient, well-planned subdivisions. A surveyor's seal and registration number must be affixed to every plan submitted to a planning board for approval.

I recommend that you hire a surveyor who does business in the area where your land is located, since the surveyor has the responsibility to know all about conditions and laws of the community relative to land development. A local surveyor is usually intimately and thoroughly knowledgeable of the general nature of land titles in the area, of the area's topographical characteristics and soil conditions, and of the long-standing and current development practices and strategies of the community. In short, the local surveyor knows what can and what cannot be done with your land.

A local surveyor will also have advance knowledge of the voting habits of each member of the planning board. There are rules and regulations that the planning board, as well as the developer, must abide by. But the board consists of individuals like you and me, any one of whom could let personal feelings influence his or her vote, regardless of the regulations. I've found that new members to a board, like new members to a community, are more resistant to change, preferring the "status quo." The older members are more amenable to growth and to change. This may be the reverse of what we would expect, but that's how it usually is.

If you follow the regulations and the advice of your surveyor, you shouldn't have any difficulty most of the time. Once in a while you will butt heads with a board member who will resist your efforts—*que sera.*

As I mentioned, most communities today have enacted safeguards to protect the public against unscrupulous developers and poorly developed subdivisions. These safeguards are in the form of subdivision rules and regulations. You can get a copy of them from town hall. They differ in content from state to state and from town to town, but their intent and purpose is universal: to protect the safety, convenience, and welfare of the inhabitants by regulating the design and construction of livable subdivisions. They control the development of the subdivision in all its stages. They were created not only as public safeguards, but also as guidelines to assist landowners, developers, and landscape architects in complying with the provisions of the subdivision control laws of the state.

The first step in getting approval for a subdivision is the surveyor's submission of a preliminary plan to the planning board; later, a definitive plan will be submitted.

Preliminary Plan

A *preliminary plan* may first be submitted to the board for discussion and modification if necessary. This submission is not mandatory, but highly recommended because it will clarify the problems of the subdivision, if there are any, before a *definitive plan* is prepared and filed. It's a standard procedure and you must follow the rules. Multiple copies (from three to ten) of the plan and a completed application form must be submitted to the board, with written notice of such submission made to the town clerk.

The plan can be drawn in pencil, on tracing paper, at a suitable scale and must show enough information for it to be openly discussed. The information form will include the names and location of all abutters, widths of existing and proposed roadways in the immediate vicinity, the proposed drainage system, lot lines and dimensions, and the topography of the land—including site features such as existing walls, fences, buildings, and water bodies. The applicant, or the applicant's agent, must be present at the preliminary plan meeting to discuss the subdivision. Within a period of time (usually sixty days) the board will approve the plan with or without modifications or disapprove it, stating its reasons. Approval at this stage facilitates the procedure for securing final approval of the definitive plan.

Definitive Plan

Submission of a *definitive plan* is a more formalized procedure. The plan must be prepared by a registered surveyor and drawn in waterproof ink on tracing cloth or polyester film. The original cloth and multiple copies must be submitted with a completed application form stating all easements, restrictions, and appurtenant rights. The definitive plan must evolve from field surveys and be certified by the surveyor. It will include:

1. A locus map showing the location of the property
2. Owner's name, date, and scale of the plan
3. Names and location of all abutters
4. Site features: ponds, lines of existing and proposed roadways, lot lines and dimensions, and pertinent easements
5. Location of all existing and proposed monuments
6. Location of streets in the immediate area
7. A table showing the zoning district, number of lots, total acreage, linear feet of roadway, and number of bounds to be set
8. Space for endorsements by the approving boards

Also required are multiple copies of the topographic plan showing the existing and proposed contours of the subdivision and of the abutters' land, along with a profile plan and cross section drawings of the roadway and the drainage, sewer, utility, and water systems. In some communities these plans must also be submitted to additional officials of the town, who will make their comments to the planning board. They may include, but not be limited to

The board of health to determine if any lots may be injurious to the public health if built upon

The engineering department to approve the design of the street and drainage systems

The police and fire chiefs to notify them of the intended location of hydrants, alarm systems, and the safety of road and lot layouts

The park department to notify them of your intentions for planting or removing any trees

The sewer department for approval of the design and layout of the sewer system

The water department to verify the adequacy of the design and capacity of the water system

The electric, gas, and telephone companies to review the compatibility of your plans with their respective services

The building inspector to verify the suitability of each lot as a homesite

The conservation commission for analysis of the subdivision's effect on the environment

Once all the above reviewers have studied the plan and made their recommendations in writing to the planning board, a public hearing is held with notification made to the abutters and all interested parties. The applicant, or the applicant's agent, must attend this meeting. The board will vote to approve, modify and approve, or disapprove the plan within sixty days of submission. Before approval of the definitive plan, the applicant must agree to complete the required improvements as shown on the plan by filing a surety company *performance bond,* or depositing an amount of money sufficient to cover the cost of completing the improvements.

If the applicant fails to complete the improvements within a specified time, the board will use the applicant's deposit and hire a contractor to do so. The applicant must also file a *covenant* attesting that he or she will not convey any lots until all the improvements are completed.

When all the improvements are completed, the town will make an inspection. If all is done to their satisfaction, they will release any performance bonds, deposits, or covenants, endorse the original cloth drawing, and return it to the applicant—keeping a copy on file. The approved plan and any deed restrictions must then be recorded at the registry of deeds. Once the planning board receives notice of the recording, they will place a copy of the definitive plan on file with the building inspector, who will then have the authority to issue building permits for each lot, as they are applied for.

Once the plan is approved, and before improvements are made, you have what is known in the trade as a paper subdivision. You can sell the entire paper subdivision in its existing, undeveloped condition and take your profit. The new buyer has until the specified time in which to install the improvements. This ranges from five to seven years from the date of the signed and approved plan. If the improvements are not installed within this time, then the subdivision approval runs out and is terminated and the owner of the land must start the whole procedure over again in order to subdivide the land.

Besides the time lost and the duplication of effort, there's a costly danger in letting the time expire on the approved subdivision. If your initial approval was for half-acre lots and you put the roads in within the specified time, then you're safe. If the time has expired and in the meantime zoning changes require one-acre lots, then when you resubmit for a subdivision approval you must abide by the new zoning, that is, one-acre lots. In effect, you will have lost one half of the potential yield in the subdivision. Yes, one-acre lots are usually worth more than half-acre lots, but not twice as much. Perhaps 20 or 30 percent more. After all, only one home can be built on either. You could lose a significant amount of profit in a situation like this.

If you run across the chance to buy a paper subdivision yourself, check out the approval date and find out if you have enough time to complete the improvements.

Partially developed subdivisions periodically show up on the market. By all means look into them, but I caution you to be *careful*. The partially developed subdivision may have resulted from a developer's running out of working capital (although perhaps something personal prevented completion of the job). The developer may have run afoul of the zoning ordinances or subdivision regulations and was ordered to cease by the town authorities. The roads might have been cut in the wrong place and the developer stopped before making a bad thing worse. Stay away from these situations. Usually, the cost to correct the first developer's errors will result in a loss for the entire project. You don't need headaches like these; there are too many good opportunities out there. If all the numbers and legal and physical aspects work out favorably, however, go ahead and buy the land.

DEVELOPMENT

Cluster Residential Developments

Cluster residential developments are a fairly new application to the subdividing of land. Basically, the lots are reduced in size and clustered together around various street patterns.

The cluster plan will have the same number of lots as in a conventional plan, but there will be substantial areas of common open space to enhance the development. More importantly to the developer is the welcome fact that there is much less linear feet of roadway needed. Most planning boards like the concept of cluster zoning because the subdivisions are usually more attractive and they preserve a good deal of the natural topography.

To have your land considered for a cluster arrangement, there are certain qualifications that the planning board looks for. Usually, the parcel must be at least 5 acres in size and the total number of lots cannot exceed the number that would result under a conventional arrangement. At least 30 percent of the total area must be set aside as common open space suitable for such uses as parks, playgrounds, or other recreational or conservational uses.

The planning board's determination of the suitability of the land for a cluster plan will take into consideration whether the plan is superior to a conventional plan in preserving open space, utilizing natural features of the land, providing efficient provision for streets and utilities. The means of achieving these objectives include the avoidance of frequent minor street or driveway openings onto through streets; limited physical changes of the topography, preserving the natural landscape; variations in lot sizes and building arrangements; and the utilization of open space to protect natural amenities such as streams, bogs, or scenic spots.

Planned Unit Developments

The *planned unit development* (PUD) arose from a relatively recent philosophy of zoning ordinances that was developed from the condominium cluster housing concept. This concept, which started in the 1960s, is a major advance for communities and developers in improving today's residential environments. The PUD is a development incorporating a variety of uses planned and developed as a unit.

Multiple-use zoning allows for several compatible, but different, uses in a district. Office buildings, stores, apartments, and condominiums are allowed in the same district. If you combined all these uses into one project, this would be a PUD—a sophisticated evolution from conventional subdividing that encompasses several diverse land uses—housing, shopping, recreation, business, and entertainment. In a PUD the structures are built at the same density as in a conventional development, but they are clustered and enveloped by common open space.

PUDs can be developed on as little as ten acres of land, or as much as several thousands. Columbia, Maryland, is a PUD of better than fifteen thousand acres, costing over $1 billion to develop, with a potential population of over one hundred thousand residents. The purpose of a PUD is to encourage the conservation of significant amounts of open space, while providing for a variety of housing types and characteristics, harmonious with the natural features of the land, and economical and efficient street and utility systems.

A PUD will result in several advantages in that the costs of the housing units are reduced by efficient land planning and smaller lots. Many people like smaller lots because the groundskeeping chores are minimized. The jointly owned common areas and optional amenities such as tennis courts and swimming pools are controlled and maintained by a property owners' association. PUD's are not for everyone; some people don't like the lack of privacy and the sharing of facilities common to a PUD; nor do they like to follow the rules created by the property owners' association in governing the PUD.

It will, more than likely, be quite some time before you will want to attempt a PUD. Get your feet wet first with much simpler subdivisions of land, and as you acquire more know-how and capital, then you can start delving into the more involved and expensive planned unit developments.

Streets and Improvements

The surveyor must design the streets and ways in accordance with the local subdivision regulations. Most communities require that streets be 40 or 50 feet wide, with the actual paved surface anywhere from 20 to 40 feet wide. The extra width beyond the paved surface, on either side, is for the location of the utilities, sewers, drains, sidewalks, and for the future widening of the paved surface, if traffic conditions warrant it. Many communities require that a provision be made to extend streets to the boundary of the land, so that a roadway connection can be made if and when abutting properties are developed.

The condition of the terrain will greatly determine the street layout. The planning board may require that you draw up a topographical map of the area, showing the surface configurations. The topo map will show the "roll" of the land, outlining the high and low spots and areas that need excavation or fill, irrigation or drainage.

It is not legal, by the way, to create "reserve strips" that prohibit access to streets and abutting property. For example, the configuration of your land may dictate that you run a road along one side line of your parcel with the lots extending inward from one side of the road. Since you won't have lots on the opposite side of the street, you may not feel generous enough to give the abutting property owner access to road you paid to construct. So you leave a *reserve strip* between your road and the abutting parcel. You own the reserve strip and the abutter cannot legally cross over your land to gain access to the roadway. This entire procedure is illegal and prohibited by the regulatory authorities. You cannot "landlock" an abutter if it is within your power to allow access to the abutter's property.

The streets must be designed and located so as to be continuous and in alignment with existing streets, providing adequate and safe access to all the lots in the subdivision. It is preferred that streets intersect at right angles and that the grade of any street be within certain limitations. They cannot be too steep, thereby creating safety hazards. Minor streets intersecting with arterial or collector streets should be held to a minimum so that traffic isn't pouring out onto busy streets from too many outlets. Provisions must be made for turnarounds at the end of dead-end or "cul-de-sac" streets so that vehicles can reverse their direction without having to back into a neighborhood driveway to negotiate the turn. Nor can dead-end streets be overly long, if it can be prevented. If fire apparatus or ambulances have to get down a dead-end street and the way is blocked for one reason or another, it is certainly detrimental to the public safety.

In the 18th and 19th centuries in the United States, subdivisions were laid out in a grid pattern, because the tools available to surveyors at the time made straight lines and right angles the easiest way to lay out a land pattern. When the Government Survey System was enacted in 1785, the grid pattern was extended westward from the Ohio River, forming 640-acre sections. After the Civil War, developers started laying out subdivisions taking into consideration the natural terrain and amenities of a region.

The road layout that you will use will be determined by the terrain and the shape of the parcel. There are certain standard types of road layout used by surveyors and land planners in larger subdivisions, and your surveyor will know what the local authorities prefer. Some of the standard layouts used by surveyors and land planners are: gridiron, curvilinear, radburn, and loop. (See Figure 12-2.)

Street improvements such as roads, paving, water supply, drainage, and sewers, as well as utility services, must be provided for before final approval of the subdivision. The topographical map is utilized by the surveyor and land planner in making provision for these. A rugged, rolling terrain will certainly present more development difficulties and higher costs than a fairly level parcel. Streets, water lines, and utilities can easily go up or down a hill. Surface water drains and sewers, however, can only be on downgrades.

The plan should be designed allowing for a minimum of excavation and fill. The more dirt you have to move around, the more it's going to cost you. The cost of improving your land will be determined by the soil, climate, type of development, local regulations, and your own financial ability.

If electricity, telephone, gas, and water are already installed in front of your property, you are in a favored position to start. If these services are a distance away from your property, the utility companies will install them, at your expense, and rebate an amount of money to you (from 50 to 75 percent of your total installation costs) for each home that is built and occupied within a specified time (up to five years) from the time the service is installed in the subdivision. This doesn't include all the services. Telephone, gas and electric services offer the rebate; water, sewers, and drainage are the developer's sole responsibility.

When the utility company installs poles to carry its wiring, or digs a trench to put the power underground, it does so in conjunction with the other utility companies. Either the telephone company or the electric company may own the pole. If, for example, the electric company installed the pole, then the telephone company and even the cable television company may install their services at the same time on the same pole. Easements for utility services are normally provided for along the front lot lines. In some cases they are at the rear lot lines, sparing the street frontage from unsightly poles and preventing the extreme trimming of trees to protect the wires.

Communities are increasingly requiring that utilities be beneath the ground. Placing them underground will cost you more, but they allow for a more attractive subdivision.

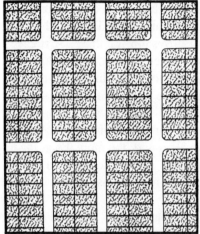

Gridiron Pattern. A widely used but unimaginative design resulting in monotonous neighborhoods.

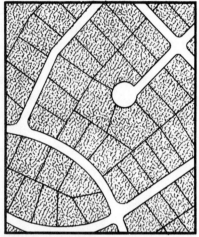

Curvilinear Pattern. Allows for attractive neighborhoods and breaks down flow-through traffic with numerous minor streets.

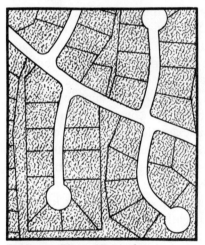

Radburn Plan. Allows for attractive neighborhoods by creating clusters of lots on cul-de-sac streets.

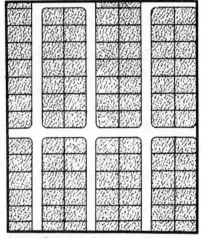

Loop Streets. Limits traffic flow through a subdivision.

Figure 12-2. Street layout patterns

Road Frontage

The amount of existing, usable road frontage is one of the more important factors that you look for in selecting a parcel of land to buy and subdivide. The more frontage the better—it's more valuable than the depth. With development costs as expensive as they are today and with roads costing better than $100 per lineal foot to pave, the usable frontage represents improvement costs that you do not have to buy. Normally, if you have sufficient paved road frontage, you simply subdivide the lots and sell them (a Form A subdivision). It could take just a couple of months from the time you bought the land. If you have to put in roads, the process could take two years.

I stress usable frontage, because you are not always allowed to fully utilize the frontage of some parcels. If, for instance, you purchase a parcel with long frontage on a heavily traveled highway or main street, the regulatory authorities may not allow you to subdivide the frontage into lots with each lot having an individual driveway exiting onto the busy highway. Concern for the public's safety may dictate that each lot will have access onto an interior road in the subdivision, which in turn will exit onto the highway.

Figure 12-3 shows an example with no lots exiting onto the main highway, just two minor access roads. This is a good design for the public's sake, but is not preferable from the developer's viewpoint. If the developer were allowed to use the frontage fully, the lots would need only to be subdivided and sold. The revenues from these sales could then finance the development of the remainder of the land.

Let's take a look at an example of a small parcel with good frontage and some of the alternatives available to you in subdividing this parcel. Assume you are buying a level, 9-acre parcel with 540 feet of usable road frontage and 720 feet of depth. The zoning calls for single-family, 1-acre lots, with 150 feet of road frontage required for each lot. All the utilities are in place, so you're saving money there. The area's 1-acre lots have been selling for $15,000, and 2-acre lots for $20,000. Lots of 3 acres are selling for $22,000.

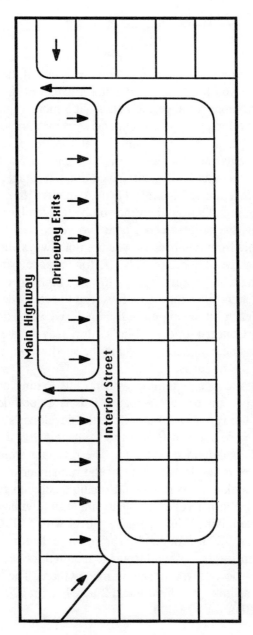

Figure 12-3. Unusable main-highway frontage

There are several ways to split this land up into lots, but you want to do it the most economical and profitable way. You could split it up into 3 lots of 3 acres each, which would sell for $66,000 total (Figure 12-4). Or you could put in a road (Figure 12-5) and get a yield of 8 1-acre lots valued at $120,000. However, on analysis, the $84,000 cost of the 700 feet of road (700 × $120) would not be worth the added investment to gain access to 6 additional lots with a total revenue potential of $90,000.

A more practical alternative available to you (Figure 12-6) is to create "panhandle" or "pork chop" lots. The name is derived from the shape of the lots, evidently. This is an ideal way to use the frontage effectively, with a minimum of development expenses to get to the back land. Not all communities allow panhandle lots, and, if they do, they often limit how many you can have in a single subdivision. The normal lot frontage requirement is waived for panhandle lots with the new frontage ranging anywhere from 10 to 30 feet. The panhandle lots in Figure 12-5 are large and may be used to better advantage than the smaller lots.

In some communities, if a 1-acre lot is required for a single-family home, then a 2-acre lot may have 2 single-family homes or 1 two-family home. You would have to gauge the desirability of two-family homesites mingled with single-family homesites. Too often, the two-family home has proven to be unpopular in new neighborhoods, particularly if an absentee owner rents out both dwelling units. Renters do not have the same caring interest in property as do owners.

Most raw acreage parcels can be subdivided in numerous ways. But what is the best way for you? Tax experts advise that at income tax time you prepare your tax statement in more than one way to see where you benefit the most—a joint return versus separate returns, for instance. So, too, can you test various layouts with your land. Your surveyor can draw up the many possible variations for subdivision, but a surveyor's time costs money. You really only need some basic knowledge to be able to lay out the various possibilities yourself. You can later discuss these with your surveyor during the preparation of a more formal plan.

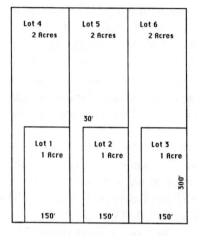

Figure 12-4. Three 3-acre lots

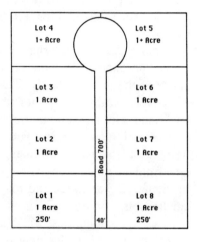

Figure 12-5. Eight 1-acre lots

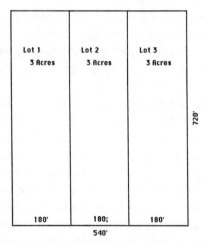

Figure 12-6. Panhandle or "pork chop" lots

Development Costs

Earlier you learned how to approximate the yield, or number of lots, that a parcel of raw acreage can be developed into. Armed with that statistic and the other factors of land developing that you've learned, you can now determine what it will cost to subdivide and develop most parcels that you look at. The costs of buying, developing, marketing, and maintaining a subdivision are numerous and varied, as this list points out:

Raw land cost
Surveying costs
   Perimeter plan
   Preliminary and definitive plans
   Topographical map
   Subdivision plan
   Lot staking
   Road and sewer design
   Road and grade staking

Development costs
   Cutting and filling
   Grading
   Sewer and water
   Paving, curbing and sidewalks
   Utility deposits

Financing costs
Taxes
Legal expenses
Selling expenses
   Commissions
   Advertising
   Brochures

Contingencies
Profit

It's going to take quite a while to collect all the cost estimates to complete the development. Again, you should have a handy "on the spot" measurement to get an early indication of how these costs will affect the profitability of each venture. Actually, there are two measurements that you will be using: (1) the engineering and legal costs per lot and (2) the per lineal foot cost of installing the roads and utilities.

Engineering and legal costs will be determined by the number of lots, since each lot will bear its own closing costs. I assign a cost factor of $500 per lot to cover engineering and legal expenses and contingencies. This has to be adjusted periodically, but for now that's enough to cover these costs.

To arrive at the per lineal foot cost of installing the roads and utilities, you first have to determine the total number of lineal feet of paved roadway that you will need. Suppose you had a projected yield of 12 lots, with a 150-foot frontage requirement for each. There is usually a lot on both sides of the road, so you would need 150 feet for each pair of lots. Six pair of lots will require a total of 900 lineal feet (6 × 150') of paved roadway with utilities. If the road ends in a cul-de-sac, the extra paved surface needed to form the large circle would amount to another 100 lineal feet. For your 12 lots you will need 1000 lineal feet of roadway. You now have to collect cost estimates from the subcontractors who will be doing the work. Add these costs together, then divide this amount by the total number of lineal feet needed. In the above example you needed 1000 lineal feet. If your cost estimates came to, say $120,000, then your per foot lineal cost would be $120 ($120,000 ÷ 1000 ft.).

Once you have accumulated your development costs, you then have to add in the cost of taxes. The town assessor can give you an idea of the taxes before and after subdividing. A 12-acre parcel will be assessed as a single parcel. Once it is approved for 9 lots, each will be assessed as an unimproved lot. When the improvements are completed, each lot will be assessed higher as a finished homesite.

To your cost structure you will also have to add the cost of borrowing the funds to buy and improve the land. Even if you pay cash, you must factor in *opportunity cost*, which is the return you would have earned had you put your money into an alternative investment. Opportunity cost would replace interest expense on your cost schedule.

The following hypothetical situation shows how all this fits together. The parcel you are considering buying is a 12-acre tract priced at $3000 per acre with taxes for one year amounting to $1500 (before and after subdividing). Zoning calls for 40,000-square-foot lots with 150-foot frontages. If we multiple the 12 acres by .75, we get a yield of 9 lots. The lots will be laid out with 4 lots on either side of the road and 1 lot at the end of the cul-de-sac; so your road requirements will be 700 lineal feet (4 pairs of lots × 150' + 100' for the cul-de-sac).

Land	(12 acres × $3K/acre)	$ 36,000
Eng./Legal	(9 lots × $500/lot)	4,500
Roads/Util.	(700' × $120/ft.)	84,000
Taxes		1,500
		126,000
Interest		9,000
Total Costs		135,000

Assume that the entire project from purchase through approval, development, and sell-off takes just one year. In practice you will actually be preselling your lots, so by the time that the road improvements are completed, the lots with luck will be all sold and waiting for a closing date. This being the case, and the fact that most of the improvements are paid for after they are completed, you would be using most of the borrowed money for less than half the year. If the annual interest rate is 15 percent of the borrowed $126,000, your interest costs will be no more than $9450 ($126,000 × 15% ÷ 2). For ease of mathematics we'll call it $9,000. You will be deducting the carrying costs of interest and taxes from your personal income tax.

With a per-lot cost of $15,000 ($135,000 ÷ 9) you now add your desired profit. Don't short-change yourself. You're taking the risks of land development and you certainly have the right to expect a higher return than had you put your money into a placid and risk-free investment like Treasury Bills or certificates of deposit where the return is guaranteed. If alternative investments are paying around 10 percent, you certainly want to do better than that for your risk-taking; plus you want to be compensated fairly for your time and efforts. Profit of 30, 40, or 50 percent is not unusual—it depends on the amount of time and effort it has taken you to get to this stage, and what you figure that time and effort is worth.

If your lot cost is $15,000 and you expect a 30 percent return, then your suggested selling price would be $19,500. If comparable lots in the vicinity are selling for less, then this will not be a worthwhile venture for you, unless you buy and develop the land cheaper, or are willing to hold the land until all the comparables are sold off. On the other hand, if comparables are quite a bit higher, you can be assured of a fast sell-off and a profitable venture. You could even increase your selling price to just below the selling price of comparables, thereby increasing your return.

CHAPTER XIII

COMMERCIAL AND INDUSTRIAL LAND

Although the subdividing of land for residential land use is stressed in this book, let's also take a look at commercial and industrial land use. You certainly don't have to limit yourself solely to house lots, particularly if a good business parcel comes your way.

Land that is zoned for commercial and industrial use has quite a wide range of possibilities for development into such uses as shopping malls, retail stores, office buildings, factories, hotels, nursing homes, gas stations, apartments, and parking lots. You have to evaluate the need for a particular use in the community at that particular location. Make a list of the potential uses that may qualify, and compare it to the site characteristics that are important to each use. For instance, a parcel that is very high and steep would not be suitable for a shopping mall because of the difficulty of entry. A shopping mall would be more readily adaptable to a fairly flat parcel of land at street level. Also, the population of the immediate surrounding area must be sufficient to economically support shopping facilities.

There are certain site characteristics that must be considered for most commercial and industrial uses. Good road frontage and accessibility and good visibility from all directions are of paramount importance. Location in a trade area or proximity to other businesses is also a factor. Population, too, must be studied, as well as local transportation patterns and access from highways. The size and shape of the parcel and its topography is critical to the end use. Uneven terrain or irregularly shaped parcels very often are handicaps to certain uses. A suitable and well-located commercial or industrial parcel of land is an ideal investment that will reap profits for the astute and creative land investor.

COMMERCIAL LAND USES

As with industrial land, commercial land brings a much higher price per unit than residential land. You have to be careful, however; just because an area is zoned for a business use doesn't guarantee anything. There must be a demand for the use. The demand is in direct proportion to the population of the area.

Naturally, as the population of a community grows, its demand for various commercial activities increases. A growing community needs drugstores, food markets, beauty parlors, restaurants, theaters, clothing and furniture stores, medical facilities, schools, churches, civic and recreational facilities, and mostly, apartments. Commercial property has great appeal to investors interested in income-producing property that can generate a steady flow of cash. However, it's not the land itself that is producing the income; it's the rentable or salable structures on the land that produce the revenues.

SHOPPING CENTERS

The explosive growth of the suburbs following World War II, coupled with the decline of downtown shopping areas, fueled a like explosion in the construction of planned shopping centers. In 1950 there were only 100 planned shopping centers in the country. In 1972 there were 12,000. Today there are over 20,000, accounting for 50 percent of all retail sales. A planned shopping center is a multi-store shopping area designed to house certain types of compatible retail establishments, as opposed to downtown shopping areas, which grew haphazardly with no plan. There are four categories of shopping centers: neighborhood, community, regional, and super regional.

The Neighborhood Shopping Center

The smallest, and the one closest to your home, is the *neighborhood shopping center*. It serves a trading area of up to 10,000 households living within a 5-minute drive. It will have 10 or 12 stores providing for the sale of convenience goods (foods, drugs, and sundries) and personal services (beauty parlor, laundry, hardware, etc.) for the day-to-day needs of its clientele. The principal tenant is usually a supermarket of about 20,000 square feet; the total for the entire center runs less than 50,000 square feet on a 5- to 10-acre site.

The Community Shopping Center

Next in size is the *community shopping center*, which includes most everything that a neighborhood center offers, plus providing for the sale of soft and hard lines (clothing and appliances). The prime tenant is a junior department store, variety store, or discount store of 25,000 to 90,000 square feet, as well as a supermarket. The selling area of about 30 stores totals from 100,000 to 400,000 square feet on a site of 15 to 20 acres. It serves a trading area of less than 100,000 persons within a radius of 15 minutes driving time.

The Regional and Super-Regional Shopping Centers

Within a half-hour's driving time of a trading area of up to 250,000 people is the large *regional shopping center* of 40 to 100 stores including one or two major department stores of 100,000 square feet each. A center of this size has a total store area of up to 750,000 square feet on a 50- to 100-acre tract of land with parking for over 1000 vehicles.

Then there is the *super-regional shopping center,* which is all that the regional is, and then some.

Investing in Shopping Centers

Needless to say, we're talking about a great deal of money when developing a shopping center. The beginning land investor certainly cannot get involved in ventures of this scope and complexity—at least not at the early stages of investment activity. Shopping centers, particularly the larger regionals, are developed by large, well-organized syndicates and real estate trusts, with the financial backing of major insurance companies and the like. The neighborhood shopping center is more reasonably within the reach of the individual investor.

You may want to invest in an existing shopping center, neighborhood size, or whatever. If you do, take into consideration the following:

1. Is the location good? Is it in a growth or declining area?
2. Is the center constructed soundly? Are you going to have to spend a lot of money to maintain it or to bring it up to standard?
3. Are the leases good? Long-term? Profitable?
4. Are the tenants compatible without being unnecessarily duplicated (two drugstores in the same center)?
5. What of existing and future competition in this trading area?
6. Is parking adequate?
7. Is there undeveloped land in the complex?
8. Are taxes at acceptable and manageable levels? Are there increases pending?

A new shopping center has to go through a long period of maturing before it is accepted by the local buying public. It could go belly up during this maturing period. An existing center, too, may have many built-in problems. It could be in a saturated area with too many stores and not enough customers. Shopping center investment and development is a highly specialized field and you would be wise to consult the professionals in this field before you dare to tread into it.

Keep in mind as a land investor that shopping centers usually increase the overall value of an area. Many fortunes have been made by persons who have had advance knowledge, or inside information, on where and when new shopping centers were to be located and built. If you can get information of this sort, or even if you can predict or estimate future shopping center locations, you can get a leg up on other land investors in the area by buying property next to the proposed center or in the immediate area. There's many a case where land next to a center has jumped in value forty-fold in a short period of time.

Once a center is developed, satellite businesses spring up around it. Use your imagination; it's the wise investor who sees and takes advantage of this potential.

INDUSTRIAL LAND USES

Industrial land is property used for manufacturing purposes. This could range from a small building in your back yard where you design and assemble wooden toys to a large steel mill covering many acres. Research and development facilities and warehouse complexes are additional industrial uses.

Most towns look on industry as an asset to the community, primarily for economic reasons. Industry creates jobs. This is of particular importance in smaller towns where very often the young people have to leave their community to seek employment elsewhere if there isn't enough work to go around. A community has a significant investment in its youth. Their leaving town because of a lack of jobs is an economic waste and loss to the community. As the youth leave, the potential labor force shrinks, discouraging new industry from locating there and often forcing existing industry to relocate.

Industrial property has a high value for taxation purposes, with minimal demand on community services. It's cheaper for the police and fire departments to protect an industrial property valued at several million dollars than it is to protect multiple residences with a similar aggregate value.

Industry is moving out of the crowded city locations that it has been relegated to. Abundant and less expensive land, less congestion, excellent transportation systems, pleasant surroundings and a better quality of life are available in the suburbs. And the suburbs want industry. Many towns offer specific incentives to entice industry to locate within their borders. Tax breaks, favorable zoning, land donations, and financial assistance are some of the inducements offered by aggressive, industry-seeking communities. Utility companies too often join with municipalities in an effort to attract industry. Lower utility and energy costs are their contributions in the effort.

Communities want industry that is clean, nonpolluting, and inoffensive to the senses. We're becoming increasingly aware of how some industries have polluted their environment, causing danger and hardship on towns. Nonpolluting industry connotes "light" manufacturing. This type of industry usually rents space in existing buildings rather than buying industrially zoned land and building a manufacturing plant.

On the other hand, "heavy" industry usually buys land outright and builds its own plants. This requires a large investment besides the land and buildings; there's investment into production machinery, materials handling equipment, storage facilities, distribution systems, and fire and security systems to name just the basics.

Today, the trend for industry is to build a one-story plant on a large parcel of land. This allows the plant to be designed for efficient use of space, smoother production flows, and reduced production costs. Heavy industry tends to locate close to its source of raw materials to keep distribution costs low. Paper mills and lumber processing plants are near the source of their raw materials, trees, so they can develop the end-product and not ship a lot of weight that is processed off during the manufacturing process. Soft drink companies ship their syrup to regional bottlers so that the bulk of the product, water, can be added to the syrup and then bottled. There's no sense in paying transportation charges for water and bottles when they can be added to the product locally. If the product gains weight while being manufactured, then the plant is located near the marketplace.

The investor in industrial land has to take all the above into consideration. The rewards are high with income-producing industrial land, but so too are the risks. These types of properties are unique to particular users and are therefore highly illiquid; that is, there isn't a broad market for them when they are put up for sale because they are built for a specific purpose and are not readily adaptable to other types of manufacturing uses. A bottling plant is built for a bottler and cannot very easily be used as a furniture manufacturing plant without a lot of retooling. You do indeed have to analyze the situation carefully.

Besides finding suitably zoned land, you have to determine if there is a demand for it. Will it be more attractive to heavy or light industry? Will you be buying a large parcel for resale to heavy industry, or will you subdivide the land to sell individual lots to light industry? Why would industry want to locate here in the first place? There are a number of factors that industry must weigh in their location or relocation decisions:

1. Quantity and quality of the labor force
2. Proximity to their markets
3. Availability of necessary raw materials
4. Acceptance and cooperation of the community, including financial inducements
5. The quality of life in this area such as education, recreation, and religious facilities
6. Transportation, shopping, labor, utilities, energy, and materials costs in the area

Industrially zoned land is an area that is overlooked by many land investors. It's fraught with numerous dangers and risks, but to the well-initiated, those that take the time and effort to learn the essentials of the business, it yields high rewards.

PARKING LOTS

There are almost as many motor vehicles of various kinds as there are people in this country. Our roadways are becoming increasingly congested and businessmen and merchants in central shopping districts of every major city are very concerned about the availability of parking for their customers. The shortage of adequate parking is a primary factor in the decline of the central business district of many cities.

As I mentioned earlier, land usually does not produce income; there are some exceptions, however. Strategically located vacant lots in high-density areas can serve as income-producing parking lots. The open parking lot is the most common facility found in the city. There are minimal improvements to the land, which keeps maintenance costs down and allows for easy development of the land in the future, if necessary.

With a bit of investigating, you can learn enough about the parking lot business to make it a profitable endeavor for you. You can, of course, build a multi-story parking garage on your vacant lot, but you would then be getting into high finances. Let's stick with a vacant lot for now. You can own the land and operate it as a parking lot, or you can turn it over to a parking lot operator and collect a percentage of the parking revenues.

The simplest and least expensive operation is an unattended lot in which spaces are rented monthly to renters who park and lock their own cars. Without an attendant, however, you have to contend with free-loaders who park illegally and self-parkers who will not park close enough to adjacent vehicles, wasting a lot of valuable space. Studies have shown that with unattended lots, 300 to 350 square feet is used per car. A lot with an attendant who will "close up the ranks" will require only 200 to 250 square feet per car. If you are purchasing a 10,000-square-foot lot, you can expect to accommodate 50 cars with an attendant or 35 cars without an attendant.

Parking lot locations are usually determined by the walking distance from the lot to the final destination of the driver. The final destination is most often a shopping district, an office building, theater, hospital, hotel, restaurant, or other similar attractions. Most persons hesitate to walk farther than a city block (500 feet) and will pay a high parking fee not to. A two-block distance of 1000 feet is considered the maximum distance that an individual will walk from a parking lot to his or her final destination.

In searching for a vacant lot to use as a parking facility, it is particularly advantageous to be near a main activity center, or a "traffic generator," like a large office building or department store. These facilities will create a lot of business for you during the daylight hours. A nearby hotel or theater will create business both day and night.

MOBILE HOME PARKS

The mobile home is the fastest-growing segment of the single-family housing industry, with between one quarter and one half million units built and sold annually. Better than 90 percent of all new homes sold for prices below $15,000 are mobile homes.

There are two types of mobile homes: the less expensive travel trailers and campers that measure less than 29 feet in length, which can be towed by an automobile; and the larger modern mobile homes, which may have as many as four bedrooms and two baths, measuring up to 14 feet wide and up to 70 feet long. The travel trailers, which include many of the features of an automobile, are considered personal property. The modern mobile homes, many of which are permanently affixed to the ground, are being considered realty in an increasing number of states.

A mobile home will range in price from $12,000 to $25,000 for 800 to 1000 square feet of living space, or roughly $15 to $25 per square foot. Much less than the $60 and up per-square-foot costs for conventionally built houses. Most mobile home parks are concentrated in Florida, California, and the Sun Belt. Generally, mobile parks are located on the outskirts of urban communities where raw land costs run between $3000 and $5000 per acre. Mobile home spaces can be sold outright or, as is normally the case, rented at prices ranging from $100 to $300 per month (depending upon the facilities offered), not including electricity, gas, or water, which are paid by the user. A park owner can earn additional revenues from vending machines, coin-operated laundries, and the sale of bottled gas.

Those that buy mobile homes as their residences are military personnel, retired persons, construction workers, lower-income families, and vacationers. They are mostly two-person households with incomes just below the national average. Mobile homeowners find the financial terms for mobile homes more suited to their financial abilities.

An increasing number of people are using their mobile homes as second, or vacation, homes set in a recreational environment. Retirees, too, are increasingly seeking out mobile homes because they are more affordable and also because they want the smaller living areas with reduced housekeeping chores. Many retirees like to travel often, returning periodically to their smaller, less demanding mobile home base. While they are away, they know the neighbors will keep an eye on their property in the close-knit mobile home community.

The need for mobile home parks around the country has far outstripped the supply. One reason for this shortage is the attitude of towns towards the parks. People still think of the parks as unattractive and unwanted additions to their community and have enacted zoning ordinances preventing, or severely limiting, their development. However, there are many exclusive parks today that are the equal of the communities in which they are situated.

The travel trailer and camper has also become a popular means of travel and vacation for many Americans. A park suited specifically to these campers will pay dividends to the land investor. Campers usually stay overnight, or at most two weeks, at such facilities, which are usually located near tourist attractions. While a mobile home park allocates 8 to 10 spaces per acre, the travel trailer park can handle 25 to 30 spaces per acre. Rates run from $5 per night and up. The facilities are less elaborate than in a mobile home park and consequently much cheaper to develop and maintain. Restrooms, laundry, power hookups, and an office are your primary necessities.

If you find a suitable parcel and an agreeable community, you can assure yourself of high and continuous profits far into the future. Naturally, an investment in either a mobile home park or a travel trailer park will demand a great deal of your time—time that you may not be able to give. In fact, you will find that most investments in real estate of a business or commercial nature will demand much of your time, whereas simply speculating in lots needn't be time-demanding at all.

CHAPTER XIV

HOW TO SELL YOUR LAND

METHODS

Now you are finally at the stage where you are ready to reap the benefits of all your efforts. You have found and purchased your land. You may have subdivided it. Now you are ready to sell it and earn a profit. Unlike most commodities, land can actually be sold with little, or no, advertising exposure. Just cleaning up a parcel will make it more noticeable and may result in a sale. If there's any junk on it, take it away. Remove the dead and fallen trees. Rip out the weeds and thorn bushes, fill in holes and gullies and plant grass if needed. This will often do the job.

If the land is located in a sparsely traveled area, then you will have to use additional methods to make potential buyers aware of your land. Word-of-mouth advertising is one inexpensive way for you to sell your land. Tell your friends and acquaintances about it and tell them to inform their friends and acquaintances. Improving the land by cleaning it up and making it presentable and word-of-mouth advertising will sell a lot of land for you. However, there are methods that you can use as supplements should you need them. For-sale signs, newspapers, direct mail, telephone, and real estate brokers are proven sales methods used by most investor-developers.

For-Sale Signs

The easiest way to sell your land is to simply place a for-sale sign on it. Placed in the ground, or nailed to a tree, a for-sale sign informs passersby that the land is for sale. If they are not interested, they may pass on the information to acquaintances that may be looking for land. Earlier I mentioned that people often pass a vacant parcel without taking any particular notice of it. The final line of the Henry Woodward poem "I Am Real Estate" points out the lament of the vacant, passed-by parcel. A sign forces people to notice it. I've done the same thing many times; I've driven by a parcel, over and over, without paying it much heed. Once a for-sale sign went on it, I immediately became more interested in it. I will say from experience, however, that there aren't very many parcels that I pass by now without considering their potential.

A for-sale sign can serve as a location device for you. If you run an ad in the newspaper and a prospect calls, you can give the directions to the parcel using the for-sale sign to pinpoint the location. The for-sale sign also works as an instrument for creating prospects for other parcels you may have for sale, or for building a prospect file for future land you make available.

Real estate brokers put signs on a lot to attract phone calls, not only for the subject lot, but also for other properties that they have in their inventory. A for-sale sign is an inexpensive way to have their names continuously in front of the public. It works seven days a week, all year long.

I AM REAL ESTATE
by Henry Woodward

I am the basis of all wealth, the heritage of the wise, the thrifty and the prudent.

I am the poor man's joy and comfort, the rich man's prize, the right hand of capital, the silent partner of many thousands of successful men.

I am the solace of the widow, the comfort of old age, the cornerstone of security against misfortune and want.

I am handed down to children through generations as a thing of greatest worth.

I am the choicest fruit of toil. Credit respects me, and yet I am humble.

I stand for every man, bidding him to know me for what I am and possess me.

I grow and increase in value through countless days.

Though I seem dormant, my worth increases, never failing, never ceasing, for time is my aid and population eats upon my gains.

Fire and elements I defy, for they cannot destroy me.

My possessors learn to believe in me. Invariably they become envied.

While all things wither and decay, I survive.

The thriftless speak ill of me, the charlatans of finance attack me, yet I am trustworthy, I am sound. Unfailingly I triumph, and my detractors are disproved.

Minerals and oils come from me. I am the producer of food, the basis for ships and factories, yes, the foundation of banks.

Yet I am so common that thousands unthinkingly and unknowingly pass me by.

If you are selling several contiguous lots, you could put a for-sale sign on each lot, but too many signs give an area a cluttered and unattractive appearance. Instead, put up one sign saying "Lots for Sale" and place smaller lot-number signs on the other parcels. Many developers put a diagram on each lot showing the size and dimensions of each parcel.

This is very informative to the prospect, but it could very well give enough information that the prospect needn't contact you.

Some lots will sell themselves, but most often you have to do the selling and you can't do it until you face the prospect in person. If the prospect got all the necessary information from the sign, he or she may not call you. Most prospects need a little encouragement—a little assistance and assurance from the seller or broker that they are doing the right thing. You can't tell them that they are doing the right thing unless you face them. You can't do it over the telephone either. The purpose of having them call you is to arrange for an appointment for you to "walk the land" together.

Don't try to sell over the phone, because you'll strike out every time. Would you buy a piece of land over the telephone? Certainly not, and neither will your prospects. Get their name, address, and telephone number and make a definite appointment. You will get a lot of calls from people that cannot afford the lot or are simply curious about it. Screen these calls so that you are not running out every other day on wild goose chases. Give just enough information so that they become interested in seeing the features you stressed.

Naturally, if you don't have the time to be showing the lots, then you have to give all the necessary facts over the phone or hire a real estate broker to handle the showings for you. Ten percent of the selling price is the traditional commission paid to real estate brokers selling land. This is not a fixed percentage, but rather a negotiated fee. Since you will be supplying qualified prospects, you can arrange to pay a lesser commission if the showing results in a sale.

Don't put up a home-made sign. Do it right. Have a professional sign maker design an attractive, eye-catching sign for you. Zoning will dictate the size and type of sign you can use and your sign maker will be aware of the local sign codes. Use attention-capturing colors, such as red or black on white. Limit the words. Too many words make it difficult for drivers to read. In addition to the words "Lots for Sale," your telephone or address should appear. You may want to use the words "For Sale by Owner." I don't know why, but a for-sale-by-owner sign seems to imply a possible bargain in many a prospect's eye.

Perhaps it's the fact that there's no middleman involved. In any event, it works, so try it.

Classified Advertisements

When you initially decided that you wanted to buy land, what did you do first? You went to the classified ads section of your newspaper, didn't you? Everyone is familiar with, and uses, the classified ads whether they are looking for a used typewriter, an apartment to rent, or a piece of land to buy. The classified ads are the most productive and most widely used selling method in real estate. Newspapers reach more prospects per advertising dollar than any other medium. Some communities have but one newspaper, so your ad may very well reach the majority of the land-seekers in the area where the paper is distributed.

You could actually forget all other selling methods and be highly successful just using classified ads. The other selling methods—mail order, real estate brokers, sign programs, telephone solicitations—are all supplements to the classifieds for the beginner. Initially, you may want to stay with newspapers only.

As your experience and confidence grows, however, you'll be buying more properties and you will have to develop a complete marketing program using the other selling methods in conjunction with newspaper advertising.

You can also use display ads which are the larger advertisements spread throughout the newspaper. Certain sections of the newspaper are made up of display ads selling a particular product class. The real estate section consists of display ads on homes for sale, apartments for rent, condominiums, land, mobile homes, and various building services.

In my own experience, however, classified ads beat out the larger display ads in the number of qualified prospects they attract. They reach more prospective buyers per dollar expended. The classifieds are the "Sugar Ray" of real estate selling. Pound for pound, dollar for dollar, they are the best around. It's not uncommon for a $10 ad to sell a

$1 million parcel. The real estate buying habits of the American consumer are oriented to the classifieds. Everyone interested in buying land will automatically go to the classified section. It is so widely used that it is broken down into types of property for sale and geographical location to aid readers. If you're interested in buying land only, you simply look under the "Land for Sale" section of the classifieds. If you want to sell your land, you'll place your ad in the same classifieds. This section will prove, time and again, to be the most successful for you, but you may want to test your ads under the general real estate section where houses for sale are listed, or even under business opportunities, or investment opportunities, where would-be entrepreneurs always look.

If you're running ads in more than one newspaper, keep track of which newspaper is producing the most inquiries so that on future sales campaigns, you'll know best where to put your advertising dollars.

The best ad is the one that creates sales for you. It isn't necessary for it to be long and overly descriptive to be effective. A short, punchy ad will have better results than a long-winded, rambling ad. Get your message across about what you are selling, but don't tell the whole story. You want to create enough excitement for a prospect to be interested enough to call you.

Look in the papers at other land-for-sale ads and at ads that real estate brokers run. Are there any features, or words, that could be incorporated into your own ad? Keep in mind when reading the real estate broker's ads that they are designed to keep the phones ringing in the broker's office to provide customers for salespeople. Yes, they want to sell the subject land, but they must make their ads do double and triple duty, so they will also try to sell any of the dozens of other parcels they have in their inventory. Your ad must be specifically geared to the one property you have for sale.

The classified ad department at the newspaper can help you to compose an effective ad. You may also want to write a series of ads, changing or alternating them every other week or so. An effective "land for sale" ad should include the price, terms, amenities, location, size, zoning use, and your telephone number or address. The following are a few examples of some prospect-creating ads:

BREWSTERVILLE
1-Acre Homesites

Fine residential community. 20 minutes to Memphis. Near shopping and schools. All utilities underground. Call 4-7 p.m
Phone #

DERRYTOWN

Estate Sized

House Lots

$12,000.
Owner
698-3761

Five Acres
Magnificent mountain views. Level & wooded. Next to new lake community. $16,000. Owner financing available.
Phone #

HAMILTON
34 Acres
Over 1,100 ft. frontage on Rte. 65. Nr. exit 12E Zoned commercial. Terms.
Phone #

ATTN. BLDRS.
23 acres with pond. Lincoln Center. Gd. for Condos.
Phone #

PARSONFIELD
Owner must sell. 16 acres. Surveyed. Paved rd. frntg. $14,000. $1,400 dwn.
Phone #

Naples, Four 35-45 ac. parcels —3 mi. to ocean. Surveyed & soil tested. $1,200 per acre. Terms.
Phone #

Plymouth
Lge lot w/private beach rights. Nr. Marina. Phone #

NEDDICK, 7 lot subdiv. mtn. views. 2-4 acres each. $9,000-$12,000. Write: Box K, Neddick

Cape Moody—4 lots. One acre each, town water. Priv. rd. with views of river.
Owner Phone #

WESTWOOD
19-acres surveyed into 3 lots.
$9K per lot. $25K for all three.
Phone #

Ames-12 choice ½ ac. lots,
$16,900 each.
Owner Phone #

Attn. Sportsmen

14-Acres	$ 9500
32-Acres	$20000
39-Acres	$20000

Heavily wooded, rolling terrain. 2 hrs. to Boston. Terrific hunting and fishing.
Phone #

Direct Mail

Often overlooked as a sales tool is the United States Post Office. Use the postal system as your personal sales force in getting your sales message to your prospects. You can do this effectively through a well-conceived direct mail program.

There's nothing mysterious about direct mail. You're involved in it in one way or another. Each day you receive mail from direct marketers who are trying to interest you in purchasing their goods and services. Direct mailers get their message directly to selected prospects. I say selected, but it's not really predictably and precisely selected. Many direct mailers use the "shotgun" approach by sending out countless mailing pieces to a wide audience hoping that some pieces will land into the hands of interested prospects, or at least create interested prospects. These mailings are actually going to "suspects." They are trying to create a prospect from a suspect.

The shotgun approach is actually a "numbers game." From experience, mailers know that for every so many pieces that they send out, they can expect a certain percentage of response; like a shotgun shell, just aim the gun in the general direction and something is bound to hit home. Though this may seem haphazard and unscientific, it does indeed work.

With the rising costs of direct mail, most direct mailers are refining their mailing techniques. The costs of postage, printing, artwork, and copy, as well as the cost of physically putting the mailing together, are all increasing. Direct mailers have to improve their percentage of return to compensate. Not too many years ago, Sears sent their catalog out to anybody who wanted one and to many that didn't. That big catalog became very expensive to create, so Sears drastically reduced their mailings and you'll find it not as easy to get one of their catalogs today. You have to be a fairly active customer, or be willing to pay four dollars to get one.

Sears went from the shotgun approach to the "rifle-shot" approach, as have many of the larger direct mailers. They are aiming their mailings at audiences that they expect to have more than a passing interest in their product. They want to increase the percentage of return on their mailings. If the product is inexpensive, say less than ten dollars, then a high return is a must. Enough products must be sold to cover the cost of the mailing and a profit to boot.

If the product sells for several hundreds of dollars, then a smaller percentage of return can be acceptable. A $200 or $300 retail price can cover a lot of costs.

At one time, when postal costs were cheaper, mailers readily accepted low returns on many of their mailings, since each mailing eventually added names to their mailing list. This is a highly mobile country, people move often. A mailing list deteriorates by at least 20 percent each year. If a mailer is losing 20 percent of the list each year, it won't take very long for the list to be worthless. New names must be constantly added to the list, replacing those lost.

Mailing thousands of pieces in a direct mail campaign is not only costly, but also time-consuming. As a beginning land investor, you may have a limited supply of both time and money. You must be selective in choosing your target market by mailing only to those prospects that you think may have more than an average interest in your land. You'll never know the exact degree of their interest, but you must make some educated guess and use, as well as possible, the rifle-shot approach.

In planning your direct mail program you have to decide who you are going to mail to, who your target audience is, and what the contents of the mailing will be. Let's first go with the contents of the mailing. You'll want to mail it first class and limit the weight to under one ounce so that you need only one first-class stamp. Most people like to see a plot plan. Besides graphically depicting the land, it seems to have an intrinsic value to them. When I receive a mailing package on the sale of land, I spend a lot of time looking over the plot plan, if one is included. I look at the size and dimensions of the individual lots, or the entire tract as the case may be, the topography, if shown, the land's locus or relationship to surrounding parcels and amenities. You should include a plot plan of the land you are selling in your mailing. A fact sheet will sometimes suffice, but the graphic presentation of a plot plan will make more of an impact. Most plot plans are very large and would be cumbersome and costly to mail. A local printer can reduce the plan to a reasonable size so that you can place it in your mailing envelope. Don't reduce it to the extent that you can't read the dimensions of the lots, and make sure the reduced copy is neat and legible.

You may want to design an all-purpose brochure or flyer. A method that I have used successfully many times is a simple self-mailer type of flyer. A self-mailer is a flyer or brochure that can be folded, stamped, addressed, and mailed as is, without being inserted into an envelope; it is itself an envelope. It has to be of a somewhat heavier stock of paper so that it will hold up in the mail and won't flop around limply in the reader's hand.

In your initial mail campaigns your budget will dictate what your flyer will cost. Printing costs add up very rapidly. Multi-colored advertising pieces make for a good presentation, but are expensive. If you use a colored stock—beige perhaps—with a brown or blue ink, your flyer will look as though it is multi-colored when it is only one color of ink on a contrasting-colored, but complementary, stock.

Perhaps the simplest flyer you could use is a standard-sized 8½ × 11 inch sheet with the plot plan printed on one entire side and folded in half, or in thirds, with the selling copy printed on the reverse side. You simply fold, staple, address, and stamp it and put it in the mail. It can be an information-packed promotional piece or it can have a coupon that the addressee can fill out and mail back for additional information. Included in the copy should be directions on how to get to the subject land.

Printing the prices of the lots on the flyer is a personal choice. If you do print the prices and later have to increase them, the flyers are useless to you. You don't want to junk up your flyer and make a poor impression by crossing out old prices and writing in new ones. I don't like to see one price tag over another in a supermarket, though I realize that prices do increase. I would like it even less on a promotional flyer for land. I would get the distinct impression that I missed out on a golden opportunity at the lower prices and the new prices are not such a good deal.

A self-mailer can also be inserted into an envelope if you want to send the mailing out more formally, or along with other selling materials. It can also double as a "take-one" flyer that you can place in strategic spots. Perhaps a general store, or a restaurant in the area where your land is located, will allow you to put a supply of flyers in a conspicuous spot. A cover letter is a widely used insertion in many direct mailings.

For the next week or two save all the mailing pieces that you receive, and open them all on the same day. You'll notice that there is a format, a tested and workable pattern, that most mailers use. Each mailing packet will include a cover letter, a flyer or brochure, a return envelope or business reply card, and an exhortation for you to take some action. This works for the large mass-mailers, but it doesn't necessarily mean that it will work for you. You have to find what works for you by making test mailings and measuring the response. Even the mass-mailers test, test, and test again. When you do find a successful mailing package, that does not mean that it will be successful on future mailings too. There is no perfect mailing package that works every time. That's the nature of direct mail—you keep testing and trying.

Timing   The purpose of sending a mailing piece to a prospect is to acquaint him or her with your land and to introduce yourself. The right time to do this is critical and can determine the success of your mailing.

Mass-mailers have a large volume of pieces in their mailings and keep a record over several years in order to develop meaningful and useful statistics. They know what months, what states, even down to what ZIP codes are the most productive for them at various times of the year.

In selling a limited number of lots, you won't get to the point where you will need the large quantity of mailing pieces, nor the sophisticated mailing techniques, of the mass-mailers. You do, however, have to consider what the best time will be for you to send out your direct mail pieces. This will be determined somewhat by when your land is ready for sale, but there are other obvious considerations too. If you're selling property in a summer resort area you will want to time your mailings to just before or during the season, when most of your prospects will be travelling toward the resort area.

In most cases, especially in the northern part of the country, the deep winter months are the least responsive. It's hard to get the prospects away from their warm hearths to walk through the snow and ice a hundred or more miles away. This doesn't apply if you're selling ski resort land, naturally. Conversely, many of the mass-mailers find the winter months to be their most responsive—in particular, the catalog mail order houses. People are indoors during the winter months and will take the time to flip through the pages of an interesting catalog. In the summer when they are more mobile and their interests are in the great outdoors; they won't pick up the catalog then.

The best days for prospects to receive your land promotion are Tuesday, Wednesday, and Thursday. Monday they're too busy recuperating from an active weekend, and Friday they have already made plans for the upcoming weekend. You should follow up your mailings with a phone call within 48 to 72 hours of mailing it. This gives the prospect time to receive and read the material, but not time to forget it.

Target Market   First decide who your target market is and then build a mailing list. Your market will be partly decided by what you are selling. Are you selling the entire tract as raw acreage? Are you selling an approved paper subdivision? Are you selling lots on an individual basis? Once you determine this, you can then proceed to build a workable mailing list.

After you have been buying and selling land for a while, you will have accumulated quite a few names. These names are the nucleus of your mailing list. They are persons, whether buyers or sellers, that have shown an interest of some kind in land. If they are sellers of land, whether it is a tract of raw acreage or a single house lot, they may one day be a buyer of one of your parcels. After all, they have already been through the process (in some manner they had acquired the piece of land that they are selling, either by inheritance or by outright purchase). They may want to do it again in the future. Everyone that calls about your for-sale sign or classified advertisement is a prospect and should be added to your mailing list.

You can refine their interests by categorizing them into specific types: single-lot buyers, multi-lot buyers, raw acreage buyers, builders, developers, investors, etc. If you buy and subdivide a parcel of waterfront property, for instance, you can immediately contact the prospects on your mailing list that expressed an interest in waterfront land.

Since direct mail is a numbers game, as I mentioned earlier, the more names you mail to, the greater the chance of selling something. This is particularly so with a list built through land inquiries, because of the fact that the prospects inquiring about your land qualified themselves as interested parties. They aren't cold prospects. If they don't buy from you on the first contact, they may in the future if you keep them informed of what you have for sale. The primary thing to keep in mind about mailing lists is that the more current the names, the better the response is likely to be. The longer the period from the time of the latest contact, the less responsive the list will be. A mailing list cannot lie fallow—it has to be used periodically to keep the prospect's interest from waning.

By the same token, the longer you wait after the time of inquiry, the less responsive the prospect will be. When someone contacts you, whether from your mailings, for-sale signs, or classified ads, get right back to him or her before interest cools. With a commodity like land, interest can cool off very quickly. If someone sees your ad, they may have a sudden impulse to find out more about the parcel right away. If you don't get back to that prospect in a reasonable amount of time, he or she may start to rethink his or her interest and come up with any number of reasons not to buy land at this time.

Many thousands of lots are sold each year to buyers who have no immediate use for the land. They bought it because it was a good deal, or they had some cash to invest, or a friend bought in the area, or they are speculating. Maybe next year they will build something on it, or give it to their son or daughter, or use the lot as a forced savings towards a child's college education. Any number of reasons, but none of them concrete enough to make it a must purchase.

When you receive an inquiry from a prospect, you must build interest enough to make the prospect act—to make him or her want to buy your land. If the interest wasn't sparked by impulse only, and the prospect is looking for a lot to build on now, he or she may look elsewhere if you are tardy in responding. If the prospect is not interested in what you have for sale now, say that you will put him or her on your mailing list and keep him or her informed of what you will have for sale in the future.

To strengthen the quality of your mailing list, you should keep a little history on each of your prospects. A 3" × 5" card with the prospect's name, address, phone number, land interests, how he or she contacted you, and a running history of your contacts with him or her will prove very useful.

In the early stages of building your mailing list, doing this will be very easy because your list will be small and manageable. As the list grows, you will have to develop efficient ways to manage it. Personal computer manufacturers have designed mailing list maintenance programs that can be used for this purpose.

When your list is small, you may want to type each prospect's name and address onto a multi-copy mailing label. The most common types of labels come in 8½" × 11" sheets of 44 labels per page with carbons so that you can get up to five or six copies of each label you type. When you get beyond five copies, the labels become harder to read. It's best to use no more than four or five copies of each label and retype new labels as you need them. Prospects for land, and most other commodities for that matter, like the personal touch. A blurry or smeared sixth copy of a label blatantly informs them that they are just a number on a large mailing list and they may become turned off to your direct mail promotion.

If your land is a long distance away from where you live and you don't want to personally take, or meet, every prospect there, then your marketing effort can lean heavily on mail order selling. You can promote and sell the lots without going to the land itself. I don't fully recommend this type of selling, but if circumstances dictate then you have to do it.

Before doing this, however, you should take into consideration that the land buyer will not be as familiar with the land as you are. Maybe the buyer will walk the wrong lot. Include a provision in your sales material, that once a lot is chosen by a prospect, the prospect and you, or the prospect and your agent, must physically walk the lot together. Walk the lot and its entire perimeter, point out all the bounds and amenities, and explain fully any covenants or restrictions. Later you won't have to worry about a buyer claiming that the lot he or she intended to purchase was a lot different from the one described on the deed. It does happen.

You have to make it easy for the prospect to find the land. Your mailing should include directions to the land, a plot plan, a copy of the restrictions, and your phone number. You can also install directional signs on roads leading to the land. Have each lot staked with easy-to-spot markers on all four corners and put a number sign in a conspicuous spot on each lot. If you make the buying experience easy for the prospect and handle the transaction honestly and efficiently, that sale may result in further sales to the buyer's friends and family.

Your list doesn't necessarily have to be built of names of prospects that have contacted you. You could build a list from unsolicited names—directories, phone books, and the like. You can compile a list from your local telephone book, for that matter, or perhaps a list of doctors and architects or other professionals in high-income jobs. You could even compile a list of persons living in expensive residential areas. You are the judge on who you are going to send your mailings to and with skill and luck the addressee will have a better-than-average interest in what you are selling.

Be selective when compiling lists from directories. There are such a large number of names in most directories that you can get carried away by mailing to many hundreds and thousands of people who don't have the slightest interest in your land. It would be wise for you to test-mail to a reasonable sampling of names from each directory that you use. For example, if you have a directory of doctors in a specific geographical area, you may want to mail to say 10 or 20 percent of them and measure the response. If the test is successful, then mail to the remainder of the directory. If not, move on to another source of names.

Using the Telephone

I did say earlier that you cannot sell land over the telephone, and I'll stick to that statement. Consumer products like magazines, newspapers, and many products sold to business and industry very often can be sold over the phone. In fact the telephone industry is playing this up big with their telemarketing programs. Land, however, cannot be sold over the telephone. It's too expensive, too legally involved—the prospect will want to see and walk the land, and well he or she should. Yet you can use the telephone to help you to sell land. Notice, I did not say to sell, but to help sell. As a beginning investor, and perhaps part-time to boot, your time to sell land will be limited. The telephone, used properly, will prove to be an invaluable tool for you.

When a classified ad, a for-sale sign, or a direct mail piece carries your telephone number, you are going to get phone calls. The first thing the caller is going to hear when you answer is you, of course. The tone in your voice and your attitude will greatly determine if you can make a solid prospect of this caller. Yes, the prospect does have an interest in your land or wouldn't have called you in the first place. But if the reception the prospect receives from you over the phone is gruff or condescending, the interest will assuredly dissipate.

Visual communication is lost over the telephone. You can't see your prospect, and you can't read his or her body language nor see the enthusiasm or lack thereof in his or her eyes. You have to compensate for this with oral skills and good listening habits. Take a look at your telephone—it has two ends; a good salesperson uses them both. A good salesperson is a good listener. You don't have to do all the talking—let your caller do the bulk of it.

Listening requires patience and concentration. If both parties are talking, nobody is listening. Plutarch put it succinctly: "The talkative listen to no one, for they are ever speaking. And the first evil that attends those who know not how to be silent is that they hear nothing." Most of us are bad listeners. This is so true of many salespeople who prefer to talk to their prospects rather than listen to them. They think they have to keep talking to draw the prospect out. Too often they talk themselves out of a sale. If you engage in active listening, the prospect will tell you what you want to know with little effort and coaxing by you. When you receive a call, introduce yourself and let the caller take over. Don't interrupt. You may annoy him or her or make the prospect lose the point of his or her conversation. Here are a few examples of poor listening. See if any of them hit home:

Talking while the caller is talking

Impatience at the caller (for whatever reason)

Rushing a slow-talking caller or finishing sentences for the caller

Trying to educate the caller over the telephone, resulting in the salesperson doing all the talking

Trying to sell the land over the telephone instead of setting up an appointment to show the land

By listening attentively you will be able to draw out all the information you want to know about the prospect. Your voice will reflect your personality. It's not what you say, but how you say it. I know of several telephone sales organizations that place a mirror on the wall in front of each of their phone solicitors with a sign over the mirror that says "smile." Indistinct as it may be, a smile can be sensed in your voice.

When the caller says he or she is calling about your classified ad, smile as if the caller is in the room with you. Say you're glad he or she called and that you'll answer any questions and also send a plot plan, price list, and directions to the land. This last comment is a chance for the caller to give you a name and address. Now you know to whom you are speaking. Most callers are reluctant to give their names over the phone. Your offer to send some material will take away this reluctance.

Your next objective is to arrange for an appointment to show the prospect the land. You cannot show the land to everyone who calls, especially if you are kept busy with inquiry calls. You will have to qualify the sincerity of the caller's interest. If this is a qualified prospect, in your mind, then go for the appointment.

If you're doing this part-time, then weekends are probably the only time you have available, and most likely this will be convenient for the caller too. You'll find it easy to make the appointment, but you'll still have to go for it in an aggressive and positive manner. In setting the appointment you can't ask the caller "What's a convenient time for you?" The prospect will be noncommittal to a question like that. Rather, give a "guided" alternative. "Would Saturday morning or afternoon be better for you? Say, ten o'clock? Fine, see you then." By guiding a prospect with questions like this, you are forcing him or her to make minor commitments. The more you can make the prospect say "yes" to minor commitments, the easier it will be for the prospect to say "yes" to the major commitment—"Do you want to buy this land?"

Sometimes you will be the one to initiate telephone contact with prospects. It would be a serious mistake for you to telephone a prospect and start talking before carefully planning what you are going to say. The first twenty or thirty seconds are critical and can make or break the call. You don't want the prospect to think that he or she is getting a "canned" presentation, but there are several elements to the call that you can prepare so that your phone call will be effective. Those elements are: an opening statement, qualifying the prospect, and setting an appointment.

Your opening statement should be designed to introduce yourself and to build a friendly rapport that will catch the prospect's interest so that he or she will want to hear more:

> Hello, Mr. Rogers, this is James Sheerin. I recently sent you some information on an exciting parcel of land that I have for sale on Walton's Mountain.

Once you've piqued the listener's interest, your next objective is to qualify him or her. You want to know if the prospect has any interest at all in land. The purpose of qualifying the prospect is to save you time so that you won't be wasting it by showing land to someone whose interest is nil. Many people can't say no to a request. This type of prospect will accept even if he or she hasn't the slightest interest in, or financial ability to buy, your land. Yet, you can't be too selective in qualifying because you may eliminate possible buyers. You have to turn the suspect into a prospect, then into a buyer.

> Mr. Rogers, do you own any land now? Did you know that land on Walton's Mountain is in high demand and is becoming scarce?

In addition to receiving inquiry calls from your promotional efforts, you'll be initiating follow-up calls to those that haven't responded to your direct mail promotion. If you mail to a list that you compiled from a directory, you can expect to get a very small percentage of response, perhaps three or four responses for every hundred names. Rather than just forgetting the remaining ninety-six or ninety-seven persons that didn't call you, you should follow up with a telephone call. If you can create three more prospects from your follow-up calls, you have, in effect, doubled your response from this mailing.

Your call should be within seventy-two hours of when you sent the mailing out so that the information will be fresh in the prospect's mind. You'll find that the follow-up effort will produce more prospects than relying solely on the direct mail. You are contacting the parties twice; once with the mailing and again with the follow-up call. The mail introduced you to the prospect so that your follow-up call won't be a completely cold call—the prospect will already be familiar with you.

If your budget is limited for telephone calls, you may want to follow up only on those names located within your own area code. As you progress, you might look into an 800 number, which allows the prospect to call you toll free. You'll be pleasantly surprised at the number of calls you will get when it's your dime. I ran an ad continuously in the classifieds of a major city newspaper with an 800 number and my phone was constantly ringing. I received from 25 to 100 calls per week. With this many calls you can see the necessity of qualifying the callers.

Clean Up the Premises

Too often I've seen tracts of land that have become dumping grounds for lazy and inconsiderate persons. Maybe the town landfill was too far away for them, or perhaps it was closed for the day and they found it more convenient just to dump their debris on someone else's property. Builders hire helpers to clean up the scrap building materials at a site and take them to the town dump. Sometimes the less responsible types just find a convenient, inconspicuous vacant parcel, unload their rubbish, and save themselves a little time and trouble.

Roll up your sleeves and collect all the rubbish that nature hadn't intended to be on your land. Collect it into trash bags and take it to the landfill. (Don't just drop it on someone else's land!) You can rent power equipment that will remove the underbrush and thorn bushes. A "brush-hog" will shred and spread the undergrowth that it chews up. Prune the dead, low-lying branches from the trees, cut down leaning and dead trees, and remove all fallen branches from the ground.

If you hire a local landscaper to do this work for you, the charge will be about $1 per square foot. A 1-acre lot will cost about $400 to $450. It's best to hire the landscaper in the off-season when you will get a better price because the landscaper wants to keep the crew busy. Many land developers "grub out" only along the frontage to a depth of about 50 feet or so to give the parcel a spruced-up appearance.

If you have a lot of heavy work to do, you could hire a local contractor with a bulldozer. A machine and driver will cost about $200 per day and will do plenty of value-adding work in an eight-hour period. The dozer can level abandoned buildings, rip out old fencing, uproot stumps and dead trees, bury heavy items like abandoned automobiles and building foundations, pile up junk for removal, fill depressions, clean up approaches to the property, and regrade dirt roads and paths. After this is done, you can plant quick-growing ground covering such as rye grass in the disturbed areas.

A land-investor friend of mine always installs a white-rail fence along the frontage of the parcels he buys. The fence is attractive and attention-getting and distinguishes his property from abutting parcels. If you have a lot of frontage, though, fencing can be very costly. You may want to install ten or twenty "L-shaped" feet of fencing at the two front corners, and perhaps a 30 foot strip of fencing, with a gate, in the center of the frontage.

The same clean-up principles will increase the value of a vacant lot in an urban area. Clean it up, fill it in, level it off, fence it, repave the crumbling sidewalk in front of it, and you'll get inquiries right away. Check with town authorities as to what permits you will need to carry out the clean-up activities. Anything that you can do to improve the land's appearance will add value to it. People believe what they see, and "eye appeal" will play a significant role in the success of your selling efforts.

INTERIM USES

Land by itself does not make money for you until you sell it. During this interim period, you must pay the normal carrying costs of interest and taxes, besides having working capital tied up in the value of the land. If you plan on a long holding period for the land, perhaps until the surrounding area develops more fully, then carrying costs will be eating into your potential profit.

Successful land investors have often utilized the inherent value in raw land during long holding periods to generate some income. Sometimes enough to cover carrying costs. Sometimes not. But any income is better than none. The natural amenities of the land may be employed in some interim use that will provide income for the user—as well as the owner if they happen to be different persons. Land can be rented or leased for a variety of uses, some of which are far removed from the eventual end use. You have to determine what uses of the land are allowable under the zoning by-laws. A visit to the municipal authorities will let you know if any particular uses that you have in mind will be approved.

You are going to have to take the initiative to make the interim use happen. If the land is suitable for farming, for instance, you'll have to promote it as such. Nobody is going to come beating on your door to use it as a farm. You will have to go out and find someone and sell the idea. This will be the case with whatever interim uses are being considered. Don't assume that the use will be as obvious to everyone else as it is to you. Let it be known that the land can be leased for particular uses. You can run an ad, notify brokers and potential users, and you can install a sign on the land.

If the parcel is heavily wooded, and for your eventual use it would be best if it were cleared, you can sell the timber to do-it-yourself wood-cutters for firewood. With firewood selling for $100 to $200 per cord, a low retail price would assure that your land will be cleared for you by firewood seekers. After the timber has been sold, you can have the tree stumps removed and the land graded and seeded.

If the land is cleared suitable for agricultural purposes, you could then lease it to local farmers for raising crops or for grazing farm animals. Terrain is an important consideration for agricultural users. Rocky, hilly, marshy land would be of little use to them. Flat, dry, cleared land, preferably rectangular in shape, is the least costly to cultivate. Location, too, is of prime importance, as is proximity to markets. Soil and availability of water are other requisites for using the land for agricultural pursuits.

Hunting and fishing leases are good sources of income for large parcels in rural locations. Outdoorsmen will travel a long way to pursue their hobby and will return year after year if the fishing was good. Wildlife is attracted to areas that have favorable conditions for feeding and watering. Some landowners sow grain to attract wildlife and leave high pasture grasses to provide cover areas. Ponds can be stocked with a variety of fish native to the area. The fish and game department can advise you on how to do this if you have these intentions. You could lease the land to a single lessee such as a sportsman's club for hunting and fishing or as a shooting range for its members. Though there are plenty of public lands available for sportsmen, many prefer private hunting grounds.

Proceeds from the sale of sand and gravel to area contractors and road builders can be quite lucrative. Both commodities are needed for the production of concrete and asphalt. Excavation of these materials does devastate the surface of the land, but after the resources are removed the land can be returned to normal use by grading and landscaping.

In many parts of the country waste disposal is becoming a critical issue. The ecology movement eliminated refuse burning. Development of landfill disposal methods has created many opportunities for landowners. Municipalities, private waste haulers, and industrial waste disposers are constantly in search of suitably located land for this purpose. Substandard land with little development value can be converted to valuable commercial property after the landfill use is completed. One community has built a little league baseball field over an old town landfill. Old gravel pits have good landfill potential. The superintendent of public works will let you know of the landfill possibilities in the area.

In parts of the country where coal, oil, gas, or other minerals are produced, the right to extract these resources can be leased. You will want to have the lessee return the surface of the land to its original condition after all the minerals have been removed.

As mentioned earlier, the mobility of many Americans has sparked a boom in travel trailer use. Most municipalities have laws prohibiting parking in the streets or in driveways. Spaces in mobile home parks are in great demand. You can lease your land to a mobile home park operator to use for mobile home sites or for off-season storage of idle mobile homes. Campsites and picnic areas are other income-producing recreational uses.

It's not just the larger parcels that have income-producing capabilities. With a little thought, small plots of land, and vacant lots in the city, can be put to work for you. A strategically located downtown lot can be used as a temporary parking lot, or to sell Christmas trees in season and nursery items year round. Fruit and vegetable stands, a used car lot, trailer and boat sales, billboards, a miniature golf course and driving range are some other uses. You are limited only by your imagination and, of course, municipal approval.

TAX TACTICS

Installment Sales

The profit on the sale of a parcel of land is usually a considerable amount, often enough to push you into a much higher tax bracket. An installment sale can alleviate this problem. In addition to deferring tax payments on monies not yet received, an installment sale can also save you money by spreading out the gain over a number of years.

Suppose you sell a parcel for $50,000, earning a handsome profit of $25,000. If it isn't an installment sale, you must pay the taxes in the year of the sale on the full $25,000 profit, regardless of how much of the sales price you receive. Additionally, the $25,000 will push you into a higher tax bracket for that year, costing you additional taxes. If, however, you ask for a down payment of $10,000 (20 percent) and equal payments of $10,000 per year for the next four years, you'll be in a more favorable tax position.

To be eligible as an installment sale, payments in the year of the sale must not exceed 30 percent of the selling price, and payments must be made in two or more installments. If more than 30 percent is received, the full gain must be reported in the year of the sale and taxes paid accordingly. Both the down payment and any periodic or installment payments in the first year are included in this 30 percent.

Tax-Deferred Exchanges

One way of saving on taxes is to defer payment of them. This can be done through property exchanges. Exchanges are often thought of as being tax-free, but they're not. The parties to the exchange are simply postponing the tax payments until each eventually sells his or her property. The federal tax code allows those who want to exchange their property for another person's property of equal or higher value to defer the payment of taxes on the profit. The tax is not eliminated, it is deferred. The new property acquired in an exchange is considered to be a continuation of the old investment. You can continue exchanging property, upwards in value, indefinitely. Your heirs can carry on with the same exchange and tax-deferment privileges.

The IRS is alert to the growing popularity of exchanges and all transactions must meet specific and strict requirements to qualify. The properties exchanged must be held for business or investment purposes, and must be "like-kind" properties. "Like kind" is based simply on the distinction between real and personal property. Real property may be exchanged for other real property, and personal property may be exchanged for other personal property. Real estate is like (in kind) other real estate, and personal property is like (in kind) other personal property. A warehouse can be exchanged for a shopping center, an apartment house for a tract of land.

Obviously, most trades are not on an even basis. If your land is worth $30,000, odds are you will not find another willing exchanger with property also worth $30,000. Typically, one of the parties will have to include additional capital or personal property to equalize the trade. This, or "unlike" personal property, is referred to as "boot" and is taxable in the year the exchange takes place, if it is recognized as a gain.

There are three kinds of exchanges: a two-party exchange, a three-party exchange, and a multi-party exchange. The two-party exchange is a simple, even transaction in which both parties like and want the other party's property. A three-party exchange is a bit more involved.

If you owned a ten-acre parcel and a local builder wanted to buy it from you, you would have to pay taxes on the sale. Instead, you could seek out an owner of an investment parcel that appeals to you and swap properties with that owner and have him or her then sell your old ten-acre parcel to the builder. A multi-party exchange is an extension of the three-party exchange. In the three-party exchange above, if the new owner of your ten-acre parcel did not want to sell, but also wanted an exchange, another party would be brought into the transaction. This can go on to include up to a dozen or more exchangers. A real estate broker involved in the process would collect a commission on each transaction. In fact, if the broker were also the end-buyer, the one who eventually pays the cash to buy the ten-acres, his or her ultimate purchase would have set all the previous exchanges in motion.

LAND SALES FULL DISCLOSURE ACT

Since World War II, the sale of lots for residential and recreational use has grown tremendously. This rapid growth has attracted some undesirable types into the lot sales industry. To protect the public from fraudulent acts and practices, Congress passed the Interstate Land Full Disclosure Act in 1968. The act requires developers to file a statement of record and a property report with the federal government if they sell lots in a subdivision of 50 lots or more by mail or any means of interstate commerce.

The filing must be made with the Office of Interstate Land Sales Registration (OILSR), a division of the Department of Housing and Urban Development (HUD). The statement of record must include facts and conditions about the property that would be of interest to prospective lot buyers such as:

- The name and address of the owner of the property
- A statement of condition of title, including liens, easements, and taxes
- A description of the subdivision with a plan showing lot sizes, streets, and distances from amenities and municipalities

- A statement of the status of existing and proposed utilities and completion dates
- A statement of the selling terms, conditions, prices, and refund policy
- Copies of all forms of conveyance used in selling the lots

The property report must include all the essential information about the subdivision that is listed in the statement of record, as well as any unusual conditions relative to the location of the property. These conditions include distances over paved roads to nearby communities, limitations on the property such as pollution from nearby industrial plants or noise from airfields, and any dangers of flooding.

The property report must be given to a prospective buyer at least three business days prior to the signing of a sales contract, or the buyer can cancel without liability. Failure of a developer to comply with this act can result in a penalty of up to five years imprisonment and a $5000 fine. Because of the risks, costs, and time involved in the registration process, many developers purposely limit the size of their subdivisions to 49 lots or less, or limit their marketing efforts to intrastate only, thereby avoiding the necessity of registering with HUD.

After reading about this act, I'm sure you're a bit worried about it. Don't be overly concerned; most, if not all, of your parcels will contain fewer than 50 lots, and the bulk of your marketing efforts will be intrastate, not interstate. Selling within your state borders, you can have up to 300 lots in a single subdivision without being required to register with HUD. Also, lots of five acres or more are exempt from this act, as are lot sales to builders for constructing homes. In any event, if you do get to the stage where your subdivisions are as large as 50 or more lots, you will probably be a successful developer at that point and can certainly afford to hire an attorney to help you to register. I hope you do get this successful.

CHAPTER XV

THE BROKER'S ROLE

You cannot function in the real estate business for any length of time without dealing with real estate brokers. A discussion on how real estate brokers operate will help you to use their services more effectively, and this knowledge will help you prosper in buying and selling land.

After you have been buying and selling land for a period of time, you will have met many prospects and buyers. You will also have developed a long list of properties that you did not buy for one reason or another. You may want to put a buyer and seller together on some of these parcels and collect a commission for your efforts. However, all states have laws that prohibit unlicensed persons from dealing in real estate that is not their own property. Why let these potentially high earnings slip through your fingers? It will prove worthwhile for you to obtain your real estate license and capture these commissions for yourself. You may find that your land investment income and commissions will surpass what you have been earning in your current field of endeavor, and you may want to get more deeply involved in real estate. Let's look at what a real estate broker is, and does, and how you become one.

THE LAW OF AGENCY

Basically, a real estate broker's function is that of a negotiator. They are licensed as agents to negotiate to buy, sell, lease, or exchange property with third parties on behalf of a principal. The person for whom the agent acts is the principal, who promises to pay the broker a fee for the consummation of these services.

The law holds that whatever one may legally do for oneself, one may also do through another. A capable person may appoint another capable person to act for him or her. A real estate broker acting as an agent on behalf of a principal has a unique arrangement, termed a *fiduciary relationship,* that is governed by the requirements of the *law of agency.*

The law of agency concerns the legal rights and duties of a principal, agent, and a third party. The agent must at all times act in accordance with this trust when representing a principal. This trust prevents the agent, for example, from buying the principal's land through a third party to resell at a profit later; and from other actions contrary to the interests of the principal.

An agent is classified as either a *general agent* or a *special agent.* A general agent has broad powers to represent and bind a principal in all matters concerning particular areas of a principal's business. A special agent is authorized to represent a principal to transact one specific piece of business. The real estate broker, or salesperson, is a special agent contracted by a principal to find a buyer (or seller) for a piece of land.

Although the real estate field is a profession in and of itself, it consists to a large extent of individuals from other fields. To be an architect, a journalist, a surgeon, or a chef, you must acquire an impressive education in your chosen field and serve a lengthy apprenticeship. This is not so with the real estate business. You don't have to be a college graduate, nor do you have to serve a long apprenticeship. You simply pass a test relative to the real estate laws and practices in your state. You can buy a manual from your local real estate board, study it, and take the test. If you fail, you take the test again. If you pass, you may enter the field.

It's an easy profession to get into. Many retirees, after serving in their chosen fields, obtain a license and become brokers, most often working part time. Numerous housewives too, become licensed and each day after the kids are sent off to school they go to work for a few hours returning by two or three o'clock to retrieve their children from the school bus. They are referred to, not unkindly, as "kitchen brokers." Perhaps because the amount of time they spend in the office during the working hours of the day equals the amount of time spent at home. The profession needs them because the turnover in personnel is so great.

Like the restaurant business, it's an easy field to get into, but difficult to succeed in. The average broker does not make a lot of money and must cope with a lot of disappointments for what money he or she does earn. To be fair to the "professionals" in the business, that is, those that have stuck it out, learned the fundamentals, and succeeded, their success was earned with a lot of effort.

The real estate business is in a state of flux; it is trying to improve the quality and professionalism of its members to protect the public from fraud, dishonesty, or incompetence in buying and selling real estate. All fifty states, the District of Columbia, and Canada require that real estate brokers and salespeople be licensed. The license laws differ somewhat from state to state, but they are similar in most respects. They all require that the applicant meet certain personal and educational qualifications and must pass a written test to show adequate knowledge of the business.

Many states now require that applicants for a license must first take several courses in real estate practices, law, and mathematics. After satisfactory completion of the courses, they can then take the examination as a real estate salesperson. After serving a sales apprenticeship and taking additional courses, they can then apply for and take the more difficult broker's examination. Once in the field, the on-the-job training and studies continue.

Most of the real estate franchisers, such as Century 21, ERA, or Better Homes and Gardens, offer a continuing and diverse program of instruction to their salespeople and brokers. All for the good of the profession, and all for the good of those seeking the services of reputable real estate professionals. Too long now, brokers have been maligned. And too long have they been the "goat" of real estate deals that have not gone as the buyer or seller wanted them to go.

I've heard, over and over again, statements that unjustly point blame at the broker for "souring" deals. "The broker told me that the roof did not leak." "He told me that the burner was in good condition." Take into consideration that the broker is not only the agent for the principal, but in matters relative to the property for sale also the principal's spokesperson. The statements the broker makes about the property are usually made from information garnered from the seller. Yes, it's the broker's responsibility to make sure that the seller's claims are valid, but quite often a broker has no choice but to rely on the seller's statements. How many property owners tell the truth 100 percent of the time, if that truth adversely affects the sale of their property? Not a great many, I assure you.

If the basement leaks during heavy rainfalls, or the noise from passing traffic is unbearable at times, or flocks of sea gulls periodically congregate on the roof, human nature being what it is, do you think this information will be readily volunteered by the seller? No sir. They'll let it be sold, and if a problem comes up later it's the broker who often absorbs the blame.

Periodically, the media reports on polls and surveys taken on how the public perceives certain professions. Brokers don't fare very well in these surveys. Often they are just below the medicine man, and a step above the used car dealer and the attorney. At other times they are rated below the attorney and used car dealer, but the standing is usually not too lofty. There are good and bad, quality and less than quality persons in every profession. The real estate profession is making strides in improving its performance and credibility to the public, more than many other professions.

DUTIES AND RIGHTS OF THE PRINCIPAL

The principal's primary responsibility is to compensate the agent as agreed upon in the listing agreement. Compensation is normally an agreed-upon percentage of the total amount of the transaction. A typical fee is 6 to 7 percent for the sale of a residence, and 8 to 12 percent for the sale of land.

The fee is a negotiated percentage in every transaction. Keep this in mind when you are dealing with a broker. Any attempt by brokers to set uniform commission rates in their area is a violation of state and federal anti-trust laws. If no amount of commission is stated in the agreement, then custom usually prevails. If a broker has to sue to collect an unspecified commission, the courts will determine a reasonable amount by the customary commissions in the community.

If the seller defaults, the broker is still entitled to a commission. The seller may have a change of heart about selling the land, or the seller's may refuse to sign the deed, or there may be a defect in the title, or the buyer and seller may mutually agree to cancel the sale; the broker is still entitled to the commission.

The commission is earned when a seller accepts an offer from a ready, willing, and able buyer. The commission is due upon delivery of the deed to the buyer. The principal is responsible for giving the agent full honesty and cooperation in any dealings with the broker. In other words, the seller cannot willingly conceal a fact that if known would detrimentally affect the sale or alter the broker's efforts in selling the property. The principal is liable for all agreements made by the agent working within the authority given to the agent. The listing agreement should clearly spell out the authority given to the broker.

DUTIES AND RIGHTS OF THE BROKER

In performing his or her duties, the broker has certain obligations to the principal. Primary among them is loyalty. The broker is given the principal's trust and confidence and is not allowed to benefit through a hidden profit. Unless otherwise agreed upon, the broker's compensation is to be paid by the principal only. If the broker thinks the principal's land is worth much more than the asking price, the broker cannot buy it through a third party "straw" to sell it at a later date. If the broker wants the land, he or she must disclose this fact to the owner.

The broker must not represent both the buyer and the seller, nor collect a commission from both without their full knowledge and consent. The reason for this is that the broker cannot faithfully perform for both parties; a broker cannot get the highest possible selling price for the seller, while at the same time obtain the lowest possible buying price for the buyer. A broker cannot share or split the commission with an unlicensed person. Neither can the broker give gifts and inducements or finder's fees. The broker, to earn the commission, must show that he or she is licensed, had an agreement with the seller, and was the procuring cause of the sale.

The broker must "give notice" to the principal any information received relative to the property. If an offer is made, no matter for what amount, it must be communicated to the principal. It is the principal's right to accept or refuse any offers made, not the broker's.

The broker is working in a fiduciary capacity and at all times must act accordingly, for the principal's interests. The broker must account for all money or property upon demand from the principal. No personal funds of the broker's may be commingled with any money held for the principal. Real estate brokers open special *escrow accounts* in a bank so that clients' money can be kept separate from their own. Commingling of funds is a serious offense that could cost a broker his or her license.

The listing agreement contains the instructions a broker must follow and it is the broker's duty to obey these instructions. The broker must not make any statements misrepresenting material facts, nor make extravagant statements that would lead a buyer into a misunderstanding.

CHOOSING A BROKER

You will be selling much of your land by yourself, but you will eventually get to the point where you will require the services of a broker. A couple of pages back I said that you cannot function in this business without dealing with a real estate broker at one time or another. You will have to make sure you select a good one to work with.

Because of the nature of their business and the number of contacts that they develop, brokers know who is buying land and who is selling. They keep files of buyers that are looking for specific types of land. It's common for a broker to sell a parcel of land within a couple of days, and even hours, of the first listing. Certainly, a quick sale can be beneficial in keeping the seller's carrying costs at a minimum.

There are certain criteria that you must look for in selecting a broker to work with. All things being equal—assuming that the broker is capable and reputable—you will want a person who does business in the community where your land is located. I've often seen brokers' signs on property that is far removed from the brokers' sales office— several counties away in some instances.

With the price of gasoline being what it is, a broker is not going to be too enthused about showing a distant property. The broker isn't going to want to waste time and gasoline on "maybes," even though some maybes do buy. Even "sure things" won't entice every broker into driving a long distance.

For that matter, how familiar with the community could he be? Will the broker know the comparables so that he or she can advise you on a fair market price for your land? (If your land is too expensive it won't sell; if too cheap, you're the loser.) The broker has to know the community and competing properties. Practically every area of the continental United States is serviced by a knowledgeable local broker. Employ a local broker who is familiar with the land in your community.

If the broker belongs to a multiple listing service, you know that your land will get as broad a coverage as is available in that community. Is the broker aggressive? Will the broker and the broker's salespeople use their best efforts, coupled with some creativity, to market your land? You have to be able to make a value judgment in this regard. If the broker has a reputation as a "go-getter" and of being successful, then your decision on whether or not to select him is an easy choice. But, if it appears as though his firm is a "sleepy" office, one in which the broker and salespeople seem a little less enthusiastic about your land than you would want them to be, then you should look elsewhere for a more effervescent attitude.

Many brokers are aggressive with listings and worry little about sales. They live on their listings by letting other brokers sell the property. Ask the broker a few questions that will help you to decide if he or she is the agent you want:

What is your specialty?

Do you sell much land? What types?
How many salespeople do you have?

Do you belong to a multiple listing service?

How will you serve this listing? What types of promotion and advertising will you use?

Do you have prospects for this land in your files now?

What do you think my land is worth?

Let the broker know that you intend to be a "squeaky wheel" and that you will be calling often for an activity update. And do just that, call often. If you don't, then your land will be just another listing among many.

Besides choosing a broker to sell your land for you, consider also the employment of a buyer's broker. A buyer's broker is one contracted to find land for a principal to buy. His or her efforts will be on the buyer's behalf and will be compensated by the buyer. Chances are, you will get a better deal having a broker search and negotiate for you than if you do it for yourself.

If you've selected a productive broker for selling your land, the same broker could be looking for land for you to buy too. It would be better, however, to have a separate broker for each function, one as a seller's broker, one as a buyer's broker. If you're looking for land over a broad geographical area, more than one broker would be a better choice. The more people that are looking for land for you, the greater the chance of finding what you want.

THE LISTING AGREEMENT

Real estate is the inventory by which a broker earns commissions. To have the right to sell a piece of real estate, the broker must obtain permission from the property owner in the form of a listing agreement. The listing agreement is the employment contract authorizing the broker to act as agent for the owner-principal, using his or her best efforts to find a buyer for the principal's property. If the broker performs his or her duties as required, the owner will pay an agreed-upon commission.

Most states allow an oral listing, while 15 states require a written agreement. To avoid misunderstandings, I recommend that all listing agreements be in writing, as should any transaction that you conduct in real estate or in any business deal for that matter. Don't be coaxed by casual statements like: "We're friends, we don't need to sign anything." Or the infamous "My word is my bond." Or "A handshake will do." If you accept oral agreements, you will one day regret it.

A listing agreement includes certain elements that describe the rights and duties of the principal and agent. The listing must present enough facts so that both parties understand fully what is being sold, by whom, for how much, for how long, and for what fee. The agreement should include:

1. The names, addresses, and signatures of the seller and the broker
2. The starting and ending date of the agreement
3. A legal description of the property
4. The complete terms of the sale including the sales price and any financing terms that are offered
5. The type of listing: open, exclusive agency, exclusive right to sell, net, or multiple
6. Agreement to pay a stated commission
7. Full description of any personal property that is included in the sale; if the property is a home, then such a list may include appliances, television antenna, rugs and draperies, or any other included items

Types of Listings

All listing agreements must include the preceding elements. There are, however, variations in the agreements relative to the rights of the principal to simultaneously attempt to sell the property, or to list it with other brokers. There are five commonly used variations of the listing contract: (1) Open Listing, (2) Exclusive Agency Listing (3) Exclusive Right To Sell Listing, (4) Net Listing, and (5) Multiple Listing.

Open Listing   An open listing exists when an owner-principal allows several brokers the opportunity to sell his property. The broker who successfully sells the property earns the commission. The owner reserves the right to personally sell the property with no liability for a commission to any broker. The sale of the property automatically terminates all outstanding listings.

Exclusive Agency Listing   An *exclusive agency* listing is the hiring of a single broker to sell the principal's property for a commission, exclusive of other brokers. The principal may retain the right to personally sell the property without payment of a commission. Included in the listing agreement is the wording *exclusive agency,* along with the name of the broker. If a different broker sells the land, a commission must still be paid to the listing broker. The purpose of the exclusive agency listing is to give the listing broker protection from other brokers so that the listing broker can use his or her best efforts without competition from other brokers.

Exclusive Right to Sell Listing   An *exclusive right to sell listing* is similar in all respects to an exclusive agency listing except that the owner gives up the right to sell the land personally. This is preferred by brokers over all other listing types, since it gives them full protection. (Figure 15-1).

Think of the broker's viewpoint. A broker may spend a lot of time and money to market a property and then be unable to deliver title because another broker (or the owner) sold it first. Wouldn't you be disinclined to spend advertising dollars and valuable time if you weren't sure your efforts would produce a commission?

Exclusive Right
To Sell Agreement

THIS IS A LEGALLY BINDING CONTRACT. IF NOT UNDERSTOOD, SEEK COMPETENT ADVICE.

Agreed pursuant to normal Real Estate buying and selling procedures, all Real Estate Listing Agreements shall be in writing. This is an Exclusive Right To Sell Agreement.

1. I hereby grant the Broker listed below, for the period designated, the exclusive power and authority to sell the property described herein, for the price and upon the terms herein set forth, or any other price or terms acceptable to me and in consideration of the acceptance by you of this agency and of your efforts to secure a buyer for the property, I agree to pay a commission stated below, on the amount of the sale price, whether such sale be made by you or by me or sold by any other person acting for me or in my behalf.

2. I agree to direct all inquiries concerning the property to you during the period of your agency.

3. I further agree to pay a commission if a sale, exchange, lease for a period of more than 12 months, or other transfer of said property is made within SIX (6) months after the termination of this authorization, to persons with whom Broker shall have negotiated during the term hereof and whose names the Broker shall have submitted in writing by certified mail to Owner within TEN DAYS after termination of this authorization.

4. I agree to furnish a warranty deed showing a merchantable title. All items of income and expense shall be adjusted pro rata as of date of delivery of deed.

5. You are authorized to relist this property on said terms with any other Licensed Broker.

6. You may accept a deposit of earnest money in my behalf and should the purchaser fail to complete the purchase, you are to retain one-half of the deposit in payment of advertising, services and other expenses as Liquidated Damages up to an amount not to exceed the full commission.

7. Owner warrants the accuracy of the information furnished herein with respect to the below described property and agrees to hold the Broker harmless from any liabilities or damages arising out of incorrect or undisclosed information. The undersigned Owner warrants further that he is the owner of record of the property or has the authority to execute this agreement.

I hereby Grant _____ Broker for the period of _____ Months not to exceed ONE YEAR (12 months) from this date the Exclusive Power and Authority to sell the property described herein.

I agree to pay a _____ % commission on the amount of the sale price.

TERMS _____ SELLING PRICE _____

PROPERTY DESCRIPTION AND LOCATION

ADDRESS: _____

Taxes _____	Size of Lot _____	Roads _____
Assessment _____	Power _____	Sidewalk _____
Water (Source) _____	Number of Rms. _____	School _____
Sewer (Type) _____	Bathrms. _____	Construction _____
Type of Heat _____	Garage _____	Age _____

THE UNDERSIGNED OWNER (SELLER) HEREBY ACKNOWLEDGES HAVING READ AND UNDERSTANDS THE FULL TEXT OF THIS CONTRACT, AND HAS RECEIVED A COPY HEREOF.

.... OWNER
Date

.... OWNER
Accepted   BROKER

THIS AGREEMENT EXPIRES _____

Figure 15-1. An exclusive right to sell agreement

Net Listing

A *net listing* is an arrangement whereby an owner sets a minimum acceptable price for the property, with any amount in excess of this to be the broker's commission. It may take the form of an open listing, an exclusive agency listing, or an exclusive right to sell listing.

The concept of a net listing is questionable, both legally and ethically. Some states frown on its use, while other states outlaw it completely. To illustrate some of the difficulties that could arise, consider an owner who decides that he or she wants $50,000 for a piece of land, with the excess over this amount to be the broker's commission. If the broker advertises the land for $55,000 and a prospect makes an offer of $50,100, the broker must, by the law of agency, present the offer to the owner. If it is accepted, the broker will make just $100 for the time and expenses in marketing the property. Hardly fair to the broker.

Conversely, a less than honorable broker could convince an unsuspecting owner to list the land at far below its actual market value, sell it for a high price, and earn an unreasonable commission.

Reputable brokers avoid a net listing, not only because of its dubious nature, but also because it can be a source of misunderstanding between brokers and sellers, and cause a lot of unwanted trouble and poor public relations.

Multiple Listings

A *multiple listing agreement* is used by brokers who are members of a multiple listing service (MLS). A multiple listing agreement is generally an exclusive right to sell listing, with a provision that any member of the MLS may also sell the land and share the commission.

Members of an MLS are obligated to notify, within a specified period of time, the multiple listing organization of the listing so that the information can be disseminated to all other members. When the land is sold, the commission is divided between the listing broker and the selling broker, with a fee going to the MLS organization. If the listing broker makes the sale, he or she retains the entire commission, minus the MLS fee.

It is usually to the benefit of a seller to have land listed with a member of an MLS because it will be given broad exposure. The more people trying to sell the land, the better the chances for a sale.

The National Association of Realtors has developed a 14-point multiple listing policy that its members must follow:

A multiple listing service shall not:
1. Fix, control, recommend, suggest, or maintain commission rates or fees for services to be rendered by members.
2. Fix, control, recommend, suggest, or maintain any percentage division of commission or fees between cooperating members or non-members.
3. Require financial support of multiple listing service operations by any formula based on commission or sales prices.
4. Require or use any form that establishes or implies the existence of any contractual relationship between the multiple listing service and the client (buyer or seller).
5. Make any rule relating to the posting or use of signs.
6. Make any rule prohibiting or discouraging cooperation with non-members.
7. Limit or interfere with the terms of the relationship between a member and the member's salesmen.
8. Prohibit or discourage any members from political participation or activity.
9. Make any rule granting blanket consent to a selling member to negotiate directly with the seller (owner).
10. Make any rule regulating the advertising or promotion of any listings.
11. Prohibit or discourage a member from accepting a listing from a seller (owner) preferring to give "office exclusive."
12. Adopt any rule denying a listing member from controlling the posting of "sold signs."
13. Refuse any exclusive listing submitted by a member on the basis of the quality or price of the listing.
14. Adopt rules authorizing the modification or change of any listing without the express, written permission of the listing member.

A listing agreement terminates upon the sale of the subject property. It can also be terminated by: (1) mutual consent of the parties or revocation by either party, (2) expiration of the agreed-upon period, (3) destruction of the property, (4) death, insanity, physical incapacity, or bankruptcy of either party.

WRAP-UP

Now that you've finished reading this guide, do you fully understand all there is to know about investing in land? The answer is a resounding NO. I didn't expect it to be otherwise. I don't know of anyone who could reply positively to this question no matter how many books they've read on the subject or how many years they've been investing in land. There's just too much to know and to keep abreast of.

Do you, at least, feel more confident of your chances to profit in land since you have read this guide? I hope you do. My goal in writing this book was to give the novice investor (the old pro, too) enough of the basics to enable him or her to proceed intelligently into land investing. Certainly you won't remember all that you've read; but keep the book handy as a reference tool. If you want to know about ownership rights, look it up and reread it. Easements, liens, financing terminology—look it up.

From page one to here I've taken you through the entire process. The early pages provided you with enough facts to show you that land investing can be profitable. I attempted to reduce the terminology of the trade to humanly consumable levels. You now know what a landowner's rights and responsibilities are, and how to protect and perform them. I warned you of the pitfalls and how to avoid them. In truth, I've written this book mostly out of the trials and tribulations and mistakes that I've made in land investing over the past two decades. I want you to be aware of them and avoid them as much as you can.

You know what to look for in assessing a parcel's potential, how to put a value on it and negotiate its purchase, how to finance, subdivide, and resell it for a profit. You know where to get the information, guidance, and assistance you need. All you need now is the actual experience—go do it and profit.

GLOSSARY

Abandonment. Vacating or giving up the use of, or rights in, real property.

Absolute fee simple title. An estate that is free from all encumbrances or conditions; the best title obtainable.

Absorption. The rate at which real property will be sold over a period of time.

Abstract of title. A condensed history of the title to a particular parcel of real estate including all subsequent conveyances and encumbrances.

Abut. Be next to or to touch.

Acceleration clause. A clause in a mortgage or note that gives the lender the right to call all monies owed to be immediately due if the borrower defaults.

Accretion. The increase in the size of land by the gradual action of bodies of water.

Acknowledgment. A formal declaration made before a notary public or other official that the signature on a document is genuine.

Acre. A measure of land area containing 160 square rods, or 4840 square yards, or 43,560 square feet.

Ad valorem. According to valuation.

Administrator. A person appointed by a probate court to settle the estate of a deceased intestate person.

Affidavit. A written declaration or statement of facts given voluntarily and under oath before someone who has authority to administer such oath.

Agent. A person authorized to act for another.

Air rights. The right to use the space above the surface of the land.

Alienation. The transfer of property from one person to another.

Alluvion. Soil deposited by accretion.

Amenities. Qualities that are pleasant and enjoyable that increase the value of realty such as a scenic view or water access.

Amortization. The liquidation of a financial debt by periodic installment payments.

Annexation. The attachment of personal property to land in such a way that it becomes a part of the real property.

Appraisal. An estimate or opinion of value made by a qualified person.

Appreciation. An increase in the value of property.

Appurtenance. An incidental property right such as an easement or right of way that passes with the land when title is transferred.

Assessed value. The value placed on property by an assessor as a basis for taxation.

Assessor. The government official who determines the assessed value.

Assignee. The person who receives assigned property.

Assignment. The transfer of a right from one person to another.

Assignor. The person who assigns or transfers property.

Assumption. An agreement by one person to assume the obligation of another; for example, the assumption of a mortgage.

Attachment. Seizure of property by court order so that it will be available to satisfy a judgment against the owner.

Attractive nuisance. Something dangerous that would attract a person to it, such as an open pit that children might explore and risk danger to themselves.

Avulsion. The sudden removal of soil from one parcel to another.

Balloon payment. The unamortized final payment on a note, which is usually larger than the preceding installment payments.

Base line. An imaginary east-west line used by surveyors to find and describe land locations.

Bench mark. A permanent marker used by surveyors to measure elevations.

Bequeath. To transfer or make a gift by will.

Betterment. Improvements that add value to real estate such as paved sidewalks or roadways.

Bill of sale. A written agreement that transfers ownership of personal property from one person to another.

Binder. A receipt of the buyer's deposit pending the final closing of the transaction.

Blanket mortgage. A single mortgage covering more than one parcel.

Block. A rectangular parcel in a city surrounded by streets.

Bona fide. In good faith, without fraud.

Bond. An obligation written under seal by a third party insurer that it will make good in case of default by the bonded party.

Boot. Cash or its equivalent given in a property exchange to balance equities.

Breach of contract. The failure to live up to the terms set forth in a contract.

Broker. One who acts for another for a fee.

Buffer strip. A strip of land separating parcels.

Building codes. Local or state ordinances regulating the construction of buildings.

Building line. A line set by the building codes establishing the distance from the street and sidelines beyond which no structure can be built.

Bundle of rights. The group of interests and rights vested in the owner of a parcel such as the right to sell, mortgage, lease, will, or to build upon real property.

By-laws. Rules governing the organization and authority of a group.

Carrying charges. Costs incidental to holding property such as taxes, interest, and insurance.

Glossary

Caveat emptor. Let the buyer beware.

Chain of title. A history of all transfers and encumbrances affecting a title.

Chattel. Personal property.

Clear title. Title free of any encumbrances.

Closing. Bringing a transaction to a conclusion.

Closing statement. A summary of the financial adjustments between buyer and seller at the closing.

Cloud on the title. An outstanding claim or encumbrance that impairs the title. It usually pertains to nuisance claims that can be cleared by court order.

Clustering. The grouping together of homesites surrounded by common areas.

Collateral. Security given on a note.

Collateral heirs. Relatives not lineally related to a decedent—uncles, aunts, nephews, nieces.

Commingling of funds. The illegal act by a real estate broker who mixes buyers' deposits with his or her own funds.

Commission. A broker's compensation for services—often a percentage of the sales price.

Community property. Equal interest of each spouse in all property acquired through their joint efforts during marriage.

Comparables. Properties equivalent to the subject property.

Condemnation. The process through which private property is taken by eminent domain for public use.

Confiscation. The right of the government to take the property of enemies during a war without compensation.

Consideration. Anything of value given or received in a contractual agreement.

Contingencies. Terms and conditions in a contract that must be performed.

Contiguous. Adjoining.

Contract of sale. An agreement between a buyer and a seller.

Conveyance. The means by which interests in real estate are transferred—a deed, mortgage, or lease.

Covenant. A written agreement or promise in a deed to do or not to do something.

Cul de sac. A dead-end street ending in a large turnaround.

Curtesy. The right a husband has in his deceased wife's estate.

Damages. The indemnity or compensation for a loss resulting from a breach of contract.

Dealer. A person who buys and sells real estate as a business rather than as an investment.

Decedent. A deceased person.

Deciduous trees. Trees that lose their leaves in the winter.

Dedication. A gift of property by its owner to the public for some public use.

Deed. A written instrument that transfers title to real property.

Default. Failure to perform an act or obligation as required in an agreement or contract.

Deficiency judgment. A judgment against a debtor that allows a creditor to collect against the personal assets of the debtor if proceeds from a foreclosure sale are insufficient to satisfy the debt.

Depreciation. The loss in value of real property because of age, deterioration, or functional or economic obsolescence.

Descent. The transfer of ownership according to inheritance laws if an owner dies intestate.

Developer. A person who subdivides land and constructs buildings.

Devise. The transfer of property by will.

Dower. The right a wife has in her deceased husband's estate.

Duress. Forcing someone to do something against his or her will.

Earnest money. A payment of part of the purchase price as evidence of good faith to purchase real property.

Easement. A right, privilege, or interest one person has in the land of another.

Economic life. The period of time during which a property may be profitably utilized.

Economic obsolescence. Loss in property value from external forces such as zoning ordinance changes or a deteriorating neighborhood.

Emblements. Crops produced on leased land.

Eminent domain. The right of the government to take private property for the good of the public upon payment of just compensation.

Enabling acts. Authority permitting municipalities to establish planning agencies or activities like land-use planning and zoning.

Encroachment. The projection of a structure or other object that intrudes into or overhangs upon property of another.

Encumbrance. Anything that interferes with or affects the title to property—liens, easements, mortgages, and restrictions.

Equity. The value an owner has in land over any mortgage amount.

Equity of redemption. The right a mortgagor has to prevent foreclosure by paying off the full debt.

Erosion. The decrease in size of a parcel of land through the natural action of wind, ice, or water action.

Escalator clause. A clause in a contract that provides for an adjustment.

Escheat. The reversion of property to the state when there are no legal heirs to the land of an intestate deceased person.

Escrow. The instrument, monies, or item of value deposited with a third party to be delivered upon the fulfillment of a condition.

Estate. The interest that one has in real property.

Estoppel certificate. A written and signed statement that prevents the signer from disavowing the facts.

Et ux. And wife.

Et al. And another.

Et als. And others.

Exclusive agency. The relationship in which the broker has the right to sell exclusive of all other brokers. The owner may also sell the land.

Exclusive right to sell. The relationship in which only the broker may sell the land.

Executor. A person named in a will to carry out its terms.

Extension agreement. An agreement to extend beyond the original termination date.

Farmers Home Administration (FHA). A federal agency that grants loans for agricultural purposes.

Feasibility study. An analysis to determine whether an investment should be undertaken.

Federal Deposit Insurance Corporation (FDIC). The federal agency that insures deposits in federal and state chartered banks.

Federal Home Loan Mortgage Corporation (FHLMC). An agency authorized to buy and sell conventional, FHA, and VA loans.

Federal Housing Administration (FHA). The federal agency that insures home mortgages.

Federal National Mortgage Association (FNMA). Fannie Mae—a privately owned agency authorized to buy and sell FHA and VA mortgages.

Federal Savings and Loan Insurance Corporation (FSLIC). The federal agency that insures deposits in federal- and state-chartered savings and loan association.

Fee simple. The largest estate in ownership of real estate without restrictions or limitations on how the owner may dispose of the property.

Feudal system. A system of land ownership used in pre-colonial England in which the king owns all rights.

Fiduciary. A relationship of trust and confidence between an agent and principal.

Final plat. The surveyor's subdivision plan approved by the planning board.

Finder's fee. A fee paid to a broker for obtaining a mortgage loan or for locating a property for the buyer.

Fixture. An item of personal property that has been attached to land or buildings in such a way as to be considered part of the real property.

Flaw. A gap or break in the chain of title.

Flowage easement. The right to flood and maintain property such as drainage from an abutting pond to flood a cranberry bog.

Foreclosure. A legal procedure in which property used as security for a debt is sold to pay off the debt.

Glossary

Foreshore. The land between the high-water mark and the low-water mark.

Forfeiture. The loss of anything of value due to default or failure to perform.

Fraud. Misrepresentation or concealment of a material fact with the intent to mislead.

Free and clear. Property free of liens and encumbrances.

Freehold estate. A fee simple interest in land held for life.

Front foot. A measurement 1 foot long along the frontage of a property.

Functional obsolescence. Loss of value due to outdated design and fixtures.

Funnel development. A development method whereby a small waterfront lot provides water access for several inland lots.

Gap. A defect in the chain of title.

General contractor. A contractor who hires and coordinates the services of subcontractors in developing a project.

General lien. A lien on all personal and real property of a debtor.

General partner. The managing partner in a limited partnership.

Gift deed. A deed that transfers ownership with love and affection as the consideration.

Government lot. A fractional section in the government survey system that is smaller than a full-quarter section.

Government National Mortgage Association (GNMA). Ginnie Mae—an agency of the federal government that buys and sells mortgages on the secondary mortgage market to support low-income housing programs.

Grading. The moving of earth to acquire the desired topography in a subdivision.

Grant. To transfer a legal interest in property.

Grantee. The person to whom an interest in property is conveyed.

Grantor. The person conveying the interest in property.

Habendum clause. The "to have and to hold" clause in a deed that defines the extent of the ownership to be conveyed.

Headright system. A reward of a grant of land in colonial America for persons responsible for a new immigrant.

Hectare. A metric measure of surface area, 2.471 acres.

Hereditament. Any property that is capable of being inherited.

Highest and best use. The most profitable use of land.

Homestead. Real estate occupied as a home.

Homestead exemption. A statutory right that gives limited protection of the family home from creditors.

Hundred year flood plain. Land that the federal government projects may flood in the next hundred years.

Hypothecate. Give something as security without giving up actual possession.

Implied contract. A contract evidenced by one's acts and conduct.

Improved land. Land that has had roads and utilities installed.

Improvements. Structures on a parcel of land including buildings, fences, sewers, water pipes, and roadways.

Inchoate. A wife's interest in the real property of her husband during his life. Upon his death it becomes a dower interest.

Incorporeal. Intangible rights such as an easement.

Indenture. Any written legal instrument.

Injunction. A court order ordering a person to do or not to do something.

Installment contract. The purchase of land on the basis of specified payments made periodically.

Instrument. A written legal document.

Interest. A right in property ownership.

Interest rate. The price charged for the use of money.

Intestate. Without a will or last testament.

Involuntary lien. A lien against land without the consent of the owner such as that for tax or that for a betterment charge.

Joint tenancy. Real property owned by two or more persons with the right of survivorship.

Joint venture. The joining together of two or more persons to conduct a specific venture.

Judgment. The determination by a court establishing the rights and claims of the parties to a court action.

Junior mortgage. A mortgage subordinate to any prior recorded mortgages.

Just compensation. Payment made for property taken in a condemnation proceeding.

Key lot. A lot with the rear of other lots abutting one or more of its sidelines.

Laches. An unreasonable delay or negligence in asserting one's rights causing the loss of such rights.

Land contract. A contract used in the sale of land in which title remains with the seller until completion by the buyer of all installment payments.

Landlocked. Property with no rights or means of access.

Lease. A contract creating a landlord-tenant relationship.

Legal description. A property description sufficient to locate the boundaries and property lines.

Lessee. The tenant.

Lessor. The landlord.

Leverage. The use of borrowed funds to finance the greater portion of an investment.

Levy. To place a tax on a property.

License. The right granted to use the land of another.

Lien. A claim or encumbrance on land as security for a debt.

Lien theory. The concept in which title is held by the mortgagor with the mortgage serving as a lien on the property.

Life estate. An ownership interest in land limited to the duration of a certain individual's lifetime.

Lineal heirs. Direct line descendants—children and grandchildren.

Lis pendens. A recorded notice that there is a suit pending against the land.

Listing agreement. A contract of employment between an owner and a real estate broker.

Littoral rights. An owner's rights to use the waterways adjacent to his land.

Market approach. A method of appraising land by comparing it with comparable properties.

Market price. The actual selling price of a parcel.

Market value. The price that a parcel is expected to sell for in the open market.

Marketable title. Title that is free and clear of objectionable defects and encumbrances.

Master plan. A comprehensive plan covering the long-term physical development of a community.

Mechanics' lien. A lien placed on property by those that have supplied materials and labor and have not been paid.

Meridians. North and south lines used in determining boundaries in the government survey system.

Metes and bounds. Measurements and boundaries; the boundary lines of a parcel with terminal points and angles.

Monument. A fixed, natural or artificial, object used in a metes and bounds description.

Mortgage. A pledge of real estate as security for a debt.

Mortgagee. The lender.

Mortgagor. The borrower.

Multiple listing. A listing that is available to all the brokers in the multiple listing association.

Multiple nuclei theory. A theory of development in which several business districts combine to form growth.

Multiple-use zoning. Zoning that allows for diverse but compatible zoning uses.

National Association of Realtors.® A national real estate organization.

Neighborhood. A community of homogeneous groups and businesses.
Net listing. A listing in which the seller sets a minimum acceptable net price.
Nonconforming use. A land use that does not conform with current regulations.

Obsolescence. Loss in value because of physical, economic, or other changes.
Open-end mortgage. A mortgage that permits a borrower to borrow additional funds after part of the loan has been reduced.
Open listing. An agreement between a broker and a principal in which the owner as well as several other brokers may sell the property.
Option. A right to purchase land within a specified period of time.
Optionee. The person who holds the option (the prospect).
Optionor. The person who gives the option (the owner).
Ordinance. A law passed by a governing body.

Package mortgage. A mortgage that includes personal and real property as part of the security.
Parcel. A portion of land.
Partition. The dividing of jointly owned real estate so that each owner may own a specific portion.
Partnership. An association of two or more persons acting as co-owners of a business.
Partywall. A wall built on the line between two parcels for the use of both owners.
Percolation test. A soil test for drainage.
Performance bond. A surety bond guaranteeing that the bonding company will complete construction of a project if the contractor defaults.
Permeability. The rate at which water will filter through a saturated soil.
Personalty. Any property that is not realty.
Planned unit development (PUD). A single parcel in which diverse land uses are combined into one development or subdivision.

Plat. A map showing the planned use of a parcel of land including all dimensions, property lines, and easements.

Plat book. The public record book where all plats are kept.

Plottage. The combining of two or more parcels resulting in an increase in utility and value.

Point of beginning (POB). The starting point that a surveyor uses under the metes and bounds description method.

Points. A one-time fee charged on the origination of a mortgage loan. One point equals 1 percent.

Police power. The power of the government to impose laws to protect the public welfare.

Possessory interest. The right to occupy and use real estate.

Power of attorney. A written instrument authorizing one person to act as another's agent.

Prepayment penalty. A penalty that a borrower must pay to pay off a mortgage before its due date.

Prescription. Acquiring title to property through adverse possession.

Prescriptive easement. An easement acquired by adverse use.

Prima facie. Evidence sufficient to establish a fact.

Prime rate. The lowest interest rate that commercial banks charge their best customers.

Principal. (1) The employer of an agent. (2) the amount of a loan.

Prior appropriation. A concept of water ownership.

Probate. Establish the validity of a will.

Profit. The right a person has to enter another's land and remove something.

Prorate. To adjust costs between buyer and seller.

Prospect. A person who may be interested in buying.

Puffing. Exaggerated statements of opinion.

Purchase money mortgage. A mortgage given to the buyer from the seller.

Quadrangle. A tract of land in the government survey measuring 24 miles square.

Quiet enjoyment. The right to enjoy one's property without interference.

Quiet title suit. A court action that removes any defects or clouds on the title.

Quitclaim deed. A deed granting only the interest that the grantor has in the land.

Range. A tract of land in the government survey six miles wide running north and south.

Real property. Real estate.

Realtor.® A registered trademark used by real estate brokers who are members of the National Association of Realtors.®

Realty. Real estate.

Recording. Entering a legal instrument into the public records.

Rectangular survey system. The government survey system for describing and locating land.

Redemption. The right to recover one's property for a limited time after it has been sold through foreclosure.

Refinance. Paying off an existing loan with a new loan.

Regulation Q. A regulation of the Federal Reserve System establishing maximum interest rates that commercial banks may pay depositors.

Regulation Z. The Truth in Lending Act of 1969 that requires lenders to inform borrowers of all costs relative to a loan.

Remainder. The interest in an estate that is left after the termination of a life estate.

Remainderman. The party that acquires a remainder interest.

Restriction. An encumbrance or limitation to the use of land.

Right of way. The right to cross over another's land.

Riparian. An owner's rights to abutting waterways.

Rod. A measure of length: 16½ feet.

Satisfaction piece. An instrument acknowledging the payment of a debt.

Seal. An impression made on a document to attest to its execution.

Section. A tract of land in the government survey system 1 mile square (640 acres).

Setback. The distance that any structure must be from the property line.

Severalty. Ownership of realty by one person.
Specific performance. A legal action requiring a person to carry out the terms of a contract.
Speculator. A person who buys and sells land in anticipation of profits.
Spot zoning. A use inconsistent with zoning in the area.
Statute of fraud. The state law that requires real estate contracts to be in writing.
Straw. One who buys property for another concealing the identity of the true buyer.
Subdivision. A tract of land divided into lots.
Survey. The process of locating and measuring land areas and dimensions.
Syndicate. A joint venture of two or more persons.

Tax sale. The sale of property because of nonpayment of taxes.
Tax title. Title acquired at a tax sale.
Tenancy at sufferance. Possession of real estate after a lease has expired.
Tenancy at will. Possession of real estate without a fixed term duration.
Tenancy by the entirety. Ownership between married persons with the right of survivorship.
Tenancy in common. Co-ownership of an undivided interest in real estate without the right of survivorship.
Testate. Leaving a valid will.
Title. Ownership of real estate.
Title insurance. Insurance that protects the owner against losses resulting from past unknown title defects.
Title search. An examination of the public records to determine the status of ownership.
Topography. The nature of the land surface.
Topographic map. A map showing elevations of the land and all natural and artificial features such as rivers, roads, and structures.
Torrens system. The registration of land with the Land Court to correct title flaws and omissions.

Township. A tract of land in the government survey system 6 miles square.

Tract. An area of land.

Trade fixture. Items of personal property attached to leased property used by a tenant in his business.

Usury. Interest on a loan that is higher than permitted by law.

Utilities. Services such as electricity, water, telephone, gas, and sewage disposal.

VA loan. A low interest loan guaranteed by the Veterans Administration.

Valid. Legally sufficient.

Value. The worth of something. The amount that real estate will sell for in the open market.

Variance. Permission to deviate from the zoning laws.

Vendee. The buyer.

Vendor. The seller.

Vested. Bestowed upon someone.

Void. Not enforceable.

Voidable. Subject to being void.

Voluntary lien. A lien created by an agreement such as a mortgage.

Waiver. The surrender of a claim or right.

Warranty deed. A deed in which the grantor guarantees good clear title.

Wraparound mortgage. A second mortgage that includes a first mortgage.

Yield. Return on investment.

Zoning. A municipal process that controls land use for the good of the public.

Index

Abandonment, 68
Abstract of title, 88
Abstractor, 88
Acceleration clause, 153
Acre, 49, 215
Accretion, 31, 80
Actual notice, 84
Ad valorem, 96-97
Adverse possession, 67, 81-82, 89
Affirmative easement, 66
Agency, law of, 300-302
Agent:
  general, 300
  special, 300
Agreement of sale, 180
Air rights, 29
Alienation, 79-84
  involuntary, 79-82
  voluntary, 79, 82-84
Ambessi, Guisseppe, 85-87
American Farm Digest, 201
Amortization, 148
Angle measurement, 47

Appraising, 117-127
  purpose, 119-120
  value, 118-119
  location, 119-120
  market value, 120
  social forces, 120
  economic forces, 121
  physical forces, 121
  governmental forces, 121
  neighborhood desirability, 121-124
  economic principals, 122-124
    anticipation, 122
    balance, 122-123
    change, 123
    competition, 123
    contribution, 123
    conformity, 123
    diminishing returns, 123
    highest and best use, 123-124
    substitution, 124
    supply and demand, 124
  approaches to value, 124-127
    market data, 124-125

Index

income, 125-126
cost, 126-127
Aquifiers, 32
Area, 49-50
Articles of Incorporation, 74
Asking Price, 129
Assessment:
process, 97
tax rate, 98-99
special, 100
exemptions, 99
assessed value, 99
Assignee, 168
Assuming a mortgage, 146
Axial theory, 109

Babcock, Frederick, 102
Babcock, Richard, 107
Baby boomers, 189
Bail bond lien, 62, 64
Balloon payment, 148
Banks, 155-156, 197
Bargain and sale deed, 175
Bargaining, 128
Base lines, 40
Benchmark, 38, 49
Beneficiary, 149
Betterment charges, 100
Bill of sale, 24
Binder, 172
Blanket mortgage, 152
BLM, 190-192
Bonds, 146-147
collaterial, 146
promissory note, 147
Boot, 293
Bounds, 37
Broker's commission, 91, 302-303
Budget, 98
Builders, 197
Builders acre, 49, 215
Building codes, 110-113
Bundle of rights, 35, 61
Buyer's fever, 135-136
Buyer's market, 137
Buyer's fees, 91

Canned presentation, 286
Carlyle, Thomas, 6
Carrying costs, 18
Casey, William J., 231
Certificate of title, 82
Chain of title, 85, 175
Chattel fixtures, 25
City planning, 103
Civil War, 5
Classified advertisements, 273-276
Clay, 212
Closing, 89-92
documents, 90
statement, 91
seller's fees, 91
buyer's fees, 91-92
Cloud, 86
Commercial land uses, 256
Commission, 302-303
Community property, 58, 70, 75-76
Competent parties, 166
Compound interest, 148
Concentrate, 222-223
Concentric circle theory, 102
Condemnation, 80
Conditional fee estate, 57
Confiscation, 80
Consideration, 167, 176
good and valuable, 176
Constructive notice, 84
Contract for deed, 92, 144, 172
Contracts, 165-173
law of, 165
essentials of, 166-169
types of, 169-173
express, 166
implied, 166
bilateral, 166
unilateral, 166
discharge, 168
Conventional life estate, 57-58
Corner markers, 50
Corporation franchise tax lien, 62, 65
Correction line, 45
Co-ownership, 58, 69-76
severalty, 69

Index

Estates, 55-61
 freehold, 56-59
  fee simple, 56-57
  qualified fee, 57
  life estate, 57
  legal life estate, 58
 leasehold, 59-61
  for years, 59-61
  periodic, 60
  at will, 60
  at sufferance, 60-61
Estimate, 118
Exchanges, 293
Exclusive agency, 308
Exclusive right to sell, 308

Farmers, 184
Farmland, 184
Federal Land Bank, 157
Fee, 57
Fee simple, 56-57
Fee simple absolute, 57
Fees:
 seller's, 91
 attorney's, 91
 mortgage, 91
 recording, 91
FHA, 149, 157, 194
FHLB, 155
FHLMC, 159
Fiduciary relationship, 300
Field survey, 47
Fixtures, 25-27
 trade, 25
 chattel, 25
 of realty, 25
Florida, 183
FNMA, 158-159
For sale signs, 270-273
Forced sale value, 190
Foreclosure, 152-155
 default, 152
 acceleration clause, 152
 redemption rights, 153
 strict, 154
 entry and possession, 154

judicial, 154
nonjudicial, 154
deficiency judgement, 154
friendly, 154
Form A lots, 229, 245
Form C lots, 229
Fourteenth amendment, 106
Fraud, 169
Freehold estate, 56
Frontage, 216, 245, 255
FSLIC, 155
Further assurance, 175

Gap, 85
General liens, 62
General contractor, 62, 63
General warranty deed, 174
General partnership, 70
Geodetic survey, 219
GNMA, 159
Government survey, 40, 242
Grantee, 57, 86, 176
Grantee index, 85-86
Grantor, 57, 176
Grantor index, 85-86
Greeley, Horace, 8
Gridiron pattern, 244
Groundwater, 32
Growth theories, 101-103
 Concentric Circle, 102
 Axial, 102
 Sector, 102
 Multiple Nuclei, 103
 path of, 182-183
GSA, 193-194

Habendum clause, 176
Harris, C. D., 102
Health & Human Services, Dept. of,
 195
Homestead, 58
Homestead Exemption Law, 58
Homesteading, 59
Hong Kong, 60
Hoyt, Homer, 13-14, 102
HUD, 149, 188, 294
 OILSR, 294

Index

Index